Naná Vasconcelos's
Saudades

33 1/3 Global

33 1/3 Global, a series related to but independent from **33 1/3**, takes the format of the original series of short, music-based books and brings the focus to music throughout the world. With initial volumes focusing on Japanese and Brazilian music, the series will also include volumes on the popular music of Australia/Oceania, Europe, Africa, the Middle East, and more.

33 1/3 Japan

Series Editor: Noriko Manabe

Spanning a range of artists and genres—from the 1970s rock of Happy End to technopop band Yellow Magic Orchestra, the Shibuya-kei of Cornelius, classic anime series *Cowboy Bebop*, J-Pop/EDM hybrid Perfume, and vocaloid star Hatsune Miku—**33 1/3 Japan** is a series devoted to in-depth examination of Japanese popular music of the twentieth and twenty-first centuries.

Published Titles:
Supercell's *Supercell* by Keisuke Yamada
Yoko Kanno's *Cowboy Bebop Soundtrack* by Rose Bridges
Perfume's *Game* by Patrick St. Michel
Cornelius's *Fantasma* by Martin Roberts
Joe Hisaishi's *My Neighbor Totoro: Soundtrack* by Kunio Hara
Shonen Knife's *Happy Hour* by Brooke McCorkle
Nenes' *Koza Dabasa* by Henry Johnson

Forthcoming Titles:
Yellow Magic Orchestra's *Yellow Magic Orchestra* by x
Kohaku Uta Gassen by Shelley Brunt
Yuming's *The 14th Moon* by Lasse Lehtonen

33 1/3 Brazil

Series Editor: Jason Stanyek

Covering the genres of samba, tropicália, rock, hip hop, forró, bossa nova, heavy metal, and funk, among others, **33 1/3 Brazil** is a series devoted to in-depth examination of the most important Brazilian albums of the twentieth and twenty-first centuries.

Published Titles:
Caetano Veloso's *A Foreign Sound* by Barbara Browning
Tim Maia's *Tim Maia Racional Vols 1 & 2* by Allen Thayer
João Gilberto and Stan Getz's *Getz/Gilberto* by Brian McCann
Gilberto Gil's *Refazenda* by Marc A. Hertzman
Dona Ivone Lara's *Sorriso Negro* by Mila Burns
Milton Nascimento and Lô Borges's *The Corner Club* by
    Jonathon Grasse
Racionais MCs' *Sobrevivendo no Inferno* by Derek Pardue
Naná Vasconcelos's *Saudades* by Daniel B. Sharp

Forthcoming Titles:
Jorge Ben Jor's *África Brasil* by Frederick J. Moehn
Chico Buarque's *Chico Buarque* by Charles A. Perrone

33 1/3 Europe

Series Editor: Fabian Holt

Spanning a range of artists and genres, **33 1/3 Europe** offers engaging accounts of popular and culturally significant albums of Continental Europe and the North Atlantic from the twentieth and twenty-first centuries.

Published Titles:
Darkthrone's *A Blaze in the Northern Sky* by Ross Hagen
Ivo Papasov's *Balkanology* by Carol Silverman
Heiner Müller and Heiner Goebbels's *Wolokolamsker Chaussee*
    by Philip V. Bohlman

Forthcoming Titles:

Modeselektor's *Happy Birthday* by Sean Nye
Various Artists' *DJs do Guetto* by Richard Elliott
Bea Playa's *I'll Be Your Plaything* by Anna Szemere and András Rónai
Los Rodriguez's *Sin Documentos* by Fernán del Val and Héctor Fouce
Mercyful Fate's *Don't Break the Oath* by Henrik Marstal
Massada's *Astaganaga* by Lutgard Mutsaers
Nuovo Canzoniere's *Bella Ciao* by Jacopo Tomatis
Czesław Niemen's *Niemen Enigmatic* by Ewa Mazierska and Mariusz Gradowski
Amália Rodrigues's *Live at the Olympia* by Lilla Ellen Gray
Ardit Gjebrea's *Projekt Jon* by Nicholas Tochka
Vopli Vidopliassova's *Tantsi* by Maria Sonevytsky
Édith Piaf's *Recital 1961* by David Looseley

Naná Vasconcelos's *Saudades*

Daniel B. Sharp

Series Editor: Jason Stanyek

BLOOMSBURY ACADEMIC
NEW YORK • LONDON • OXFORD • NEW DELHI • SYDNEY

BLOOMSBURY ACADEMIC
Bloomsbury Publishing Inc
1385 Broadway, New York, NY 10018, USA
50 Bedford Square, London, WC1B 3DP, UK
29 Earlsfort Terrace, Dublin 2, Ireland

BLOOMSBURY, BLOOMSBURY ACADEMIC and the Diana
logo are trademarks of Bloomsbury Publishing Plc

First published in the United States of America 2021
Reprinted 2025

Copyright © Daniel B. Sharp, 2021

For legal purposes the Acknowledgments on p. x constitute
an extension of this copyright page.

All rights reserved. No part of this publication may be reproduced or
transmitted in any form or by any means, electronic or mechanical, including
photocopying, recording, or any information storage or retrieval system,
without prior permission in writing from the publishers.

Bloomsbury Publishing Inc does not have any control over, or responsibility for,
any third-party websites referred to or in this book. All internet addresses given
in this book were correct at the time of going to press. The author and
publisher regret any inconvenience caused if addresses have changed or sites
have ceased to exist, but can accept no responsibility for any such changes.

Whilst every effort has been made to locate copyright holders, the publishers
would be grateful to hear from any person(s) not here acknowledged.

Library of Congress Cataloging-in-Publication Data
Names: Sharp, Daniel B., author.
Title: Saudades / Daniel B. Sharp.
Description: New York : Bloomsbury Academic, 2021. | Series: 33 1/3 Brazil |
Includes bibliographical references and index. |
Identifiers: LCCN 2021022813 (print) | LCCN 2021022814 (ebook) |
ISBN 9781501345715 (hardback) | ISBN 9781501345708 (paperback) |
ISBN 9781501345722 (epub) | ISBN 9781501345739 (pdf) |
ISBN 9781501345746
Subjects: LCSH: Vasconcelos, Naná | Percussionists–Brazil–Biography. |
Popular music–Brazil–History and criticism. | Berimbau. |
Vasconcelos, Naná. Saudades.
Classification: LCC ML419.V238 S53 2021 (print) | LCC ML419.V238 (ebook) |
DDC 786.8092—dc23
LC record available at https://lccn.loc.gov/2021022813
LC ebook record available at https://lccn.loc.gov/2021022814

ISBN: HB: 978-1-5013-4571-5
       PB: 978-1-5013-4570-8
       ePDF: 978-1-5013-4573-9
       eBook: 978-1-5013-4572-2

Typeset by RefineCatch Limited, Bungay, Suffolk
Printed and bound in the United States of America

To find out more about our authors and books
visit www.bloomsbury.com and sign up for our newsletters.

Contents

List of Figures ix
Acknowledgments x

Introduction 1

1 **From Bossa to Tropicália: Naná in Recife** 27

2 **Dictatorship and Counterculture: Naná in Rio de Janeiro** 47

3 **The Enchanting and Revolutionary Berimbau: Naná and Glauber Rocha in New York City** 59

4 **Naná and Don Cherry** 71

Interlude: Edition of Contemporary Music Records (ECM) 89

Interlude: Creative Music Studio (CMS) 95

5 **Naná and Egberto Gismonti** 99

6 **Utopia, Caricature, Satire, and Therapy: Naná in France** 113

Interlude: Naná's Place Within the *Fourth World* 129

7 Race, Primitivism, and Counterculture 135

8 Voice, Body, Rhythm, and Special Effects 149

9 *Saudades* and Saudades 169

Epilogue: After *Saudades* 195

Notes 211
List of Interviews 227
Audio, and Film, TV, and Video 229
References 235
Index 247

Figures

0.1 Photo of Naná Vasconcelos playing berimbau. Courtesy of Teca Calazans. 2

1.1 Naná Vasconcelos with Trio Nordeste and Edy Star, 1968. 42

4.1 Don Cherry and Naná Vasconcelos. Photo by Dominique Fradin. 72

4.2 Don Cherry and Naná Vasconcelos at the 1972 Chateauvallon jazz festival during the years of the Organic Music Theatre. Photo by Guy Le Querrec/ Magnum Photos. 81

4.3 ECM Records promotional photo for Codona: Don Cherry, Collin Walcott, and Naná Vasconcelos. Photo by Roberto Masotti. Courtesy of ECM Records. 84

5.1 Naná Vasconcelos and Egberto Gismonti. Courtesy of Roberto Masotti. 100

7.1 Naná Vasconcelos, Paris, August 1976. © Alécio de Andrade, ADAGP, Paris 2021. 136

8.1 From left to right: Naná Vasconcelos, Manfred Eicher, Pat Metheny, and Jan Erik Kongshaug. Photo by Deborah Feingold. 155

8.2 *Saudades* back cover detail of Naná playing berimbau and tabla. Photos by Roberto Masotti. Courtesy of ECM Records. 164

Acknowledgments

Let me start by saying *muito obrigado* to Naná's widow Patrícia Vasconcelos for supporting this project, and for her tireless work making sure that the world is aware of Naná's legacy.

When I contacted Naná's collaborators, friends, and family out of the blue, I never expected that nearly everyone I approached would be willing to talk to me about his life and work. Thank you for your openness and generosity—this book comes alive because of your words: Arto Lindsay, Egberto Gismonti, Merrie Robin Monroe, Melvin Gibbs, Teca Calazans (that scrapbook is an incredible resource!), Geraldo Azevedo, Helder Aragão, Renato L, Cyro Baptista, Joyce Moreno, Fabiano Canosa, Pat Dillett, Pablo Lopes, Ricardo "Bolo" Bolognini, Vincent Segal, Adam Rudolph, Rev. Dwight Andrews, Nelson Angelo, Julie Fraad, Vinicius Cantuaria, Sergio Cassiano, Marcelino Buru, Janet Grice, Richard Bear Graham, and Jon Appleton. And thank you to N. Scott Robinson and Greg Beyer for asking Naná such insightful questions so that his own words live on in print.

Thank you to Carlos Sandroni not just for your support and mentorship through the years and your key insights on the manuscript, but also for your hospitality in Recife and Paris.

Thanks to Jason Stanyek, Justin Patch, Michael O'Brien, Chris Dunn, Joel Dinerstein, Schuyler Wheldon, Micheliny Verunschk, Rose Mary Gomes de Souza, Sonia Gaind, and Ryan McCormack for your thoughtful comments as I finished and revised the manuscript. I would also like to acknowledge Matt Sakakeeny,

Jane Mathieu, Ana Sánchez-Rojo, Courtney Bryan, Rebecca Atencio, Kyle Decoste, K Goldschmitt, Lauren Romaguera, Webb Haymaker, and Derek Gripper for your enthusiasm and support surrounding this project during the last few years. I have a deep debt of gratitude to John Siqveland, for sustaining my thinking about and playing music all these years.

Many thanks to Charlie Hayes and Michael Batt for your steady hands in working with me to run the Music Department at Tulane University while I finished this book. Thank you to Amy Medvick, Leticia Ferreira Nakatani, and Naomi Langlois for your hard work in transcribing interviews in English, Portuguese, and French (and, in one case, all three at once). I also wanted to acknowledge the insightful comments and copy-edits of my Spring 2021 Latin American Popular Music seminar. And thank you to Leah Babb-Rosenfeld, Rachel Moore, Louise Dugdale, R.I.M. El-Eini, Merv Honeywood and the rest of the team at Bloomsbury Publishing.

Many thanks to Justin Wolfe for starting the Social Distance Writing Group, meeting on Zoom to write every weekday morning. Julie Velasquez Runk, Sharina Maillo-Pozo, Beth Manley, Linda Kerber, Edie Wolfe, Rosanne Adderley, Alexandra and Tom Piñeros Shields, Ben Chappell, Robin Visser, Avi Chomsky, Elysa Hammond, Nadia Yaqub, Kristen McCleary, Karissa Haugeberg, Robin Visser, Emma Banks, and Nina Dayton. Your morning camaraderie made the pandemic more bearable. I would never have made my pre-pandemic deadline for this book without you all.

Thank you to my family: first, to Laura Wolford, not just for careful copy-editing but also, well, everything and everything. And Arthur and Elio, too. Arthur (age 9), thank you so much for working so hard proofing the last paragraph of the book, and to Mom, Dad, and Kris for being so supportive.

This project was generously funded by Tulane University, in particular the School of Liberal Arts Lurcy Grant, a Carol Lavin Bernick faculty grant, and faculty research-funding from the Stone Center for Latin American and Caribbean Studies. Many thanks to Brian Edwards, Tom Reese, and Carole Haber.

Introduction

eita velho de ouvido atento ao tempo
    damn, this guy really hears time
                    YouTube comment about Naná[1]

Ch ch ee ee ah ah ah ah. There is a recurring detail in the extensive discography of Afro-Brazilian percussionist Naná Vasconcelos that illuminates his sense of time. In my notes, I named it "parallax," because, through it, Naná establishes a three-dimensional stereo field for his sounds to move within. The parallax gesture doesn't follow a steady metronomic pulse. When Naná plays it on berimbau—a one-stringed musical bow with a gourd resonator—it resembles the feeling of an archer pulling an arrow back onto a bow (Figure Intro.1). As he plays, he reinforces the sounds of the berimbau string with his voice. *Ch ch ee ee ah ah ah ah.* Time stretches as the tempo downshifts from fast to slow. The pitch of the string plots a U-shaped curve, starting a bit higher, before going slightly lower, and then venturing higher again. Naná leans into the microphone and then out again, so that the curve of pitches matches the curve in how loud or soft the berimbau sounds. As he does this, he sways slightly between the left and right channels, placing the instrument within the stereo field. And by moving the open end of the gourd resonator toward his stomach and away from it, he creates a filter that adds to the sonic illusion that an object is moving toward and then away from the listener and into the distance.

Figure 0.1 *Photo of Naná Vasconcelos playing berimbau. Courtesy of Teca Calazans.*

The parallax gesture establishes that Naná's time breathes and stretches. He doesn't need to be tied down to an unforgiving click track in the recording studio. He assures the listener that he is not afraid to include silence in his tracks, using it as the sonic equivalent of negative space in visual art. He asserts that percussion instruments are not merely timekeepers, but timbral and melodic instruments in their own right. And by approximating the doppler effect, he establishes a stereo field that doesn't only span left and right, but also near and far, with a perceived vertical axis as well. In the many tracks where he uses the parallax gesture to invoke an outdoor environment, it has the added effect of simulating and stimulating the "causal listening"[2] of a person using sound to determine whether an insect whizzed past or a rattlesnake slithered by them through the grass.

A Chano Determined to be His Own Dizzy

Naná was a Chano Pozo determined to be his own Dizzy Gillespie. The parallel I see between the two percussionists is that they were both experts in Black musics from elsewhere in the Americas before significantly contributing to jazz. Like Naná, before moving to New York City, Chano Pozo was an accomplished percussionist, with a background in both ecstatic religious contexts and dance bands. Chano had enjoyed an illustrious career in Cuba before moving to Manhattan and teaming up with jazz trumpeter Dizzy Gillespie. The Afro-Cuban jazz that they created together—cubop—transformed the form and the rhythmic foundation of modern jazz. Chano and Dizzy set several precedents for subsequent collaborations in jazz, bringing together distinct Afrological musical practices, including "the insertion of nonjazz repertoires into jazz" and "the accommodation of instruments not typically found in jazz ensembles."[3]

Naná followed a parallel path, moving from Brazil to New York City and Paris, a generation later. His work drew upon Chano and Dizzy's precedents, while pursuing his own path, loathe to stay too long in someone else's project. His resulting career calls into question commonly understood boundaries between jazz, Western art music,[4] traditional music, the avant-garde, and the then emerging category of world music. Naná contributed to an astonishing number of music scenes on three continents: post-bossa nova MPB (música popular brasileira) and Tropicália in 1960s Brazil; music in Paris in the 1970s; European jazz, as the most sought-after percussionist on ECM (Edition of Contemporary Music) records during the label's fertile mid-1970s to mid-1980s period; post-punk New York in the late 1970s–80s; the community of musicians involved in the Creative Music Studio in upstate New York during that same time; and Recife, Brazil's innovative mangue beat scene in the 1990s and early 2000s.

In this book, I center Naná's 1979 record *Saudades* on ECM in an effort to trace how he accumulated extended techniques and navigated umpteen musical genre boundaries on the way to showcase his expansive vision. Throughout, two parallel shifts—one technological and the other sociopolitical—accompany his story. Between 1964 and 1979, Naná established himself on three continents just as the advent of hi-fi, stereo, headphones, electronic instruments, and multitrack recording deeply transformed musical production. And as Naná experimented with sound amidst these technological shifts, fundamental geopolitical shifts were also underway. As many African, Caribbean, and Asian nations fought for and won their long-overdue independence from European colonial powers, critical postcolonial perspectives from the global South were becoming more audible in Europe and North America. In the midst of all of this, Naná worked to counter dehumanizing, hierarchical notions of the primitive and the civilized through his music.[5]

There is a specific recording of Naná's, made a few years before *Saudades*, that is particularly illustrative of this counterargument. It provides a glimpse into his life, his artistic vision, and his priorities, even though the actual recorded sounds remain lost. While living in Paris, sometime between 1974 and 1976, Naná received a commission from the French Ministry of Culture to compose the music for a filmstrip on the influence of African art on Cubism, consisting of a series of photographs with music and narration. The project placed him, an Afro-Brazilian musician, in a mediating role between African and European visual art at a 1970s moment when the early-twentieth-century notion of the primitive as inspiration for modern art was being critically reassessed. He traveled to the Royal Museum for Central Africa in Tervuren, Belgium, and spent time comparing the African masks with Picasso's cubist paintings. Right there in the museum, he took out his berimbau and registered his vibrating musical response to this resemblance and its implications. When he returned home to Paris after a long day, his then wife Merrie Robin Monroe told me, his inspiration was electric:

> Naná arrived really late. He saw those images and the music just flowed out of him. He would go to the bathroom at night—tiny little bathroom. He had a tape recorder in there, and would sit in the bathroom and do the recordings. It just came out, and it is some of the basis of his most popular work, it's so exquisitely beautiful.

Despite Merrie's and my best efforts, unfortunately, neither of us have yet been able to locate this recording. Being the soundtrack to an educational filmstrip, its humble format hastened its obscurity. In the absence of the recorded sounds, I can only imagine what is found in that late-night bathroom recording session that later made it into future projects.

The fact that Naná was so energized by the assignment makes sense, however, as it brought together several of his longstanding concerns. Throughout his life, Naná played with the boundaries between European and African creative forms, explored the relationship between the sonic and the visual, and worked to dismantle the dishonest division in the arts between what is considered erudite and what is considered primitive. For Naná, accomplishing this goal meant entering and leaving his mark within elite spaces. Sounding his artistic response within a hushed, hallowed European museum space represented one such fulfillment of this aspiration. The way Merrie describes it, the lost recording represents a kind of key to understanding Naná's creative output in the years to come, the musical ideas found within serving as seeds for subsequent recording projects such as *Saudades*.[6]

The album *Saudades* most notably centers around tracks featuring berimbau accompanied by orchestra. Naná was pleased that through the album, he was able to bring the Afro-Brazilian musical bow "front and center"[7] as a solo instrument. He recorded it in March 1979 at Tonstudio Bauer, one of ECM's principal studios in Ludwigsburg, Germany, just outside of Stuttgart. The strings of the Radio Symphony Stuttgart accompanied him for the session, conducted by Mladen Gutesha, who had previously worked as an arranger for jazz icons such as Miles Davis, Keith Jarrett, and Benny Goodman. Naná's longtime collaborator and fellow ECM recording artist Egberto Gismonti was also pivotal to the project and present at the recording session, playing guitar on a duet with Naná on the track "Cego Aderaldo." Bridging oral and written musical practices, Naná sang melodies to Egberto for several nights on the tour bus as they traveled throughout Europe from one gig to the next. Egberto would, in turn, write down Naná's melodies so that they could become the string arrangements for the album.

Saudades is a word in Portuguese that apprehends loss and bittersweet longing. On the album, Naná reflects on Brazil from afar. The Brazil heard on *Saudades* is not just a Brazil remembered firsthand that he had left seven years before. It is also the Brazil covered on the international news at the time. By painting with sound in an idiosyncratic, personal, nearly wordless fashion—this isn't a straightforward protest record, by any means—Naná powerfully evokes scenes of a Brazil fifteen years into a military dictatorship, blindered to issues of racial justice, and moving ahead with massive hydroelectric projects, creating the world's largest artificial lakes and displacing whole towns of people. On *Saudades*, Naná expresses what Svetlana Boym refers to as "reflective nostalgia," a longing with room to be at the same time "homesick and sick of home."[8]

Naná's prominence as a Brazilian percussionist in jazz during the last half century is rivaled only by Airto Moreira, who played with Miles Davis, Return to Forever, Hermeto Pascoal, and Flora Purim. The annual Critics' Poll of the jazz magazine *Down Beat* voted Naná best percussionist nine years running (1983–91). He won eight Grammy awards, and his home city of Recife commissioned a statue of him atop a pedestal of maracatu drums, prominently displayed in the state capital's historic district (and recently donned with a mask to update it for the COVID-19 pandemic). Nonetheless, outside of the city of Recife—where he is hailed as a local hero—he is a highly respected musicians' musician, not a household name. I mention this not to minimize his accomplishments, but rather to point to the paradoxical role of percussionists and drummers in setting the pace and leading the proceedings while often staying in the back or on the side of the stage.

So, even with Naná's overflowing accomplishments in mind, this book shares the aims of the documentary film *20 Feet from Stardom* that centers Black backup singers such as Merry Clayton and Darlene Love whose voices are recognizable from pop hit after pop hit, but whose names and faces remain largely obscured. Naná's story is the story of a restless percussionist who refused to resign himself to being an anonymous timekeeper. This refusal spurred him to rethink the accompanying role of the percussionist and center himself within the stereo field, literally and metaphorically. Out for sushi in New York City with Arto Lindsay and Caetano Veloso, Naná once exclaimed, with a lot of emotion, that he just didn't want to do "xique xique xique" for big pop stars anymore, imitating with frustration the sound of simply keeping time with a shaker. He insisted on following his own vision.

An alteration Naná made to his signature berimbau signaled this desire to take the instrument beyond its traditional setting. The one-stringed Afro-Brazilian berimbau looks like the bow from a bow and arrow, with a gourd resonator attached. Customarily, it is strung with the wire found within a car tire, in a resourceful act of improvisation born of necessity. When Naná set out to build his own, however, he strung it instead with a single grand piano string. As his long career progressed, he succeeded in living his dream to play concert halls throughout the world with just one string.

A Life Spent Bridging Artos and Pats

Again and again, Naná paid no mind to feuds between communities of fans, crossing between musical genres and playing with musicians on both sides of entrenched divides. When he was living in New York City in the early 1980s, not long after the release of *Saudades*, even a seemingly innocent invitation to two fellow musicians to watch a basketball game on TV at his apartment illustrates this disregard. You see, Naná decided not to tell Arto Lindsay that he had invited Pat Metheny over to watch the game. And he didn't tell Pat Metheny that Arto Lindsay would be there, too. Arto laughs about it now, but remembered Naná's prank to have led to quite an awkward night.

I can think of no two guitarists working at the time as antithetical in their artistic vision and approach to the instrument as Pat Metheny and Arto Lindsay. It is a testament to Naná's musicality that he made major contributions to the work of both. The irreverent noise of Arto's anti-genre known as "no wave" rejected not just the pomp surrounding the 1970s guitar hero, but the notion that guitars should produce stable pitches and harmonies at all. Instead, Arto concentrated on extracting timbres and rhythms from his detuned Danelectro. It was as if he took the moment in Jimi Hendrix's Star-Spangled Banner where Jimi paints with noise the rockets' red glare and the bombs bursting in air, and used that as the foundation for his playing, rather than considering it merely a sound effect. At that moment in New York City, when the post-punk music and visual art underground scenes were bursting at the seams, Arto—and others, such as Glenn Branca, Rhys Chatham, and Sonny Sharrock—had no interest in playing guitar in a way that at all resembled older, more established ways of playing it. While Arto shrugs that he was "blithely unconcerned" with more by-the-book players, I imagine to many fans the squawks and scritches of Arto's guitar noise mocked the seriousness of musicians like Pat Metheny.

While Arto Lindsay was provoking audiences at the Squat Theater Nightclub, a storefront on 23rd Street, Pat Metheny was filling up stadiums all over the United States and Europe with his paintings with sound. But while Arto's sonic paintings were irreverent Never Mind the Jackson Pollocks, Pat was busy touching up meticulous and highly orchestrated musical landscapes of the North American heartland on electric and acoustic steel-string guitar. One of the bestselling artists on ECM records, Metheny bridges US and European jazz. He takes his blending of jazz and rock very seriously, honing his guitar tones to foreground the pitches that he could produce with the speed and control befitting a prodigy trained in jazz performance at the University of North Texas. The chasm in fan reception between Arto's no wave and Pat's pastoral jazz ran deep—it is safe to say that to many fans of Metheny, Arto's sounds simply wouldn't be heard as music because, in their view, he never learned to play his instrument properly. And to many of Arto's fans of no wave, Pat's sounds were at best made for accompanying an elevator ride or waiting on hold. Naná played with both Arto and Pat, as he played with many Artos and many Pats throughout his five-decade career.

Naná was born Juvenal de Holanda Vasconcelos in 1944 in Pernambuco, Brazil, and came of age in the late 1950s–early 1960s. In his teens and early 20s, he played cymbals in the municipal symphonic band, participated in left-wing activist music theater and played in his father's Latin big band, playing mambos, cha-cha-chas, and boleros (Chapter 1). In Rio de Janeiro during a repressive dictatorship and the countercultural efflorescence alongside it, Naná met a wide range of musicians, leading to touring with militant folksinger Geraldo Vandré and also to recording with Tropicalist rock band Os Mutantes and singer Gal Costa even though Vandré and the Tropicalists didn't see eye to eye (Chapter 2). Granted, audiences often police musical taste more closely than the musicians themselves, and drummers and percussionists can often move from project to project and style to style more easily than other musicians. But I argue here in this book, by tracing the first phases of Naná's career, that he was an extraordinary case in this regard. The more I learned about Naná, the more I was intrigued by his ability to make his mark within such a wide variety of scenes and scenarios.

Here is a glimpse of his range: Naná recorded the conga part that kicks off the late 1960s Os Mutantes Tropicália era classic "Ando Meio Desligado."[9] He plays tabla on the striking Clementina de Jesus track "Taratá." He appeared with Arto Lindsay and Peter Scherer alongside experimental mainstays Sonic Youth and John Zorn in a documentary about New York City in the 1980s.[10] He convinced Milton Nascimento to release the 1973 album *Milagre dos Peixes* with wordless vocals replacing the original vocal tracks after the Brazilian military dictatorship censored the lyrics for all but three of the eleven songs.[11] He contributed to Paul Simon's 1990 album *The Rhythm of the Saints*, but dodged Simon's calls trying to get him to join the album's tour.[12] He acted in and played the on-screen soundtrack for the 1976 French New Wave film *Les Naufragés de l'île de La Tortue* set on a boat, almost certainly inspiring Seu Jorge's character in Wes Anderson's 2004 film *The Life Aquatic with Steve Zissou*.[13] He toured Europe in the early 1980s with The Magnificent Force breakdance crew, including Mr. Wiggles, an early popularizer of popping and locking. In 2004, he recorded with Itamar Assumpção the original version of the song "Fim de Festa" that Brazilian soul singer Liniker memorably interprets.[14]

With the wealth of experiences that Naná had on several continents in mind, it pains me that I have to limit my focus here. What about when Naná became the darling of a group of Hell's Angels that were Pat Metheny's security detail by falsely claiming to have trashed a hotel room in order to cover for the notorious biker gang? Or that time when Frank Zappa invited him up on stage unplanned, and after his berimbau solo left the audience slack-jawed, he met John Lennon in the green room afterward, but couldn't say anything to him because of the language barrier? The format of the 33 1/3 series forces me to abandon any attempt to chronicle Naná's entire fifty-plus-years career. Instead, I've anchored the text in the fifteen years leading up to the recording of *Saudades*, tracing a genealogy of his musical innovations during 1960s and 1970s, as he made significant contributions to music scenes in Recife, Rio de Janeiro, Manhattan, Paris, and throughout Europe.

Saudades proves an able anchor for this task, because it showcases how Naná developed musically between 1964 and 1979. It was during this time that he became a virtuoso on the berimbau, developing several extended techniques on the instrument; he mastered a long list of standard and homemade percussion instruments, focusing as much on melody and timbre as he did on rhythm and groove; he developed a cinematic sense of the stereo field, learning to paint with sound, and merging music with Foley artistry (cinematic sound effects);[15] he developed a new relationship between percussion and voice, where wordless vocalizing reinforced percussion sounds and invoked chattering crowds; and he found stylistic affinities between a broad range of African and Afro-diasporic styles, Indigenous Brazilian percussion, and South Asian percussion styles.

This book is a chronicle of how Naná accumulated the elements heard in *Saudades*. Telling this story sews together several scenes, cities, musical genres, and continents. I seek out connections between the sounds he made, the places he lived, the people he worked with, and the scenes and institutions he participated in. Here are the pins stuck in the map of Naná's travels: he began his career in Olinda and Recife, Pernambuco, Brazil. In 1967, after a brief stint in Portugal, he lived and worked in Rio de Janeiro for around three years. Not long after spending a couple of months in Mexico City during the 1970 World Cup gigging with Luis Eça y La Sagrada Família, a short-lived big band with doomed crossover dreams, he moved to New York City in early 1971. He lived less than a year in New York City before moving to Paris, and then back to Rio de Janeiro, and then to Paris again, where he spent five years between 1973 and 1978, visiting Don Cherry often in Sweden, and touring throughout Europe. Near the end of 1978, he moved back to New York City, where he thrived for over twenty years before moving back to Recife in 1998, where he was active until the end of his life in 2016.

In each of these places, Naná accumulated an extended network of friends, family, and fellow musicians. Several chapters focus on how his working relationships helped shape his vision and his skills. It was in Europe, not Brazil, that Naná and fellow Brazilian Egberto Gismonti discovered an explosive and complementary musical chemistry that would lead them to record and perform together off and on for decades (Chapter 5). Naná points to Don Cherry as a "walking conservatory" that opened his head to the music of the world. Don and Naná formed a similarly lasting bond that led to recordings and performances throughout Europe, the United States, and elsewhere (Chapter 4). Naná also had an important connection with filmmaker Glauber Rocha, with whom he lived in a New York warehouse loft in 1971, a pivotal time in the development of his berimbau playing (Chapter 3).

Certain friends Naná knew from previous cities reappear later, providing a throughline to his story. Teca Calazans and Geraldo Azevedo left Recife before Naná did, sending him letters to convince him to join them in Rio de Janeiro. Teca then met up with Naná a few years later in Paris and they recorded and toured in Europe. Joyce Moreno sang with Naná in Rio and Mexico City, and then recorded with him again years later in Paris. Arto Lindsay, his future apartment mate and collaborator through much of the 1980s and 1990s, grew up in Pernambuco, Brazil. They first met when Naná wandered into the rehearsal of a teenaged Arto's garage band and blew everyone away by singing Hendrix's "Purple Haze" and playing it on the drums at the same time. Naná's first wife Merrie Robin Monroe also proved pivotal in connecting the dots of his timeline and travels, since she met him during his first time living in Paris, went with him back to Rio, back to Paris, and then to New York City.

In between the full chapters, I've decided to insert a few shorter passages that clarify the importance of key institutions and recordings for understanding Naná's musical path. Two such interludes appear between Chapters 4 and 5, outlining the Edition of Contemporary Music (ECM) record label and the Creative Music Studio (CMS) in Woodstock, New York. Naná's participation in both ECM and CMS positioned him within a community of musicians from the jazz world and beyond, leading to him forming projects and exchanging ideas and techniques.

Chapter 6 traces Naná's path in France, where he thrived, building an ever-expanding network of musicians and friends, at the same time that French cultural gatekeepers drew him into projects that indexed shifts in notions of the primitive. This theme of Naná's efforts to rethink and reorder the primitive and the civilized continues in an interlude focusing on his participation in Jon Hassell and Brian Eno's speculative album *Fourth World, Vol. 1: Possible Musics*. Chapter 7 explores how

Naná's performances call for listeners to question well-worn delineations of the proper relative importance of pitch and harmony versus rhythm and timbre that date back to the nineteenth-century origins of European musicology.

In Chapter 8, I listen closely to the sounds he made, and take stock of his vocabulary of vocal and instrumental techniques, as well as his process in the recording studio. This inventory sets up the close reading in Chapter 9 of particular details heard on the *Saudades* record proper. I am guided here in telling the story of the record by the narration of Egberto Gismonti, the only person I was able to speak to who was directly involved in the recording. The book closes with the Epilogue: After *Saudades*, in which I survey a few highlights of Naná's illustrious post-*Saudades* career in the 1980s–2010s.

Figuring out why you, the reader, picked up this book, is made all the more difficult by the multiple entry points of Naná's over 35 records of his own, over 250 where he participated in someone else's project, and numerous documentary and feature film soundtracks. Those of you who know Naná because of his work with Milton Nascimento will have heard a different side of Naná's playing than those of you who know Naná because of his collaborations with Egberto Gismonti, Don Cherry, Gato Barbieri, or Pat Metheny. And all of these jazz or jazz-adjacent projects contrast Naná's playing in the pop and experimental music realms with Arto Lindsay, Laurie Anderson, Brian Eno, Jon Hassell, Talking Heads, and so many others. And perhaps some of you are interested in learning more about Naná because of a connection to Olinda and Recife, Pernambuco, Brazil, where he grew up. From his return in the late 1990s, up until his death in 2016, Naná became a mentor to younger musicians in the innovative mangue beat music scene, and one of the most important figures in Recife's Carnaval celebration. Throughout the 2000s and into the 2010s, Naná opened carnaval, conducting a massive event bringing together hundreds of participants from the city's maracatu nação groups, who commemorate the coronation of a slave king and queen through thunderous drumming and dancing. If you are reading because of a more general interest in Brazilian music, or simply an interest in Brazil, I am keeping you in mind as well while I write.

I first heard Naná's music while writing about the music scene in Recife, Pernambuco, starting in 1999. I am from the United States, live in New Orleans, and coincidentally look like Naná's white Codona bandmate Collin Walcott. Despite not being from Northeast Brazil, I have spent several years living, working, and studying there off and on, starting in 1994. During much of that time, I was researching my first book about the music scene in Arcoverde, three hours inland from the coast, on the edge of the desert sertão backlands.[16] Arcoverde is the hometown of members of Cordel do Fogo Encantado, a band with an earthshattering live show, staging an apocalyptic take on the region's folklore. Naná produced Cordel's debut record and joined them on their first tour.

At the time, in 1999, Naná had just moved back home to Recife. In the next few years, he became a venerated elder to the new scene, playing with Cordel, as well as other artists such as DJ Dolores and Maciel Salu. Naná brought his distinctive palette of percussion and voice to the mangue beat framework where local Afro-Pernambucan styles maracatu, coco, and ciranda coexist with Public Enemy-era hip-hop, Sepultura-style metal, and punk rock.

Three months after Naná passed away in 2016, I decided to start this research after electronic music producer Helder Aragão (aka DJ Dolores) told stories from Naná's long life late into the night. I was never able to speak with Naná. Our paths had never directly crossed, despite my traveling to Brazil to speak with musicians nearly every year when I didn't have teaching obligations back in New Orleans.

The unexpected path of one of Naná's instruments led me to consider the risks and rewards of writing a book like this. In an art gallery in Mexico in 2012, an unplayable replica of one of Naná's homemade seed-pod shakers sat atop an unpainted plywood bookshelf. The white plastic copy of the shaker had been created on a 3D printer. The original shaker had fallen into Arto Lindsay's possession when he cleaned out their rehearsal space. Perhaps Naná wasn't sure, at the time, that he would be moving back to Recife for good. The replica of the shaker was part of artist Rikrit Tiravanija's recreation of Arto Lindsay's Manhattan apartment as an art installation, down to the detail of readable and listenable copies of 2,000 entire books and 2,000 CDs from his bookshelf.

Writing this kind of book risks taking a once very much alive figure and creating a replica of them, like Tiravanija's replacement of Naná's shaker's seed pods that rattle independently with an inert plastic version that resembles the actual instrument from a distance but doesn't feel or sound like the original. Tiravanija waved away a concern with the impossibility of making an exact replica by inviting Arto Lindsay to "inhabit and activate" his art installation that he considered both a portrait and a collaboration. Arto set up his home studio recording equipment in the installation and worked on music there for a few days. At the opening, Arto mingled with the gallery visitors, and actual food simmered in a pot on the stove for everyone to eat.

Although I can't invite Naná to participate like Rikrit did with Arto, it is my hope that the oral histories of his friends and fellow musicians similarly inhabit and activate this book, so that the smells of Naná's famous *bacalhau* waft in from the kitchen, and squirrels skitter in and out of the open window of his New York City apartment. And whenever someone calls and Naná's not home, the answering-machine cassette plays that catchy "Leave a message" melody that he recorded. Even twenty years after leaving New York City, multiple people sang it for me as they recalled Naná.

Over the last four years, I have been able to sit down with over twenty-five of his collaborators and friends in Recife, Rio de Janeiro, New York, Paris, and on Zoom, including Arto Lindsay, Egberto Gismonti, Merrie Robin Monroe, Fabiano Canosa, Geraldo Azevedo, Teca Calazans, Joyce Moreno, Adam Rudolph, Ralph Towner, Melvin Gibbs, and many others, who were generously willing to share what they remember of Naná as I worked to piece together important moments in his story. In addition to these oral histories, Naná's own words on a wide range of topics can be found in decades of interviews published in newspapers, magazines, online sources, academic works, and on television. N. Scott Robinson's and Greg Beyer's thoughtful questions led Naná to speak more specifically and in depth than other published interviews I've found in the process of this research. Several direct quotes of Naná's found throughout this book come from their interviews.

He was Pretty Much Like His Music Sounded

I talked to bass player Melvin Gibbs in 2018 in a Williamsburg, Brooklyn, loft more reasonably sized than the cavernous warehouse space in the East Village where Naná worked out his berimbau chops in 1971. Melvin, who recorded with Naná on several of Arto Lindsay's albums in the 1980s and 1990s, is one of the few working musicians who are longtime residents still somehow eking out an existence in a Williamsburg now transformed by capital, with sky-high rents. A veteran performer, Melvin was a cofounder of the Black Rock Coalition. In addition to playing with Arto and Naná, he has performed and/or recorded with his band Harriet Tubman, Henry Rollins Band, Ronald Shannon Jackson, Defunkt, Marisa Monte, Caetano Veloso, and many others. Drawing on his experience touring and recording widely, Melvin is a conceptual theorist of Black music from throughout Africa and the African diaspora. The conversation ranged from far-reaching questions of culture and politics surrounding world music, to subtle musical questions of time, groove, and feel. When I started writing later, I found myself returning to his insights again and again as I worked to make sense of Naná's music.

Melvin sees Naná and Don Cherry as "the original kind of world music guys, but in a different way than people thought of it." Listening to Naná's band Codona, which he found mind-blowing at the time in the early 1980s, was a combination of elements that was "respectful and forward moving, you know?" In 2018, with questions of cultural appropriation circulating as a prominent public conversation, he reflected that Codona's Collin, Don, and Naná "really had a respectful attitude towards what they were doing, yet they were able to move that thing forward in a way that made it really interesting for everybody involved." He pointed out how the berimbau was "a really respected folkloric, really deep instrument that couldn't be fucked with." It is an instrument associated with Afro-Brazilian cultural resistance and the neo-African martial art capoeira. Yet it was also "this kind of toy that people outside of that culture didn't really respect at all. And Naná took both aspects of that and raised it up to a whole other level. It's like he just made it a whole. An instrument like no other instrument."

Melvin went on to elaborate that Naná navigated the "spiritual aspect and the almost trash aspect of what he was doing" in a way that "makes it even more genius." By "trash aspect," Melvin meant that Naná accomplished what he did within what Melvin wryly called Brazil's "funny relationship to its African culture." He clarified that he considered Naná's accomplishments in a context where Afro-Brazilian music and culture are exploited through their packaging as a prized export and a tourist draw while an entrenched regime of racial terror continues unabated toward the Afro-Brazilians making the music being celebrated. Melvin acknowledged how, even amidst the celebration of Afro-Brazilian music, hierarchies endure that shape perceptions of how serious different musical cultures are generally believed to be. When Naná bridged "high art music versus a kind of folk music," he was navigating those hierarchies of prestige.

Above and beyond Naná's impeccable chops, he also possessed:

> a certain mastery in politics. He did know how to be at the right place at the right time. With that ability, combined with the weight of the life he had lived, he was able to open a certain set of doors for himself that other people would not have been able to. Because the set of experiences he had—you can't buy those experiences. And then it just becomes a question of finding the people that respect your experiences.

Melvin sees being a "connector" as one of Naná's talents. "In the context of that time ... being able to make that connection between the real kind of gut level, kind of street folkloric thing, with the high art thing ... there are contexts where that would've been very compelling. He went the world around finding these contexts." And as a person, he added, "he was pretty much the way his music sounded. He was a really sweet guy, and had a really great sense of humor; I used to joke with him a lot."

Part of my impulse to trace Naná's history between 1964 and 1979 is that I see the current moment (2021) as a productive time to revisit the prehistory of world music and new age music as genre categories. Naná played on *Fourth World, Vol. 1: Possible Musics* by Jon Hassell and Brian Eno, a 1980 album that engages in a kind of speculative fiction, collapsing the categories of ethnic/folk, commercial popular, and classical music. Assessing the record's legacy forty years later, Hassell distanced himself from the Fourth World genre label he created with the quip, "I don't want to join in the herd trampling through the campsites where I delicately and respectfully visited 15 or 20 years ago."[17] But do we take Jon Hassell on his word that he was the respectful one, and others are the ones not following the campsite rule? As anthropologist Steven Feld puts it, "Everyone—no matter how exoticizing, how patronizing, how romanticizing, how essentializing in their rhetoric or packaging—declares their fundamental respect, even deep affection for the original music and its makers."[18]

The more I learned about the music of people like Naná and Don Cherry, for example, the more it struck me that placing their genre-defying work retroactively in the dusty, discarded bin of 1980s new age or world music wasn't warranted, and that their work deserved a careful listen that reconsidered previous criticisms. I came to believe that dismissing music like the records that Naná and Don Cherry made was in part a result of the new age campsite tramplers that came after them, with their jungle sounds and ambient tracks made for deeply mourning the rainforest, relaxing mindfully, and commodifying religion, somehow all at once. After delving into Naná's and Don's journeys, their stories open up, linking the prehistory of world music to the search for roots by Afro-descendants in the Americas, in a way that qualifies the universalist humanism that world music as a genre implies. More specifically, the question I asked myself was, when Naná evokes jungle sounds through carefully placed Foley artistry and percussion, is he simply engaging in yet another iteration of the Western pastoral mode that romantically longs for the time before industrialization? Or are his efforts better described as giving listeners a glimpse of alternate "acoustemologies," or ways of understanding the world through sound?[19]

The conceptual frame of the anthropocene (the current moment understood as a new human-centered geological epoch), contested though it may be among geologists, has proven productive within the humanities and the arts in considering the implications of human impact on the earth, especially during the last centuries since the industrial revolution. The existential threat of climate change, and the current COVID-19 pandemic that is ongoing as I write, compel me to take another look at what it meant for Naná to take a single string, a gourd, a wire, a stick, a wicker basket filled with dried beans and a stone, and to argue through his playing that these humble ingredients could lead to music as complex and sophisticated as the ARP synthesizers that were in vogue at the time.

Was Naná being exoticizing, patronizing, or romanticizing? Was he working within an appropriative Western frame, as Feld suggests when he criticizes Naná's use of Central African hindewhu flute-and-vocal technique out of context?[20] Was Naná merely offering a 1970s countercultural extension of 1950s hi-fi bachelor-pad exotica records? I don't hear him that way. By tracing a genealogy of the early trajectory of Naná's life and musical practice, I argue instead that through performance, Naná was working to reorder ideas of the primitive with an ear toward dismantling racialized hierarchies and their underlying deception about who is civilized and who is less so, who is fully human, and who is not quite fully human.

One of the first primary sources that jazz studies students often read is a 1918 anti-jazz editorial, "The Location of Jass," from the New Orleans *Times-Picayune* that makes clear the denigrated status of rhythm within Eurological notions of music. The screed spatializes the hierarchy of musical elements as a mansion with an "assembly hall of melody," the elevated "inner sanctuaries of harmony," and the relegated "basement hall of rhythm," where one is subject to the abject other through "the hum of the Indian dance ... the thumpty-tumpty of the [Black] banjo, and, in fact, the native dances of the world."[21] As musicologist Loren Kajikawa argues, "This hierarchical picture of music mirrored a hierarchy of human types with racialized bodies at the bottom and white people on top."[22]

Even half a century later, after jazz had become a major musical phenomenon of the twentieth century, Naná still faced this relegation of the percussionist when prominent publications referred to him as "jungle man." Echoes of the hierarchies laid out in "The Location of Jass" surfaced when I interviewed both Rev. Dwight Andrews and another major former collaborator during the same week. When Naná arrived in the recording studio to work with Rev. Andrews in 1979,

Andrews immediately recognized the possibilities of Naná's percussion. Rev. Andrews was thrilled, and made Naná a full partner on the record, setting up several microphones in the studio to account for Naná's movement as he played. The other musician in contrast, waved away anything that Naná did, other than timekeeping, as merely sound effects, insisting that these flourishes had nothing to do with the disciplined hard work of their classical training.

The Overton windows of ideas accepted as thinkable are quickly shifting on many fronts. Cannabis is becoming legalized more widely, and there is a thawing of restrictions on research into the potential therapeutic benefits of psychedelics such as LSD—the substance that Naná insisted helped him to expand his musical vision. During this moment of change, it makes sense to revisit the backlash against countercultural questioning during the 1980s Reagan/Thatcher years. Melvin defends Naná and Don this way:

> There's a dichotomy between what they call new age and actual seeking, and Don and Naná were actual seekers. They were musical seekers first. If new age didn't exist, Don and Naná still would have done exactly whatever they did. They weren't following a trend—a trend happened to happen simultaneously to the fact that they were alive. Not only were they seekers, they had a very specific vision. And yet it fell into the branding of new age, because they were literally trying to bring in the new age. I mean, Don lived in Sweden, you know? They were literally trying to get beyond these barriers that the culture had put on them as individuals and us as people. So, yeah, in a sense, people who wanted to see a new age would gravitate towards them, but they were beyond.[23]

Melvin's description of Naná's and Don's actual seeking resonates with musicologist Jason Stanyek's argument that by taking into account face-to-face relationships between individual artists and situating them within the broader concerns of a given time and place, "interculturalism can be more than just a projection of First World corporate fantasy, more than just imperial cultures dreaming themselves as beneficent and universal."[24]

1 From Bossa to Tropicália: Naná in Recife

The classic 1959 movie *Black Orpheus*, filmed in Rio de Janeiro and directed by French director Marcel Camus, introduced generations of viewers from all over the world to an alluring and exotic view of Brazil.[1] Set during Carnaval, it places the Greek myth of Orpheus and Euridice onto the hilltop *favelas*. Although the memorable music, lyrics, and screenplay were created by figures closely allied with bossa nova, such as Luis Bonfá, Tom Jobim, and Vinicius de Morais, the music is a bit too busy with filigreed melodies on guitar to be considered bossa nova proper. *Black Orpheus* succeeds, though, in setting the terms within which Naná began his career (the film's use of racialized structural poverty as an idyllic setting, notwithstanding). On the soundtrack, quiet proto-bossa nova featuring one voice and one guitar appears alongside raucous polyrhythmic Afro-Brazilian samba percussion. This contrast provides the tension within which much Brazilian popular music was made in the late 1950s to mid-1960s, when Naná came of age. Born in 1944, Naná was around 15 years old when the movie was released.

In 1967, when Naná recorded an EP with the golden-throated singer, Agostinho dos Santos, heard as the voice of Orpheus in the film, it was a few years past the apex of bossa nova's reign in Brazil and beyond. From the beginning of his career, Naná navigated musical terrain in which the strongly Afro-Brazilian sounds associated with the *morros* or *favelas* were filtered through and tempered by ways of assembling harmonies and melodies drawing from Western art music (Villa-Lobos, Debussy, and Chopin) and cool jazz (1950s Miles Davis and Chet Baker). The polyrhythms of samba, imbued with an aura of national-cultural authenticity, were understood to be modernized and made more sophisticated by the first generation of hip upper-middle-class, mostly white kids to live in high-rise apartment buildings built during an economic boom.

This "apartment building samba," as critic José Ramos Tinhorão dismissed bossa nova,[2] turned thunderous layers of parade percussion into a new sound with quiet and minimal drumming to better feature the whispered and still vocals and unpredictable, dense harmonies. It is this distinctive sound that broke through to establish a global presence to this day: a precise, asymmetrical, straighter-eighths feel to contrast jazz swing. Yet, bossa nova icon Tom Jobim fought in interviews for the genre not to become subsumed within jazz. He saw it, rather, as a parallel development using the same musical/cultural flows found throughout the Americas: the musics of the African diaspora, and mid-nineteenth- to early-twentieth-century Western art music.

By the time Naná was old enough to venture forth musically, away from his father's dance band of Latin rhythms where he kept time to mambos and cha-cha-chas on bongos painted "Na" and "Na," bossa nova was fraying. The years of the bossa nova republic, as a political scientist writing about the late 1950s administration of Juscelino Kubitschek put it, were years of economic optimism. Bossa nova served as a soundtrack to high economic growth, the construction of Brasilia, with its ultramodern mid-century architecture and Brazil's first World Cup soccer win. The middle class held out hope that Brazil was on the verge of entering the ranks of the wealthy countries, deceptively categorized at the time as the "First World." This hope proved to be illusory by early 1964, as rates of inflation grew, further destabilizing the already precarious left-leaning president João Goulart at the height of Cold War anti-communism. On 1 April 1964, the military orchestrated a coup that led to the violent repression and exile of many politicized musicians, as well as the censorship of their lyrics. Over three decades after a tangle of politicians, scholars and artists all with overlapping but distinct agendas raised Afro-Brazilian samba to the status of national popular music in the late 1920s and early 1930s,[3] Brazilian Popular Music (MPB) had become an elastic category stretched to include sounds both hushed and raucous, with varying emphases on rhythm, harmony, melody, and timbre. It had become a complex field, where sounds understood as raw, authentic, and of the people, coexisted with sounds understood as modern, sophisticated, and elite.

Within this complex field of Brazilian Popular Music, Brazil's racial geography and history of labor migration shape a story where different regions of the country are assigned different roles. Concentrations of Afro-Brazilians in the former slave ports and sugarcane-cultivation zones of the Northeast of the country, most notably Salvador, Bahia, and Naná's home cities of Olinda and Recife, Pernambuco, have led musical fieldworkers to treat the Northeast as a repository of folklore and tradition. In contrast, the industrialized Southeast of the country, most notably Rio de Janeiro, stands for the place where Afro-Brazilian musical systems mixed with European ways of music-making to create the quintessentially Brazilian modern samba. Despite the best efforts of scholars to tell a more complicated story,[4] the way the history of samba is popularly understood to this day is still one in which Rio in the

Southeast is centered, while the Northeast is relegated to serve essentially as the source of raw musical resources. The advent of bossa nova in the late 1950s, as Naná came of age, only cements this imagined geography further, as bossa nova treats samba as its raw materials to transform, just as Rio-based samba had considered northeastern samba de roda. That is to say that, even before Naná left Brazil, being an Afro-Brazilian from Olinda, Pernambuco, in the Northeast, one of the first areas that the Portuguese dominated the Indigenous peoples of Brazil, and one of the first areas where enslaved Africans were forcibly brought, positioned him to be received in Rio as a bearer of age-old traditions.

Naná could and did play the role of culture bearer that, as he traveled, marked him in many contexts, from Rio to Oslo. Despite the risk of being pigeonholed as a keeper of tradition and thus having his complexly modern, cosmopolitan sensibility erased, the role of culture bearer provided him the opportunity to carve a distinctive niche in music scenes throughout the world. But the role of culture bearer was also, in certain ways, a straitjacket that he impressively managed to escape from, again and again. And when he couldn't escape from it, he tried to use it to his advantage in order to tell his story through sound, as he does on *Saudades*.

Growing up, Naná had a certain proximity, through his uncle, to the polyrhythms played by several interlocking percussion parts—conga-like ingome drums, gourd shakers, and an iron bell—that usher in ecstatic states in dancing devotees at Xangô toques at the Casa de Xambá in Recife, religious events in which percussion plays an important role in facilitating the visits of West African deities into the bodies of the initiated, as Xangô members understand it. Xangô is a variant of the Neo-African Brazilian religion Candomblé, that draws significantly from West African Yoruba religious and musical practices. It made enough of an impression on him that the full title of the centerpiece track of his 1973 record *Africadeus* was "Africadeus (Concerto pra Mãe Bio),"[5] a dedication to a matriarch and religious leader of the Casa de Xambá. So, the label of culture bearer is not wrong, although there is little evidence that he actively practiced Xangô, at least as an adult. Naná later described his spiritual practice as a more personal mixture of beliefs with aspects of Buddhism and other religions—as was said about his longtime collaborator Don Cherry, he "believed in everything."[6] But, at the same time, from very early on, the notion that Naná is merely following the strictures of traditions that were handed to him is woefully inadequate. Still a preteen, Naná was not only exposed to the ingomes at the Casa de Xambá, but he was also playing in his father Pierre Vasconcelos's dance band of Latin American rhythms.

The band, which played mambos, boleros, and cha-cha-chas from Cuba and elsewhere in Spanish-speaking Latin America, featured secular, pop versions of the same sorts of interlocking polyrhythms played on drums, shakers, and iron bells heard in the religious Xangô context. Before he was even a teenager, in order to play professionally as a minor, he received special permission from the state to play at the nightclub in the headquarters of the carnaval group Batutas de São José.[7] He was also a featured member of a samba school largely made up of university students, The Bohemians of Sítio Novo University of Samba (USBSINO), where he built up experience on a large range of percussion instruments.[8]

The secular and religious versions of West African drumming traditions transformed in the Americas were not his only formative musical experiences, however. Not all of his musical contexts were Afrological, to use George E. Lewis's term.[9] He also played cymbals in the municipal band, earning a steady income. In the band, he was exposed to Eurological musical forms and aesthetics, including the reality of playing in an ensemble, in which the written score dictates what is played; in which there is an intricate hierarchy of prestige from instrument to instrument; and in which certain players are often required to play nothing for most of a given piece.

Complementing the various contexts in which he was performing, Naná also had a voracious appetite for listening to records that put him in touch with the broader world of popular music, as well as avant-garde music like Stockhausen. In his words:

> I used to buy imported records in Recife. We had a large store where you would go to buy records. The American Center helped me a lot; I would say, "I want to listen to Thelonious," or "I want to listen to Ornette," or "I want to listen to Dave Brubeck." They helped me to find all those imported records, which were very expensive at that time. My mother used to say, [shouting angrily]: "You're going to eat albums!"[10]

Like many musicians who found themselves fascinated with Dave Brubeck and his band, famous for their hit "Take Five," counted in groups of five beats, Naná credits Brubeck, his sax player Paul Desmond, and drummer Joe Morello for sparking a lifelong interest in time signatures other than the standard divisions of 2, 3, 4, and 6. It was this facility for playing with divisions of 5, 7, 10, 11, and other time signatures that are unusual for Brazilian popular music and jazz, that helped Naná become one of the top drummers in the Recife bossa nova scene. Why, after being honored as the best bossa nova drum-set player in Recife, he made the transition away from drum-set playing and toward percussion isn't completely clear. In Rio, in 1968–70, he had a phase in which he innovatively combined playing drum-set with playing shaker or cuíca at the same time when he was collaborating with Milton Nascimento. But later, he went as far as insisting that his stage configuration was free of any chrome stands. When I spoke to Naná's childhood friend Edson Rodrigues, he suggested a possible explanation. When Naná began to play bossa nova and nightclub samba, in groups such as Os Bossanorte, Sambossa Trio, and Yansã Quarteto, there were concert gigs, which lasted 45 minutes to an hour, and dance gigs that often went several hours into the night. According to Rodrigues, Naná could handle the shorter performances on drum-set, but longer gigs would cause his ankle to cramp up. It is possible that Naná became a full-time percussionist, and not a drum-set player, at least in part because his ankle wouldn't cooperate.

Naná's Involvement in Grupo Construção and the Popular Culture Movement

Another reason why Naná is not just a bearer of tradition in any sort of straightforward sense, is because the very notion of tradition was neither straightforward nor settled in his home state of Pernambuco during his formative years. During the early 1960s, Pernambuco was a laboratory for Paulo Freire's radical approach to teaching adults literacy and critical citizenship at once, using methods that would soon become globally influential as his *Pedagogy of the Oppressed*.[11] At the time, in the Cold War context of revolutionary Cuba's successful literacy campaigns, a US State Department official in 1961 said, "This part of Brazil is presently making history."[12] While this statement can be read as praise, the US was concerned that an effective campaign to turn the illiterate masses into politicized citizens would make radical social transformation (read: communism) more probable in a land of poverty caused by a combination of stark social inequality, political corruption, and severe droughts (casting a different light on the broader motives behind the American Center's making US jazz records available to Brazilians like Naná).

In the early 1960s, when Naná was a teenager, and in his early twenties, politicians, musicians, and intellectuals in Recife, Pernambuco, interpreted popular music through the lens of social and political transformation. Left-wing organizations such as the Brazilian Communist Party supported the state government initiative to start a non-profit entity called the Movimento de Cultura Popular (MCP), which declared as its mission the intertwined goals of: "1. To interpret, to develop, and to systematize popular culture; 2. To create and diffuse new methods and techniques of popular education; 3. To train personnel to transmit culture to the people."[13] Cultural traditions were valued for multiple reasons. In Freire's egalitarian and dialogic teaching methods, oral traditions were one of the types of local knowledge that the illiterate brought with them as they learned to read. In addition, popular music that wedded traditional sounds with leftist political themes were thought of as a crucial way for a vanguard of intellectuals to engage in consciousness-raising and incite the masses into revolutionary action.

This use of folk music to further political goals is a far cry from the range of samba-to-bossa sounds featured in *Black Orpheus*. It is also quite distinct from the breezy unrequited love, hipness, and sophisticated songs contemplating nature that Jobim and Gilberto's bossa nova was becoming famous for around the globe right then. Just as bossa nova was gaining momentum outside of Brazil in the United States and Europe, the genre was splitting inside of Brazil. Singers such as Sérgio Ricardo and Geraldo Vandré with whom Naná would perform used bossa's new harmonic vocabulary together with sounds drawn from Northeastern traditions to carry messages of protest and militancy. The Pernambucan MCP served as the model for the national Centro Popular de Cultura (CPC, People's Center for Culture). Both Sérgio Ricardo and Geraldo Vandré, among many others, participated in the CPC, that enlisted popular music as part of a mission of political consciousness-raising with the aim of bringing together workers, the rural poor, intellectuals, and artists. The CPC was very concerned with the influx of cultural products from outside of Brazil, including musical styles, criticizing iê-iê-iê— Brazilian versions of early rock n' roll—as diluting musical Brazilian-ness. University students, representing a small percentage of the population (less than 2 percent of the Brazilian population had graduated from college in 1970),[14] sought to connect through protest music with a large percentage of the population excluded from educational opportunities. Within this activist student movement, a tension persisted between the college elite and their egalitarian musical nationalist vision.

I mention this broader context not simply to situate the general debates around traditional and popular music as Naná came of age. Naná stood in close proximity to these conversations. His drumming and percussion skills uniquely positioned him as a young person who wasn't a college student yet was participating in university-centered political/

cultural activities. His status as one of few Afro-Brazilians within this activist Recife scene made him an important conduit to Afro-Brazilian sounds. He emerged as someone who was ultimately more interested in the realm of sound than that of partisan politics even as he found himself often entangled in politically charged performances. He participated in the Teatro de Cultura Popular, an initiative within the Movimento de Cultura Popular that staged performances described as "research-shows" celebrating local folkloric traditions alongside dramatized scenes and literary passages recited from poetry and prose.

Right after the 1964 coup, the military stationed a tank at the headquarters of the Movimento de Cultura Popular and immediately shut it down. Many of the members, however, including Naná and Teca Calazans, who would become one of Naná's longtime artistic collaborators, regrouped to form Grupo Construção, continuing to produce activist theater productions combining traditional and popular music, drama, and recitations of poetry and prose. Grupo Construção committed to the amalgam of bossa nova and activism in vogue following the success of the show *Opinião* in Rio de Janeiro, which featured songs interspersed with spoken passages by three singers with distinct backgrounds: Nara Leão, who was from an upper-middle class family in the affluent Zona Sul of Rio; Zé Keti, an Afro-Brazilian, who spoke and sang about life in the morros; and João do Vale, who sang about his experiences living in the arid sertão backlands.

The first *Opinião*-style show that Grupo Construção produced, *Cantochão (Plainsong)*,[15] debuted in June of 1965 at the Teatro de Arena in Recife. In it, Grupo Construção followed *Opinião*'s practice of addressing Brazilian problems of race, class, and geography. *Cantochão* focuses on childhood, weaving in a critique of social class in contemporary Brazil by following one boy growing up in a favela, a second growing up in a middle-class high-rise apartment, and a third growing up in the sertão countryside.

It is in the context of addressing social questions such as these that the group valued folkloric research into local traditions. In order to properly represent the favela, the Afro-Brazilian styles played there needed to be credibly performed in their productions. The same was true of the rural sertão. In *Cantochão*, the actors sang traditional songs from the Afro-Brazilian religion Xangô. In a subsequent self-described "research-show," *Mora na Filosofia* (*Listen to my Wisdom*), performed at the auditorium of the federal university's College of Philosophy, the student philosophers learned songs, and practiced new samba steps, in an effort "to seek understanding of our lived reality." This was a well-intentioned endeavor that, like much folkloric and ethnomusicological research, risked backfiring and further reinforcing the cultural gap between the college students and the samba school performers that it sought to bridge. This friction between the group's middle-class academic demographic and its egalitarian vision, Marxian quotes and activist bent can be seen in the programs for the shows. The program for *Cantochão*, for example, is interspersed with advertisements from jewelers ("a constant presence of good taste") and elegant dining ("For you who like high-class music; For you who like to be well served in your meals; Grupo Construção suggests Lico's restaurant for after the show.").[16]

Naná was frequently called upon to bridge this divide, lending authenticity and musical knowledge to these shows. A newspaper reviewer commented that Naná, "up until then more known as a drum-set player, revealed a startling versatility: as a singer, a samba dancer, and a comedian."[17]

Fellow Grupo Construção member Geraldo Azevedo remembers that: "He presided over everyone. He had a very big stage presence."[18]

In subsequent shows, Grupo Construção collaborated with Sérgio Ricardo, continuing in this national-participatory direction of activist bossa nova and Northeastern folk-based popular music and theater. The production *Pregão* (Street Vendor's Call) included researched and performed street vendors' calls to chronicle the life of a Black shoeshiner living in Rio.[19] *Pregão*, the theatre production, grew out of a film that Ricardo had produced, in which the main character, who shines shoes, sings the lyric "esse mundo é meu" (this world is mine) to himself after being ignored by the throngs of people on the city streets. The film sound then cuts abruptly to a full samba arrangement of the tune. Ricardo's rich baritone describes the character as a person enslaved in the world he inhabits, before calling upon the orixá Ogum, a deity of the Afro-Brazilian Candomblé religion, to come and help fight this injustice, because, in shackles, one cannot love. Decades later, one reviewer of the film confirms that Ricardo's heavy-handed paternalism with regards to its dispossessed characters was off-putting.[20]

A clipping from the *Jornal do Commercio* in Recife describes *Pregão* as part of a debate about the cultural significance of "our music" that is "really Brazilian" in the face of apprehension toward the rise in popularity of iê-iê-iê (early Brazilian rock n' roll) and the possible fall of bossa nova. In the program of their other collaboration, *Cancioneiro de Sérgio Ricardo (the Sérgio Ricardo Songbook)*, Ricardo sardonically expresses his views toward the pop music trends of the day, writing: "There isn't much to say about popular music at the moment. All there is, really, is the necessity to shut up for a while, and let iê-iê-iê take care of the market until the public can no longer stand it."[21]

As a musical nationalist, he believes that the era's popular music is falling short, and blames this on a lack of field research into musical Brazilian-ness, combined with "how easy it is to import jazz and sweeten it up with samba." He calls for the middle class to shut up and listen to the "pure voices" of the humble folk who surround them, closing his hectoring with a verse from an unnamed troubadour whom he heard and recorded in Caruaru.

There is much to stop and consider in Sérgio Ricardo's statement here. It sums up the activist nationalist-participatory approach to popular music that was common in university circles, applying a critique of cultural imperialism to argue that adopting internationally popular US-based styles such as rock n' roll and jazz was a betrayal that diluted musical Brazilian-ness. This philosophy of political music-making was rewarded during the televised popular song festival competitions in Brazil that started in 1965. But, by 1967, the musical-nationalist views of Ricardo, Geraldo Vandré, and others were being questioned by artists such as Gilberto Gil, Caetano Veloso, and others, who began to espouse an approach that came to be known as "Tropicália."

By 1969, Naná had played and/or recorded with musical nationalists such as Sérgio Ricardo and Geraldo Vandré, iconoclastic Tropicalists such as Os Mutantes and Gal Costa, and Milton Nascimento, who stood in a category all of his own. During this late-1960s moment, at the height of the repressive military dictatorship, a great weight of responsibility had been placed on the pop song, and many university student fans cared deeply about their position on a particular side of this artistic schism. As part of Grupo Construção, Naná was present at the moment during which the conflict was crystallizing. Naná was there when this schism was just a conversation between musicians and intellectuals, all committed to the common goal of moving Brazilian popular music forward during a politically tumultuous time.

While Ricardo made a call for the middle class to listen to what he heard as the "pure voices" of musicians in the city of Caruaru, two hours inland from Recife, future Tropicalist Gilberto Gil was listening in Caruaru as well, but with deeply contrasting conclusions. When Gil befriended Grupo Construção and traveled with them to Caruaru in an effort to learn about the region's traditions, they heard the Banda de Pífanos de Caruaru. In the city Ricardo held up as a site for pure folkloric voices, Gil heard the Banda de Pífanos' use of parallel fourths, disregard for Common Practice harmonic resolution, bent notes, and loping polyrhythms, and responded with what journalists pinpointed as a core insight of tropicalism: "They play dissonances in their own way, like things you would hear in the most contemporary of music, and it also reminds one of things the Beatles have played."[22]

To Gil, the song he heard in the Pernambucan interior was at once folkloric and modern. By equating the local and traditional with the cosmopolitan and contemporary, Gil (in conjunction with Caetano Veloso, in future months) articulated this artistic vision of Tropicalist cultural cannibalism: the selective and critical assimilation of cultural inflows from elsewhere juxtaposed with sounds with long local histories. Gil's argument is that this juxtaposition would not threaten the integrity of musical Brazilian-ness, as Ricardo argued, but rather would reinvigorate Brazilian popular music.

At the end of Gil's pivotal two-week stay in Pernambuco, he spoke with a Recife journalist, asserting one of the earliest articulations of Tropicália's attempt to move beyond what they saw as tired binaries between politically lucid (read:

ideologically pure) revolutionary musical nationalism and politically alienated and imperialist rock n' roll. In the interview, Gil signals the combination of regional tradition (represented by the berimbau, Naná's future signature instrument) and blasphemous electric guitar he would unveil just a few months later at the 1967 Festival de Música Popular Brasileira:

> But don't forget that the sound of electric guitars is in the [Brazilian] streets. The longhaired hippies walk the streets ... it is a new expectation that puts artists at an impasse ... in the face of the audience's social conditioning, songwriters are forcefully obligated, by this expectation, to orient their artistic activity taking into account the meanings of iê-iê-iê, putting aside the banner of purity, because any good influence is valid. So, for this reason, I orient myself within this new direction without putting aside the fundamental roots of our culture, but taking into account a factor: iê-iê-iê.[23]

In 1967, Naná played percussion in another Grupo Construção-linked show, *Memórias de Dois Cantadores* (*Memories of Two Singers*), featuring Teca Calazans and Edy Souza (later Edy Star) taking turns singing and talking about the question of popular music. See Naná and Edy appearing on Pernambucan Television in Figure 1.1. *Memórias de Dois Cantadores* brought together folkloric music research from their two home states of Pernambuco and Bahia, respectively, two culturally dominant states within the Brazilian Northeast that are often depicted as rivals. Teca and Edy took a gentler approach, and a reviewer at the time wrote that despite the title's reference to traditional Northeastern song duels, the show wasn't about the rivalry between the states, but rather praise for what Bahia and Pernambuco have in common culturally.

Figure 1.1 *Naná Vasconcelos with Trio Nordeste and Edy Star, 1968.*

Articles referred to it as a research-show, as Naná, Teca, Edy, and Marcelo Melo had traveled to the backlands, as well as the Bahian capital of Salvador, gathering songs. On the cusp of the Tropicália challenge to nationalist-participatory protest song, this performance spelled out arguments surrounding musical Brazilian-ness and their mixed feelings surrounding the perceived invasion of rock n' roll. The didactic speeches are somewhat overwhelmed, however, by the strength of Naná's playing, which ably switches from one moment to the next between *pastoril* Christmas pageant songs, Afro-Brazilian sacred Candomblé rhythms and an affectionately satirical take on the Beatles. As Teca and Edy deliver a call for cultural preservation and folkloric research as a way to stave off the dilution of Brazilian musical identity, Naná pulls out a berimbau and plays it for the first time.

After hearing so many of Naná's virtuoso berimbau performances in the process of researching this book, it is jarring to hear him play it badly, albeit for just a few seconds, on a reel-to-reel tape digitized from Teca Calazans' collection. According to Teca, he had just started playing it in the month before the performance, when they went on their song-gathering trip to Bahia. Teca decided to stay in Salvador for a couple of days longer than everyone else. While she was there, she bought a berimbau from a capoeira mestre, and learned some basics from him. This was decades before capoeira became a global Afrocentric martial art, and at the time, it was largely a practice centered in the *recôncavo* region of coastal Bahia. Even in Recife, Pernambuco, relatively nearby in Brazilian terms, and part of the same Northeastern region, capoeira was not as widely practiced. Teca brought the berimbau back to Naná so that he could learn to play it for the show. Naná was never wedded to traditional capoeira musical practice, because, up to this point, he had never learned to play the berimbau, nor had he been involved in a community of capoeiristas. Although Grupo Opinião had already featured a berimbau on "Berimbau (Ritmo de Capoeira)," it was only a few months later that the instrument received exposure on national television in a pop context when Gilberto Gil featured it in his performance of "Domingo no Parque," played by Dirceu during TV Record's 1967 Festival de Música Popular Brasileira. It was through this performance, in particular, that Gil inaugurated the descriptor of Tropicália to showcase the ideas that he had formulated that year while in Pernambuco listening to traditional music in Caruaru with members of Grupo Construção.

Caruaru, a city around 120 kilometers from the state capital Recife, provided musical fodder for these pivotal debates, in part because it was just far enough from the capital to be considered remote. As Sérgio Ricardo and Gilberto Gil imagined the musical past, present, and future of Brazil, they needed a wellspring of Brazilian musicality to mull over. They used their conflicting interpretations of the music they heard in Caruaru to support their efforts to move Brazilian Popular Music in their preferred directions. Naná, as a key member of Grupo Construção, witnessed this clash before it became a national story. He was present at beginnings of Tropicália as a musical moment, and the berimbau was one of Tropicália's first sonic symbols of cultural roots—like the pífanos in Caruaru: simultaneously folkloric and modern, not just one or the other.

What did Naná absorb during his early years in Recife and bring with him to Manhattan, Paris and Oslo? He played in his father's dance band of Latin rhythms, in a samba school, in the municipal band, in bossa nova combos, and in Grupo Construção. He performed Afro-diasporic and European-based music marked as local, regional, national, and international. He played and heard styles understood as modern, traditional, sophisticated, rustic, activist, patriotic, sacred/ecstatic, and merely for entertainment. He learned a wide range of percussion instruments, from bongo and conga-like atabaques, to zabumba bass drum, ganzá shaker, berimbau, and a host of carnaval samba percussion (agogô, cuíca, tamborim, pandeiro, reco-reco, surdo, and others).

Beyond learning to play a range of instruments and styles, he learned about music as labor. In his father's dance band, he witnessed bohemian nightlife before he was able to fully experience it because the municipality only issued him a work permit as a preteen if he would stay on stage during the band's breaks. In the municipal band, he learned that playing could bring a regular paycheck. And during the songs that he sat out, he learned about hierarchies of musicians, and the relatively thankless role of playing bass drum and cymbals in a concert band.

His experiences exposed him to a gamut of rhythmic feels such as: Brazilian counterparts to jazz swing like *suingue* and *balanço*;[24] military precision; and ecstatic, interlocking polyrhythms to induce spirit possession. He absorbed cuíca squeaks; deafening surdo subwoofer frequencies; penetrating sounds of iron bells that cut through a mix; jingles and the sifting white noise of ball-bearings inside a metal shaker. Sounds understood as tame and sounds understood as wild. Sounds marked as civilized and sounds marked as threatening. Open, cyclical, Afrological forms that last as long as dancers keep dancing, and orchestral band music with fixed, unfolding forms, discrete sections, and planned transitions.

This range of gigs also exposed him to a fundamental structuring ambivalence within Brazil from the twentieth century to the present: the gap between the celebration of Afro- and Indigenous cultural flows within the stories Brazilians tell themselves about themselves, and the extreme social inequality and lopsided material circumstances along entangled axes of race and class. The activist music/theater group Grupo Construção was sincere in their efforts to highlight this indefensible gap as they pushed for revolutionary change. Naná, who worked as a butcher by day in his father's market stall, was the only person in the troupe who hadn't gone to the university. As a person with darker skin in a troupe of lighter-skinned individuals, he ended up playing a particular role. Whether the theme of the production was a philosophical take on samba and soccer, as in *Mora na Filosofia*, or the reality of living a precarious favela existence, as in *Cantochão*, the white, middle-class members of the group relied on Naná and his rhythms.

2 Dictatorship and Counterculture: Naná in Rio de Janeiro

In 1967, Naná showed his restlessness and ambition by seeking out ways to leave Recife, whether or not he had a steady gig or a support system at his destination. Sometime between March, when he appeared in a Grupo Construção production, and August, when *Memórias de Dois Cantadores* opened, he made a short-lived attempt to make it in Portugal. He arrived with the rest of his quartet without a game plan for making it. Serendipitously, they bumped into Agostinho dos Santos, the elegant crooner who was the voice (but not the face) of Orpheus in *Black Orpheus*. Agostinho was similarly in search of a project, and they put together a short-lived group:

> When I was in Recife, before going to Rio, I played with Yansã Quarteto and Agostinho dos Santos. We were vibraphone, piano, bass, and drumset; I was the drummer, and Agostinho sang. We were a very successful quartet, and then we said, [*chuckles*] like teenagers, [*excitedly*]: "Let's go to Europe!" We had no contract; we didn't know anybody; we just put the money together, and said, "Okay, let's start with Portugal," because it had the same language. We got tickets and flew from Recife to Portugal. We got there, and said, "So now, what are we going to do?" [*chuckles*]. We didn't know anybody.[1]

The Recife quartet ended up accompanying dos Santos's rich baritone on a 4-song EP *Africa Canta Agostinho do Santos* recorded in Portugal. The standout track on the EP is "Em Luanda Saudades de Luanda" (In Luanda, Longing for Luanda). Angolan artist and poet Eleutério Sanches wrote "Em Luanda Saudades de Luanda" for this project, playing with Luanda as the name of a place, and Luanda as the name of a woman, but also suggesting that one can feel longing for a place even while one is still there. Or, possibly, it refers to the back-and-forth movement of labor migration—at home, missing home, at home, missing home. On the record, Naná's drumming alternates between bossa nova drum-set playing, congas/atabaques, and agogô iron-bell patterns. Naná translates African-ness into a bossa framework, injecting just enough Afrocentric authenticity into the mix, without diverging from the smooth feel of dos Santos's crooning.

The trip to Portugal couldn't have lasted more than four months or so, based on Naná's confirmed gigs in Recife. However, it provided Naná's first glimpse of the possibilities and realities of living and performing abroad. The experience didn't scratch the itch—wanderlust remained, and he would soon leave Recife again, this time to Rio de Janeiro a year later in July of 1968. And not long after that, in early 1971, he would next leave Brazil and travel to New York City for a gig with Gato Barbieri.

Teca Calazans and Geraldo Azevedo moved to Rio de Janeiro first, dissolving Grupo Construção. Teca rented an apartment and she lived there together with Geraldo. They were sharing this apartment when Naná arrived. Geraldo had been sending Naná letters urging him to come. He took advantage of an opportunity to make the trip when Edy Star represented the state of Pernambuco at the Brasil Canta no Rio song festival, singing a Candomblé-themed song in a maracatu rhythm, titled "Dia Cheio de Ogum" (A Day Full of Ogum). According to Edy, he hadn't planned for Naná to perform with him in Rio, even though he had worked with Naná in Recife in *Memória de Dois Cantadores*. But Edy was at the Hotel São Francisco when Naná just showed up. He had arrived by bus, insisting on playing, making the argument that drummers in Rio wouldn't know how to play Pernambucan maracatu properly. So, Edy let him play his atabaques behind him as he sang, Naná in a smart, Manfred Mann-style turtleneck.[2] And after the competition, Naná stayed in Rio, not to return to Recife to live for over thirty years.

Naná Survives the "Leaden Years" of the Military Dictatorship

The orthodox left-wing nationalist-participatory vision for activist popular music began to be challenged, and ultimately eclipsed, by the more playful, surrealist, and psychedelic Tropicália. But during that turbulent shift, singers such as Geraldo Vandré steadfastly carried the torch for music foregrounding revolutionary politics made by musicians who often took style cues from Che Guevara. During this moment, near the end of 1968, even principal Tropicalists, Caetano Veloso and Gilberto Gil, with their interest as artists more squarely on the politics of musical aesthetics than on partisan protest per se, were imprisoned and subsequently exiled to London. Singers like Vandré, with his more obvious political stance, were just as imperiled, if not more so. It was during this time that Geraldo Azevedo and Naná joined forces in Rio with

Nelson Angelo and Franklin da Flauta to form Vandré's back-up band Quarteto Livre.

There are two carefree photos of Naná from December of 1968 that belie how serious the worsening political circumstances within which he found himself were. In one, Naná is sitting on the hood of Vandré's Ford Galaxie, a cigarette dangling from his mouth, his relaxed arms draped around his bandmates Nelson Angelo and Franklin da Flauta, Geraldo Azevedo posing next to them. In the other, they are in the backseat while Vandré drove, making maniacally silly faces, eyes crossed and tongues out. They look like college kids, with facial hair and men's bodies but still possessing an adolescent giddiness. The Ford Galaxie had just come out in Brazil the year before, and the coveted car would soon become a liability as they sped along backroads to the estate of renowned novelist Guimarães Rosa so that Vandré could lie low until he had the opportunity to travel to Chile into exile.

Vandré and Quarteto Livre had just begun that month's touring when they barely avoided being firebombed by the right-wing Communist Hunting Command (Comando de Caça aos Comunistas; CCC). They were in the Teatro Opinião in Rio de Janeiro, just one hour before the bomb went off. Franklin remembered it this way: "We always stayed in the theater, talking, drinking a little whiskey. That night, someone had an idea: 'Let's go eat a pizza at the Caravelle.'" And that's where the group went, to a nearby pizzeria. "We left an hour before we usually did. An hour later, a bomb placed by the CCC—happened after various threats, that never became anything more than that—exploded, blowing up the street, the theater's façade, and part of the actual theater. At the time, we were five blocks from there, savoring our mozzarella."[3]

The bombing foreshadowed the "coup inside the coup" of the Institutional Act Number Five (Ato Institucional Número Cinco), or AI-5, put into place eleven days later on 13 December 1968. The AI-5 dissolved the National Congress and ratcheted up the persecution and censorship of figures of the anti-dictatorship resistance, whether they be armed militants or outspoken political singers on the left like Vandré. Remarkably for an era when audio recording wasn't as easy or ubiquitous, a recording is available of Geraldo Vandré and the Quarteto Livre's last performance, the night before the crackdown.[4] On the night of 12 December, Vandré played in Anápolis, a city in the state of Goiás, not far from the national capital Brasília. By the time they took the stage, the meeting in Brasília approving this decree had already taken place, but word had not yet gotten out that Vandré was at risk of imprisonment and torture.

Naná signals his presence during the first song with his signature parallax gesture on congas. Beyond this, however, he is, without a doubt, a sideman on this project, and Vandré dominates, adopting a solemn register as he gives speeches to the audience between songs. At the end of the recording, Vandré speaks at length about how he wouldn't play his protest song "Caminhando" (Walking), because the military censors forbade it. "Caminhando" is an anthemic anti-dictatorship call-to-action with the refrain, "Come, let's go/because to wait is not to know/those who know choose the time/they don't wait for it to happen" ("Vem, vamos embora/que esperar não é saber/quem sabe faz a hora/não espera acontecer").[5] Instead of defying the authorities, he explains, deadpan in his usual earnest tone, he wrote a new song, "Continuando" (Continuing on) instead. The band proceeds to play this "new song," which just happens to have the same chords as the hit protest song. After spending a bit of time on the new lyrics, he stops singing and plays the chords over and over. At this point, once Vandré has established plausible deniability, the crowd begins to sing the old melody and lyrics to the new song's guitar part.

The triumph of that moment was short-lived, however. According to Azevedo, after the show, someone called Vandré's manager and told him that they had to get out of there, adding that the police had occupied his house, his father's house, and the house of his aunt, so he wouldn't be able to seek sanctuary there. Vandré and the rest of the band jumped into the Galaxie, and stuck to the backroads off the highway for the 1,000 kilometer trip from Goiás to São Paulo. But now, the flashy car was an albatross that Vandré feared would signal that they were artists. He didn't even want to stop to fill up the tank with gas.

As I learned about the most repressive years of the dictatorship, known as the *anos de chumbo*, or "leaden years," I wondered whether musicians like Naná who accompanied persecuted figures like Vandré were also vulnerable to being imprisoned, tortured, or forced into exile themselves. After hardliners took over and life got violently worse for both the militant left and the Tropicalist, carnivalesque left, there are stories that reveal a curious inconsistency. Musicians like Chico Buarque were able to get away with actions that were, in retrospect, clearly taunting the military generals, using *fresta*, or writing ambiguous lyrics that fans learned to read between the lines. A famous example can be found in Buarque's 1970 single "Apesar de Você" (Despite You), with its ingenious lyrics masquerading as a breakup song ("Você que inventou esse estado …," "You who created that state …," has a double meaning in both English and Portuguese that could be either referring to an emotional state, or the nation-state). It seemed to depend on whoever was staffing DOPS (Departamento de

Ordem Política e Social), the government office of censorship, on a particular day whether they let certain provocative lyrics through or not.

So, how guilty by association would Naná and Geraldo Azevedo be as members of Geraldo Vandré's band? After Vandré's exile, would they have to fear that they were next? I imagine that an argument like, "Look, I played with him, yes, but that doesn't mean that I agree with his politics!" would likely fall on deaf ears during an interrogation. In the spirit of creating a world with *tortura nunca mais* (torture never again), Geraldo Azevedo, fifty years after the fact, was startlingly willing to tell me about being captured and repeatedly tortured by the military police over 41 days, during his first time in prison. At one point, his torturers gave him electrical shocks in front of his pregnant wife, in an effort to get her to crack and give them information. Another time, a fellow political prisoner, Armando Frutuoso, died in the next cell over as a hooded Azevedo listened and the soldiers panicked. After that, he later faked a heart attack in order to give his torturers pause in continuing their monstrous efforts.

But even then, it was Azevedo's use of his graphic design skills to draft, illustrate, and mimeograph anti-dictatorship leaflets in his apartment, as well as his housemates' connection to a clandestine group that had taken up arms that placed him in the military's crosshairs. When the group was found out and denounced, their sympathizers (and assumed sympathizers) were rounded up as well. The whole time he was imprisoned, his torturers never mentioned his touring with Vandré. So, although Azevedo and Naná were worried that they would be considered guilty by association, they were somewhat shielded by the anonymity of being a sideman that Naná would, in subsequent years, work so hard to overcome.

Geraldo Azevedo insists that Naná had little patience for the "sometimes pretentious and arrogant side" of Geraldo Vandré.[6] But when Azevedo claims that Naná wasn't into politics, what he was saying, I believe, was that Naná was weary of the vanguardism of some sectors of the revolutionary student left. His participation in the Movimento de Cultura Popular and Grupo Construção makes it clear that he was not utterly apolitical.

Over the long arc of his career, the *Saudades* record as a key example, his work engages through sound with issues of cultural, racial, and ecological politics. Once he gained more freedom to enact his own artistic vision rather than being tasked only with enhancing that of others, his music explored race, indigeneity, the slave trade, and the Amazon rainforest, among other themes.

This impatience came to a head in the Galaxie barreling through the backroads to Vandré's exile. Despite the urgency of getting to their destination, Vandré decided to stop the car and make a speech to the rest of the band. But Naná was not as open to Vandré's speeches as Vandré's reverent audiences, and in Azevedo's account, Vandré's pomposity angered Naná. Vandré stopped the car, got up on the hood and wanted to have a political rally just for the band members. He shouted, "I'm going to enter the guerrilha!!," and Naná responded that he was going to punch Vandré because he wants to imitate Che Guevara. They never ended up coming to blows, but by the side of the road, the day the National Congress was poised to be dissolved, Naná and Vandré came close to brawling.[7]

Naná and Milton Nascimento

Before Naná had even arrived in Rio at the end of July 1968, Azevedo had sent Naná several letters telling him that he simply had to get to know Milton Nascimento, since, Azevedo had correctly predicted, the two shared a lot artistically. He talked up Milton to Naná, and Naná to Milton, so that when they actually met in the second half of 1968, both were open to what the other had to offer. The way Milton tells it, Naná marched up to him and declared that he had come all the way from Recife to play with him.[8] Naná auditioned, in a way, asking to borrow pots and pans from the kitchen, arranging them all around him, and coaxing sounds out of these everyday objects while seated in the lotus position.[9]

Milton was seeking to move beyond bossa nova, his soaring voice invoking the colonial-era churches of his home state of Minas Gerais, deeply contrasting bossa's Rio-based hip whispers. Milton is a dark-skinned Afro-Brazilian, raised by a white, classically trained choir director (his biological mother had worked in his adopted parents' home). He developed a sound that evoked the haunting melancholy of the beautiful but transforming landscape of Minas, where rural–urban migration drained small mountain towns of inhabitants as they moved to the industrial centers. His sound explored an expansive sense of space and a rhythmic vocabulary more in conversation with nueva canción protest music from Spanish-speaking South America than nearby bossa nova. Naná led Milton to significant shifts in his musical vision, offering rhythmic and atmospheric ideas that were clearly Brazilian, but didn't resemble bossa nova rhythms, drawing instead on a range of Northeastern rhythms without adhering rigidly to them. Naná's contributions counterbalanced the jazz, rock n' roll (Beatles), and bel canto sounds in Milton's work.

According to Azevedo, Milton's house in Rio became the clubhouse for Clube de Esquina musicians and their circles of friends. Several of Naná's future collaborators would regularly stop by, including Joyce Moreno and Maurício Maestro. Milton's house was so overrun with musicians that Milton once crashed at Azevedo's place for some peace and quiet. Soon after Naná arrived and won over Milton with an impromptu audition on pots and pans, he was contributing to Nascimento's recordings. Despite the mixed feelings of certain members of the Clube da Esquina regarding the newcomer from the Northeast, Milton recognized how Naná could affect his shifting sound. At a moment in the 1960s–70s revolution in multitrack-recording technology and audiophile home sound systems, Milton recorded certain albums in 4-track quadrophonic sound, an early attempt at an immersive mix like later Surround Sound. As a testament to the rising importance of Naná's contribution, on tracks like "Rosa do Ventre" and others on Milton's 1969 self-titled record, one channel was devoted to the backing band, another to a string orchestra, a third to Milton's vocals, and a full fourth channel was dedicated to Naná's percussion parts.[10]

During the period between 1968 and 1970, Naná was performing with a wide range of acts. He played with Milton, and Som Imaginário, Milton's backing band for a time. He also toured with Geraldo Vandré until the singer was forced into exile. But beyond this, Naná recorded a session with psychedelic rock band Os Mutantes that was brought into the fold of Tropicalists Caetano Veloso, Gilberto Gil and Gal Costa, playing the signature congas on the track "Ando Meio Desligado" that became so emblematic of the era. He also performed and recorded with Gal Costa, one of the best singers of her generation, capable of precise diction and delivery one minute, and a Janis Joplin-level freak-out the next. In June 1970, he was part of Os Bubbles, that later became A Bolha (The Bubble), Gal Costa's backup band for a famous two-week run at the Boate

Sucata in Rio. Aiming to create an immersive experience, artist Hélio Oiticica worked with Gal to fashion a total environment. "Entering the venue, the audience passed through, as if in a ritual of deconditioning, a dense forest of plastic filaments into a space organized into compartments by gauzelike screens hanging from ceiling to floor."[11] Naná and the rest of Os Bubbles were expressly told to wear everyday clothes, not stage costumes, and the audience sat on pillows rather than seats. Their goal was to foster "crelazer," a leisurely, creative state that he believed could be the first step toward a utopian community.

It was in this late-1960s milieu that Naná met Joyce Moreno, Mauricio Maestro, Nelson Angelo, and Novelli, all of whom he would record with off and on in different permutations, in Rio, Mexico City, and Paris. Naná played with Joyce, Nelson Angelo, and Novelli in a short-lived project called Á Tribo, before Naná, Joyce, Nelson Angelo, and Mauricio Maestro were called to play a residency with Tamba Trio pianist and arranger Luiz Eça for two months in a hotel in Mexico City during the 1970 World Cup. The short-lived Luiz Eça y la Familia Sagrada big band was a more musically adventurous version of a Sergio Mendes-style post-bossa Brazilian crossover act, as the name in Spanish suggests. The sacred family split when international success eluded them, and Naná returned to Rio before soon rushing to his housemate Azevedo and telling him the news that, "This guy wants to take me away out of Brazil!," referring to Argentinean jazz saxophonist Gato Barbieri, who would bring Naná to New York City in early 1971.

It is during this time in Rio that Naná became known as someone who contributed "special participations" on the records of others. This in-between status—more visible than an anonymous session musician but acting as a free agent working without long-term commitments—was, in part, due to a conscious decision to stay out of Caetano and Gil's direct orbit—not to accept them as his "godfather," as Merrie put it. Naná believed, rightly or not, that the exclusivity they would expect from him if he agreed to play with them would stifle his ability to make a name for himself. This insistence on independence led to lean times—when he returned to Rio briefly in 1972, Merrie recounted that they didn't always have enough to eat, sometimes relying on the charity of filmmaker Glauber Rocha's mother, who ran an inn in Rio. But it was this same stubborn independence that led him back to Europe and New York City in the years to come.

3 The Enchanting and Revolutionary Berimbau: Naná and Glauber Rocha in New York City

> Coincidentally, Glauber, Fabiano and I ended up living together, when Glauber arrived on Rivington Street in 1971–72 ... Glauber always told me "Biriba é pau, arco de São Jorge (The biriba wood berimbau is Saint George's bow). I was there studying the berimbau, Glauber was there naked, writing ...[1]

For Brazilians, as well as those interested in avant-garde film worldwide, there is only one Glauber. Glauber Rocha was one of the most important experimental filmmakers from the Global South committed to decolonizing cinema in the 1960s and 1970s. In 1971, when Naná was his roommate, his influence on the direction of world cinema was strong. He was in New York for less than a year because he was trying to get a project off the ground with Marlon Brando. The enormous loft on Rivington Street on the Lower East Side of Manhattan that Naná, Glauber, and Fabiano Canosa lived in for just $300 a month[2] brought together figures in film and music at the time, including Bernardo Bertolucci and Gato Barbieri, who were both only a year away from directing and performing the soundtrack for the controversial film *The Last Tango in Paris*, which Naná plays uncredited berimbau parts on.

Fabiano Canosa, a prominent curator of world cinema in New York City to this day, described to me the scene at the loft where Naná honed his berimbau virtuosity. Glauber would be on the phone, naked, working out the details of a film shoot in Allende's Chile—he didn't like to wear clothes when he worked at home. It was an extraordinarily creative time for Naná. He would often start the day with LSD. "It was good to take it," he later recalled. "I never took it by myself, but in the company of my instruments … When I started to feel it, the first thing I wanted to do was play. My sensibility blossomed and I found myself concentrating only on the music."[3] Armed with his berimbau and a stone to stop the instrument's string and create buzzing timbres, Naná would spend much of his days, according to Canosa, pacing from Glauber's partition at the front of the vast, empty space, to the bathroom on the other end. He would go back and forth with his berimbau, trying out new techniques. Canosa thought the whole process to be miraculous and made it a point to track what Naná was coming up with, day after day. He was working out the elements of a musical palette all his own—the rudiments that would serve him for the rest of his musical life. Canosa noticed that Naná was mastering how to use the gourd against his body to modulate the sounds in the wash of natural echo of the converted warehouse space. During that time, he was also exploring whispery, onomatopoetic vocals that merged with and reinforced the sounds of the instrument.

For Canosa, this was the soundtrack for his unrequited love for Glauber that he spoke openly about—Canosa would end up spending much of his long life as the keeper of the filmmaker's memory. He remembered that with Naná's evolving sound, they didn't need to put music on the flimsy record player they shared, with its tinny loudspeaker. That said, when Naná wasn't playing, they had the *João Gilberto en Mexico* bossa nova record that had just been released, and a Villa-Lobos record on heavy rotation.[4] The fact that Brazil's foremost canonical classical composer was played in this bohemian stronghold wasn't just the product of the three roommates' expansive musical tastes. Glauber had used Villa-Lobos's *Bachianas Brasileiras No. 5* to great effect in his most famous film, *Deus e o Diabo na Terra do Sol* (*Black God, White Devil*),[5] a kind of revolutionary Marxist Western, where Glauber combined Brechtian alienation effects and visceral Artaudian violence. Villa-Lobos's work is featured prominently throughout Rocha's films, including his last film, *A Idade da Terra* (*The Age of the Earth*)[6] from 1980, which also prominently features Naná's music. Rocha uses Villa-Lobos in his films not simply as a marker of Brazil's European colonial legacy, but to give pivotal scenes a sense of monumental weight and grandiosity.

When I first read that Glauber cheered on Naná's efforts to become a berimbau virtuoso by saying, "*Biriba é pau, arco de São Jorge*" (The biriba wood berimbau is Saint George's bow), I had no idea of the layers of meaning found within Glauber's statement. I simply thought that he was invoking the practice within the Afro-Brazilian religion Candomblé of coupling West African Orixás with Catholic Saints. But as I watched his films and read more about them, I realized how crucial the myth of St. George/Oxossi[7] is to Glauber's work, to the point that film critics such as Rene Gardie interpret his films as a whole as transformations of the myth of St. George slaying the dragon.[8]

If this religious story was so important to Glauber, and he used it to interpret Naná's berimbau playing, it makes sense, then, to take a moment to examine how he uses it in his films, and what exactly it meant to him. Critics such as Randal Johnson and others refer semi-facetiously to his "Protestantism," not just because he grew up Presbyterian, but because his films are at once a "protest against mystification, capitalism and imperialism" and "a prophecy of revolution."[9] Rocha takes myths and unpredictably transforms them, his characters often serving as "migrating signifiers," that leave no solid ground for the viewer as he thinks through a dialectics of good and evil. One moment, St. George is slaying the dragon, and the next "St. George himself is often the dragon resurrected and transformed."[10] In spite of these contradictions, in the 1969 film *Antonio das Mortes* that Rocha released just before he lived in New York City with Naná, the narrative of St. George is directed toward "the dragon of evil" of capitalism and imperialism in a somewhat more straightforward way than his previous films.[11] Rocha's throwaway comment that the berimbau was St. George's bow suggests that he heard Naná's playing of the instrument as overturning cultural hierarchies informed by European colonialism that imbue certain musical sounds with an aura of civilization and modernity, and others with an aura of a primitive past.

In the context of Rocha's militant cinematic project, he was nudging Naná to foreground the markedly Afro-diasporic and Indigenous elements of his performances in a manner that wasn't caricatured. This was a challenge as a Brazilian performing outside of South America, where, as Caetano Veloso famously put it, the ghost of Carmen Miranda was always in the room.[12] The berimbau, with its apparent simplicity giving way in Naná's hands to seemingly infinite sonic possibilities, served as an emblem of a Brazil that had managed to thrive despite the ongoing aftermath of colonialism and capitalism. By the early 1970s, Afro-Latin congas, cowbells, and bongo had all become familiar instruments in jazz and pop music in the United States, with the crossover successes of "El Manisero (The Peanut Vendor)" in the 1930s, and mambo and cubop in the 1950s.[13] But despite the fact that some jazz listeners had already heard mention of the berimbau in the mid-1960s through the composition "Berimbau" by bossa nova guitar virtuoso Baden Powell, by the early 1970s, the instrument itself remained unfamiliar to jazz audiences in the United States and Europe.[14] With its one solitary string, its gourd resonator, and its form that suggested a kind of "first instrument" that was just one step away from being a bow and arrow used in a prehistoric hunt, the berimbau made an argument for the unsung elegance of premodern technology at a moment when many were questioning the supremacy of Eurocentric cultural forms.

Naná wasn't the only musician that Glauber was urging to fly the flag of Latin American culture. Glauber was adamant that the musicians in his circle accentuate their Latin Americanness as they performed internationally. That Naná was in New York City at all was because of his playing with Gato Barbieri, and Gato recruited Naná in part because of Glauber's arguments that Gato, a jazz saxophonist from Argentina, should explore his Latin American roots rather than simply attempting to assimilate into the jazz world in the United States and Europe. In Gato's words:

> I had played in so many things—with Carla Bley, JCOA [Jazz Composer's Orchestra Association], Charlie Haden's Liberation Music Orchestra—when the Brazilian director Glauber Rocha said, "You are Latin, and you have to make the Gato Barbieri orchestra." So, I went to Buenos Aires ... and there I started my

new fusion with the Latin American instruments. This was in 1970. We didn't have a cent. I brought in Naná Vasconcelos, with his berimbau, and I used an Indian drummer who played with five *bombos indios* on the floor. He was really superb. And something new started to happen."[15]

Gato made clear in interviews that a revolutionary left politics were underlying this move to accentuate a Pan-Latin American sound, once again placing Naná in a situation in which revolutionary politics were front and center whether or not Naná preferred them to be. A 1973 article titled, "Third World Jazz," describes how Gato's group's lyrical Latin melodies change "slowly into the sound of the screaming agony being perpetuated in the people of South America. Putting his face to the microphone, Gato yells out: 'Chile. Cuba. Chile. Cuba. Aiyyyyyyy!'" Gato explains his new focus this way: "It was through playing Black jazz that I learned to express myself, but now I know I can be even stronger in that expression if I keep learning more about my own musical background in the third world,"[16] although this stance is complicated by the deep historical and cultural differences between nations such as Argentina, Brazil, Chile, and Cuba that he was attempting to bind together in the name of political solidarity. In a possible dig on Naná's less militant posture, soon after he left the group, Gato explains to the interviewer that he wants to express, through his music, "That Bolivia is under fire. That Chile is under fire. That Latin America is under fire. The people there, except for Brazil, are very political."[17]

Tracing Naná's trajectory through the key figures with whom he collaborated and cohabitated is a delicate business, because, if done wrong, it dismisses his creative agency as an artist. Just because a person lived and/or worked with someone else, doesn't necessarily mean that they drew inspiration from their roommate or collaborator. It is easy to fall into the assumption that influence flows from the more established figure to the artist starting out, even though inspiration is much more chaotic and capricious.

I found that Naná and Glauber had a reciprocal impact on each other. Rocha's thinking provided Naná with a framework for interpreting how international audiences were responding to him. For example, Glauber wrote a manifesto in January of 1965 titled, "An Aesthetics of Hunger," that decried the European observer of the art of the rest of the world (referred at the time in developmentalist language as the "Third World"). Rocha wrote that the European observer was interested in this work "only insofar as they satisfy his nostalgia for primitivism."[18]

The timing of shifts in Glauber's thinking suggests that Naná also affected Glauber. In 1971, just as Naná had arrived in New York City, Glauber amended his earlier writing with a second text he titled, "An Aesthetics of Dreams," that he presented at Columbia University. The text departs from Glauber's earlier distrust of folklore and mysticism, finding space for the argument that at least certain popular culture can be at the same time powerfully enchanting *and* revolutionary. "An Aesthetics of Dreams" reads differently if one imagines the scene of its writing in the Rivington Street loft—not Glauber's probable nakedness, but the constant soundtrack of Naná's berimbau echoing through the high ceilings of the warehouse space during most waking hours. It is there that Glauber writes:

> The Indian and Black roots of the Latin American people must be seen as the only developed force of this continent. Our middle class and bourgeoisie are decadent caricatures of

the colonizing societies ... Popular culture is not that which is technically called folklore but rather the popular language of a permanent, historical rebellion ... Revolutionary art should be a powerful enough magic to enchant man beyond the point where he can no longer keep on living under this absurd reality ... To me it is a spiritual revelation, which contributes to opening up my Afro-Indian sensibility in the direction of the original myths of my race. This poor and apparently hopeless race elaborates mysticism as its moment of freedom. The Afro-Indian gods will negate the colonizing mysticism of Catholicism, which is the sorcery of repression and the moral redemption of the rich.[19]

Turning over the terms of art and politics, of mysticism and class conflict, Rocha considers a defense of what he calls Afro-Indian popular culture, not as nostalgia for the primitive, but as a means to somehow liberate through enchantment. I can't help but ask: Who is influencing whom here? Despite its traceable African roots, the berimbau, with its resemblance to a bow and arrow, seems more available to connote both "Indian and Black roots" together in the popular imagination better than recognizably African-derived instruments such as congas. Could this insight, that Rocha calls a spiritual revelation, be at least in part sparked by the kaleidoscope of timbres, melodies, and rhythms that an acid-tripping Naná was coaxing out of this musical bow and arrow as he typed? *Biriba é pau. Arco de São Jorge.*

The more I learn about this brief moment in the respective careers of Naná and Glauber, the more I come to the conclusion that each affected the other. Glauber's imprint is strong in certain recordings of Naná's made not long after their several months as roommates. The title track of his 1973 album

Amazonas, for example, fits so closely with Rocha's defiant Third Worldist perspective that, years later, in 1980, Rocha featured Naná's music prominently in his polarizing iconoclastic and nonlinear final film *A Idade da Terra*, which songwriter and critic Capinam referred to as Rocha striving toward his "film-limit."[20] I can think of few instances in which a filmmaker gives a musical soundtrack so much responsibility for exposition (if you can call it exposition when discussing a film as fragmented and experimental as this one).

For the first four minutes of the film, the camera explores just one long, still shot of a sunrise over the Palácio da Alvorada (Palace of the Dawn), the Brazilian president's residence in the planned city of Brasilia, which had been built only two decades before. But the shot doesn't focus on the building's characteristic ultramodernist Oscar Niemeyer architecture. Neither does it linger on the beauty of the sunrise. Instead, over the four minutes, the shot focuses on focus itself, or rather the lack thereof. Artifacts from the camera lenses emerge, foregrounding the optics of the shot. Instead of a clear shot of a beautiful sunrise with picturesque bokeh, a mess of ellipses of different sizes appear, offering a glimpse into the inner workings of the camera.

This denial of illusionism and foregrounding of the process of cinematic production run through the entire film, as the camera calls attention to itself.[21] By choosing the setting of the presidential residence, but refusing to center the residence itself, Rocha sets his sights on the more ambitious goal of examining the broader history of colonization in the Americas through story of the coming of multiple Third World Jesus Christs.

Throughout this initial shot, four minutes of the title track of Naná's *Amazonas*—what film scholar Randal Johnson simply refers to as a "wild, unidentified chant"—foreshadow both Glauber's ambitions and his violently fragmented approach to this film.[22] As the viewer adjusts to this extended shot, Naná's track suggests an imagined time before, an ethnogenesis—the birth of a people—with a rising vocal drone and a crescendo of drum rolls. The split between the left and right speakers is extreme, accentuating the movement of voices making squawking bird or perhaps monkey noises, buzzing insect sounds, and crowds of chattering gibberish floating through the stereo field. Non-metrical drum patterns stretch a three-dimensional sense of the stereo field, accentuating proximity and distance as well as a wide horizon. A sonic montage of fragments of Central African-style yodeling polyphony, folk Catholic hymns, and heaving, raspy throat and chest utterances that invoke Indigenous ritual music. The culture of the Americas chaotically emerges out of a dense array of imagined forest sounds.

Naná lived in New York in 1971–2 for less than a year before touring with Gato Barbieri in Europe and ending up in Paris. But, in retrospect, it was a pivotal time. Naná witnessed Glauber at his prime, holding court with other important directors like Bertolucci, and trying to get a project with Marlon Brando off the ground. Glauber rethought the role of Indigenous and Afro-Brazilian popular culture within his vision of revolutionary Third Worldist cinema while listening to Naná explore the possibilities of the berimbau. He urged Naná to stand firm in representing "deep Brazil" to the world. Considering the political weight of the task, as Glauber formulated it, it strikes me as unexpected that Naná's sense of sonic space was also an artifact of a bygone era of New York real estate, formed in the reverb of a loft so spacious that it took time for him to pace from one end to the other.

It was during this time that Gato Barbieri introduced Naná to Don Cherry, a fellow traveler, both literally and in terms of their artistic orientation. Their musical chemistry would lead them to perform together in several projects throughout the years, most notably the Organic Music Theatre in the early- to mid-1970s in Europe, and Codona in the late 1970s to early 1980s, and the Mu Quintet in the mid-1980s. As a jazz trumpeter who got his start in Ornette Coleman's band as their free jazz forced jazz musicians to question their convictions, Don Cherry came to be an early advocate for engaging with musical traditions of Africa, the Americas, and Asia. Longtime friend and collaborator Karl Berger described Cherry as someone who carried a portable shortwave radio with him so that he could listen to broadcasts from around the world and learn the melodies he heard in order to incorporate them into his improvisations.

4 Naná and Don Cherry

A Swedish television documentary about Don Cherry ends with footage of Naná and Don walking the streets of Harlem, singing and playing the berimbau and the doussn'goni (a 7-stringed Malian instrument), creating a pied piper effect of children gathering to hear.[1] The light, portable instruments provide more rich melodies, complex timbres and interlocking polyrhythms per pound than most musical instruments. Don comments: "I hope that I can bring some kind of life, or some kind of knowledge from my travels, and I share that ... The Black people in America are now really interested in understanding their roots, and what's so incredible about that is that the children are the ones who started this."[2]

Before Naná met Don, he was already known for always carrying a berimbau with him on his shoulder everywhere he went. It turned out that Naná and Don both valued the playful interactions that would result from enchanting whomever they met on the sidewalk with unexpected sounds expertly played on an unfamiliar instrument. For Naná, bringing his berimbau with him in public became a powerful way to break the ice, to make fast friends relatively wordlessly, and to disarm racism and xenophobia, especially as he traveled far and wide. For Cherry, bringing participative musical performance to the

Figure 4.1 *Don Cherry and Naná Vasconcelos. Photo by Dominique Fradin.*

streets was almost a kind of non-denominational missionary work. Of a piece with his unease with urban modernity, he believed that it was important to show kids, in particular, what is possible to make by hand. Wherever he went, he wove this practice into his everyday life:

> I've played [in the streets] in Bombay and Japan, and in New York, in Harlem, and in Watts, in all the travels. It's good for people to see an instrument that's made by hand. Always the first reaction is "oh, this is something primitive." But then,

when the Black people I've met have heard the instrument, they can relate to it. They start singing, they start dancing.[3]

In 1970, just before meeting Naná, Don Cherry put together a job application in order for Dartmouth University to hire him. He submitted five pages, decorated with flowers, featuring the heading, "STUDENT OF LIFE and UNIVERSITY OF LIFE." Jon Appleton, a composer of electronic music and later one of the co-creators of the Synclavier synthesizer, reformatted Don's vita so that it would be recognizable to the upper administration. Laying bare the awkwardness of translating jazz criteria for establishing authority to the academy, it includes such understated lines as "1960 Private Studies with John Coltrane," "1962 Toured Europe playing with Sonny Rollins," and "1964 Private Studies with Thelonious Monk" alongside "Lived in small village of 'Sazuka' near Morocco, North Africa," and "1967 Moved to Stockholm and began studying Turkish folk music."[4]

One student in the music course Cherry taught at Dartmouth described it as the music equivalent of "a religion course taught by someone present at the Last Supper."[5] Another remembers Cherry teaching them to listen to the "specific silence" that lingered after he hit a gong. He used some of his pay to bring musicians to campus to perform and give clinics, including South African bassist Johnny Dyani and Turkish percussionist Okey Temiz. The final exam was to find an instrument and play it while parading around the campus quad. According to Appleton, 99 of the 100 students received an A, except for this one guy named Steve who he didn't like, who got a B, in a playfully capricious, inconsequential act of malice.[6]

In his Dartmouth file, there is also a letter apologizing for leaving town without returning an Indigenous flute from the university's museum collection. Ethnographic collections of musical instruments ignited his interest in learning music from Asia, Africa, and South America while he was living in Sweden as well. Cherry took to reanimating musical instruments that had been stored or exhibited as artifacts. He became a collector of wooden, metal, and ceramic flutes from around the world, as well as the doussn'gouni, which he integrated into his compositions and performances for decades to come.

What did Naná learn from Don? What did Don learn from Naná? While it isn't possible to cleanly untangle their reciprocal contributions, it is clear from their long association that the ideas and practice of each fed off of those of the other. They both were committed to exploring musical egalitarianism, a value of Don's in Ornette Coleman's band that he explored in one of his more critically acclaimed albums, *Complete Communion*, that he made with Gato Barbieri, Ed Blackwell, and Henry Grimes in 1966. *Complete Communion* meant to Don that each instrument was to be equally heard, constantly responding to the others, rather than featuring one instrument up front and relegating the others to an accompanying role.[7] In this, even before Don met Naná, they shared an inquietude around the hierarchy of roles within musical groups.

Another format that Don played with, and Naná subsequently also found success in doing, was a duet, in which the players explored several instruments within the space that is afforded by such a sparse ensemble. Don's two-part collaboration with drummer Ed Blackwell titled *Mu* found an audience as much outside of jazz as within it, appealing to fans of psychedelic rock as well as free jazz. *Mu* was recorded at Saravah studios in Paris in 1969, Pierre Barouh's studio where Naná would record his groundbreaking berimbau-centered album *Africadeus* just a few years later.[8] On *Mu*, Don plays pocket trumpet, piano, multiple flutes, bells, and other percussion, and sings in close conversation with Ed Blackwell's kinetic and responsive playing. This close, shifting conversation between two equal players with ample space to breathe is the same configuration that Naná later explores with Egberto Gismonti in their acclaimed 1976 record *Dança das Cabeças*, which I will describe in more detail in Chapter 5. The two recordings also share an alternation between familiar instruments, such as piano, trumpet, and guitar, with more unfamiliar instruments to the ears of the average jazz or rock listener, such as bamboo flutes and berimbaus.

Trumpeter Dave Douglas suggests that much of Cherry's most important work went undocumented because his stubborn commitment to having improvisation seep into the pores of the composing process doesn't lend itself to being easily captured on tape:

> He was one of the first western musicians (classical, jazz, or other) to consider absolute freedom—the total absence of predetermined music—as a process of its own, on a par with notated compositions. This belief flowed directly from Cherry's personality and lifestyle. He lived as spontaneously as the flow of his music, and that kind of improvisation is notoriously difficult to record. Freedom is not always polite, and the protean spirit does not always get to tape.[9]

Melvin Gibbs hears Don's projects with Naná as a "utopian version of what the world would be like if everybody got along." Gibbs compared Don's music to guitarist Vernon Reid's *Artificial Afrika*-themed recurring concert that focuses on the Africa imagined outside of Africa, as opposed to the Africa that actually exists. Not that Don didn't care about the musical details that he learned from his travels—he clearly did, it was just that he wasn't content to merely reproduce these other ways of playing intact.

Don's unstoppable vocation to create resembles that of self-taught visual artists who have been variously described as "outsider" or "visionary"—despite the double gesture of appreciation and marginalizing found within these labels. These community artists, like the maker of the Watts Tower near where Cherry grew up, left a strong impression on him. Cherry identifies with the irresistible impulse to follow what compels them, even if they have trouble explaining exactly why. In this, he talks about Simon Rodia, the artist who designed and built the Watts Tower, much like the way that saxophonist Albert Ayler, with whom Cherry performed, would speak about his playing:

> When I was young, I lived next to, in Watts, a man who made this tower. It was an Italian man, in the middle of a Black neighborhood, making a tower. And he made it out of seashells, and out of ceramics, and different pieces. And he made this, and couldn't ask anyone to help him, because he didn't know why he was doing it, but he had to do it. That's the same kind of energy that has been carrying this on. Like when me and Moki, [toured through Europe], working with movement, and trying to go from city to city and make happenings and things. We didn't know why we did it but we had to do it.[10]

In line with this questioning of formal artistic practice, Don and Naná became interested in involving children in music-making. In 1971, in Germany, Don held a "Free Jazz and Children" workshop, where "approximately 200 children with no musical experience were brought into a semi-classroom situation with instruments and four improvisers."[11] Oh, to be a fly on the wall at that event! In the mid-1970s, Naná worked full-time at a Paris hospital as a resident musician, working with autistic and schizophrenic children alongside a resident painter and a resident dancer. He would improvise vocal sounds without words and play with the children on percussion instruments and body percussion.

"We Can be in Tune with Time. We Can be a Slave to Time."

During the early- to mid-1970s, Don named a record *Organic Music Society* and toured throughout Europe as the Organic Music Theatre, an experience Naná would later swear led to some of his fondest memories.[12] The term *organic* means so many things in different contexts, from its scientific definition, to its current role as a ubiquitous grocery store label. So, what did Don mean by organic? The arc of the Swedish television documentary on Don offers some clues. It begins with Don playing birdcalls that echo into the forest near his converted one-room schoolhouse in rural Tågarp, Sweden. It ends with him and his family living in a loft in Long Island City, Queens, New York. Cherry has mixed feelings about this move, as he contemplates a critique of Taylorist industrial efficiency, stating: "I'm in a period in my life where I have to decide if I'm going to be a productive machine, or whether I'm going to be a human being that wants to create in tune with nature."[13] The director Urban Lasson treats rural Sweden and urban New York City as polar opposites, Cherry providing a soundtrack of contemplative trumpet melodies and birdcalls in the forest, and fragmented, dissonant playing as images of bales of garbage being loaded on a flatbed truck depict the gritty city. During the documentary, he contextualizes this rural–urban split as a struggle to minimize the feeling of alienation from nature and from his creative endeavors that he traces back to growing up where there were few forests: "I grew up in a ghetto, and I didn't know about seasons. It's flat and dry and very smoggy [in Los Angeles]. In 1940, you could see the mountains, but by 1945, you couldn't anymore ... There was not much of a feeling of nature. I wanted my children to experience that [feeling of nature]."[14]

Don's spoken word sections on the "Relativity Suite No. 1" track on the 1973 *Organic Music Society* record complement this early 1970s countercultural back-to-the-land impulse, together with an indictment of what the industrial time-clock does to one's soul: "We can be in tune with time. We can be a slave to time. We can be in total aspiration, trying to catch time. There must be a fourth way to flow with time. This is the organic way. This is the way of the organic society to flow with time." As Cherry speaks this stream of consciousness, he plays a rolling, polyrhythmic groove in a bass register on the douss'ngoni. In the pauses between spoken sections, he interjects vocables that alternate between sounding West African in melody and singing style, and South Asian, as he had recently been studying Indian Karnatak vocal music. In his quest to flow with time "the organic way," Cherry looks to regions other than Western Europe to find utopian alternatives.

Percussionist Adam Rudolph, who collaborated with Don on several projects and also performed with Naná, compares the grocery store definition of "organic" to Don's musical one, suggesting that he was striving for music without music-industry "pollutants." With the caveat that he can't speak for Don, Adam Rudolph suggested other dimensions to what he believed Don was after with the term:

> I think that's it's a philosophical idea. The idea of being present in the moment, allowing creative notions to come forth in a very natural, organic, unfettered way ... We don't have a predetermined idea of what the show is, we're not playing a set form, a *sonata allegro* form or a 32 bar form or a *frevo* either, you know, it's like, we are playing based upon the organic quality of what's happening in the moment, like our conversation. Right?

Rudolph also thought of it as including a focus on the language-like aspects of music, rather than conceiving of it as individual notes:

> Don, I think, was looking for that idea of naturalness and being close to nature, which also means being close to language. When he came to New York and did "Relativity Suite" with this orchestra, they didn't have any written music. He taught it all to them by singing. So, [it has to do with] that whole interesting idea of using written notation versus not using written notation.

There is an aspect of "the organic way," in the way that Don Cherry expresses it, that is also linked to a desire to find a place where he can be free from temptation, including, but not limited to, his struggle with heroin and other substances. Cherry himself, in an interview with the *New York Times*, later declared that, "They say the forbidden fruit was the apple, but I think it was opium," and was open about moving to San

Francisco in the late 1980s to enroll in a methadone clinic and move far from his on-again, off-again drug habit in New York City.[15] In a spoken verse in "Relativity Suite", he gives the listener advice: "how can I get free of temptation/my friend, have you tried meditation/oh, I'm still having frustration and temptation/oh my friend, you must try meditation."

Communal meditation is central to the *Organic Music Society* record. The first track, "North Brazilian Ceremonial Hymn," is Naná's first recorded collaboration with Don. Naná takes a mournful melody in the idiom of Northeastern Brazilian folk Catholic pilgrimage songs, and merges it with a South Asian religious context, the singing accompanied by the drone of an Indian tanpura, its devotional lyrics replaced by open vowel sounds "ah" and "eh" that alternate every few minutes. This West meets East (or better yet, South America meets South Asia) setting gives Naná license to play with the kinds of percussive interjections that he began performing as part of Grupo Construção—sounds as akin to Foley artistry as they are to conventional musical sounds. Gongs erupt unexpectedly and dominate the sound for just an instant, bells emerge and fade, a berimbau phrase takes focus, moves through the stereo field and then dies out. The sound models the process a teacher of meditation might describe of letting thoughts surface, and then fade away, as one returns to repeat the mantra.

In the early to mid-1970s, Don and his family toured through Europe as the Organic Music Theatre, with Naná and a rotating cast of musicians piled into a VW camper that Don had customized so that he could drive it in the lotus position, controlling the accelerator and the brake with his hands (see Figure 4.2). The recent remastering and release in 2020 and 2021 of two live Organic Music Theatre albums, *Om Shanti Om*

Figure 4.2 *Don Cherry and Naná Vasconcelos at the 1972 Chateauvallon jazz festival during the years of the Organic Music Theatre. Photo by Guy Le Querrec/Magnum Photos.*

and *Don Cherry's New Researches featuring Naná Vasconcelos* signals rising interest in this phase of Don and Naná's playing.

The performance released as *Om Shanti Om* was originally broadcast on Italian television in 1976.[16] It begins with Don, Moki, Naná, and guitarist Gian Piero Pramaggiori all seated cross-legged on the stage. Moki's brightly colored quilts are draped behind them, featuring embroidered religious mantras such as the Buddhist and Hindu invocation of peace *om shanti shanti shanti om* and the Tibetan buddhist mantra *om mani padme hum*. Presentational staged secular performance merges with participative sacred practice as they sit on the floor in a semicircle and feed off of the energy of each other's playing. Don includes his family on stage, even though the young Neneh and Eagle Eye are not (or rather, not yet) professional singers or dancers. They sing these mantras with a sense of repetition, prioritizing trance and devotion, rather than striving toward innovation and individual expression. Yet, on top of these short melodic cycles, Don does sometimes take out his pocket trumpet and play lyrical lines that soar above the looping incantations. Although this music has moved away from jazz to the point that it is largely no longer recognizable as such, Don asserts through this trumpet-playing that "jazz is the glue"[17] that holds together the Turkish, Moroccan, West African, Indian, and Indonesian musical elements that he combined throughout his career.

The ensemble alternates between familiar instruments, such as the pocket trumpet, timbales, congas, and guitar, and instruments that are unfamiliar to most audiences at the time, such as the Malian doussn'goni, the Brazilian cuíca friction drum, the berimbau, and the Indian tanpura. At a certain point, he takes out a thing-a-ma-jig that sounds like a duck call and looks like the result of fitting a saxophone mouthpiece to a complex junction of copper plumbing. No one there plays only one instrument, and everyone sings the mantras collectively. Halfway into the performance, Naná takes out his berimbau and coaxes melodies and effects out of it. The lower resolution of the 1970s television broadcast causes the berimbau's solitary string to disappear, making the sounds even more dazzling, as it appears that he is conjuring them out of thin air. There is also an element of misdirection to moments of Naná's performance. My eye moved to the baqueta that strikes the string just as Naná's other hand lightly touches the string with a stone, conjuring up a snare-drum sound.

At the end of the performance, Naná and Gian Piero lay down a looping groove while Don, Moki, and Neneh dance and spin in front of them on the stage. An empty, audience-free television sound stage isn't an easy place to conjure up the feeling of being immersed in an event without a clear audience–artist boundary, but their camaraderie and musicianship shine through, nonetheless. The Organic Music Theatre experimented with the boundary line between staged performance and ritual, and between jazz and a range of musics from around the world. Don and his family, together with Naná and Gian Piero, were playing with the limits of musical egalitarianism, professionalism, and community, breaking down boundaries between their art and their lives. As Moki would put it: "the stage is home and home is a stage."

Codona=Co(llin) Do(n) Na(ná)

The most enduring project that Naná and Don did together was Codona, that toured throughout Europe between 1978 and 1984 and recorded three records on the ECM label.[18] The name Codona derives from the first two letters of the first names of the three participants in the group: Collin Walcott, Don Cherry, and Naná Vasconcelos. The name is apt, in that it expresses the distinctive contribution of each player, while at the same time stressing how their playing together creates a sound that goes beyond their individual contributions. It is a name that precludes rotating members. Without all three stakes in the ground, this triangular tent will fall.

When Collin, Don, and Naná first came together, it was to support Collin in recording for ECM. Don and Collin had played together before, and Naná and Don had played together as well, but all three hadn't yet played together. But as soon as they started, as Naná tells it, Collin felt the musical chemistry and declared that: "This is not my album! This is not mine, this is ours."[19]

According to Naná, the group came together "all because I had a berimbau, Collin had a sanza, and Don had a

Figure 4.3 *ECM Records promotional photo for Codona: Don Cherry, Collin Walcott, and Naná Vasconcelos. Photo by Roberto Masotti. Courtesy of ECM Records.*

doussn'gouni,"[20] and they were curious to hear what they would sound like together. The doussn'gouni is from the West African region of Mali, Senegal, and the Gambia. A humbler relative of the 21-string kora, the doussn'gouni is traditionally played specifically by hunters. Its satisfying bass tone complements the crisper treble and mid-frequency attack of the berimbau, which shares a very similar structure to musical bows found in the Bantu regions of Southern Africa, in places such as Angola. The sanza, an instrument where sounds are made by plucking metal tongues, is part of a family of instruments found in Central and Southern Africa, including the mbira, the emblematic instrument of Zimbabwe.

All three instruments share rich, buzzy timbres in their respective registers. The berimbau gets its buzz from the player's manipulation of a coin or stone against the string. Don's doussn'gouni flies a banner at the top of its mast, where the crow's nest would be. His instrument's intentional buzz comes from a gently bent rectangle of tin perched atop the neck, adding noise to the basslines that orbit around the pitches of the lowest strings of a guitar or the mid-range of a bass. It is common for lamellaphones like the sanza, the kalimba, and the mbira, to be loosely affixed with small pieces of metal, like bottle caps, that buzz as the player plucks the metal tongues.

"Mumakata," on their 1979 album, showcases the blend between these three kinds of instruments, each associated with a distinct region of the African continent. Each is given ample space in the mix, Don's doussn'gouni panned hard into the left ear, Naná's berimbau panned hard into the right ear, and Collin's sanza occupying the center but at a slightly lower volume, so he doesn't dominate. The three instruments fill the frequency spectrum from bass to treble. The song shuffles at a brisk trot before all three players break into a mantra-like lyric. The distinction between pitch and noise blurs as the track throbs, each part interlocking with the others in multiple coexisting pulses. The rustling, crackling, and buzzing belies the relaxed precision of the groove, as does the casual but careful group singing, where no one voice vies for focus. Don's trumpet interjects and occasionally soars on top of the bed of buzz, reminding the listener of the performer's connection to jazz. The pristine, focused sound of Don's trumpet signals to the Western listener that this is not traditional African music, but rather represents the musical journey of jazz players that no longer feel compelled to stay within jazz parameters.

The track "Colemanwonder: Race Face/Sortie/Sir Duke" on the same album recorded in 1978, plots this debt to and divergence from jazz and pop by exploring melodies by Ornette Coleman and Stevie Wonder within new instrumentation. The track begins with Coleman's twisting and turning post-bop, free jazz, catch-me-if-you-can melody, unmoored from a jazz rhythm section. The sound of the trumpet points the listener toward jazz, but it is doubled by the unfamiliar sound within a jazz idiom of Collin's sitar. In this sparse setup, Naná is an equal participant, and he focuses on finding melodies on percussion instruments. He switches instruments every few phrases. First, he plays the cuíca (friction drum), and doubles his playing with his falsetto. Although the cuíca looks like a drum from a distance, it is played by rubbing a moistened cloth to a wooden dowel that is connected to the drumhead, to create squeaks and groans of various pitches. Next, he plays at least four pitches on multiple cowbells, before switching to a West African talking drum, an hourglass-shaped instrument where the pitch is changed by squeezing leather straps tucked under the player's arm. These transitions are all precisely arranged, in a way that is very different from the exuberant overdrive of the original free jazz context from which Don emerged.

Part of what made working with Collin and Don a peak experience for Naná was the way in which they listened so deeply to each other and cared about giving each other room to stretch out. "We listened to each other. We could listen to each other and find space. It had to do with security. When somebody doesn't feel this idea of competition. Musicians have to be flexible. They have to be comfortable with themselves."[21] In practice, this ethos is audible in small details of the record. At the end of the song "Codona," for example, Naná, playing congas, is so in sync with Collin's hammered dulcimer, that when they crescendo and change tempo together, they are lovingly attuned. This flexibility is also found in their ability to move between instruments, Don switching between pocket trumpet, various flutes, and douss'ngouni,

Collin switching between sitar, sanza and tabla, and Naná switching between his many percussion instruments.

Codona explored timbres unfamiliar to European audiences, showing that instruments from Africa, Latin America, and India were capable of the same precision as European orchestral instruments. They went about this sincerely and without caricature (unlike cartoon-y exploitative 1950s–60s exotica, for example), possessing significant knowledge of Indian, African, and Afro-diasporic musical systems, but without an orthodox commitment to performing these styles in a traditional manner. In doing so, the group brought together the ingredients of what was beginning to be labeled "World Music" in record store bins, a category with ample contradictions that would be thoroughly discussed by musicians and scholars in the decades to come.[22]

Codona's timbral range, precise intonation, and improvisations within careful arrangements fit well with the mission and branding of Edition of Contemporary Music (ECM) records. Since Don and Naná recorded on the ECM label, and both participated in the Creative Music Studio (CMS), a progressive "unmusic school" in Woodstock, New York, I want to turn briefly to profiling these two institutions before turning to focus on Naná's work with his other main ECM labelmate, Egberto Gismonti.

Interlude: Edition of Contemporary Music Records (ECM)

A successful and influential European record label focusing on both jazz and Western art music, founder Manfred Eicher's vision runs throughout ECM's catalog, from the sounds that are recorded and mixed, to the distinctive, austere visual aesthetic of the record covers, its signature stark photographs of unpopulated landscapes, many of them in black and white. An interplay between the sonic and the visual is a constant in ECM's brand, a priority that Eicher ascribes to being young and "looking to the mountains" and "listening to the birds, the sound of waves." He cites the qualities of "light, and the atmosphere inspired by its light"[1] in Oslo as the reason that he has preferred to record there. The joining of sound and vision is made more tangible in ECM artists' collaborations with avant-garde filmmakers such as Jean-Luc Godard, as the label has recorded and released many film soundtracks.

A few key moments in Eicher's musical biography confirm the label's priorities. He was trained as a classical bassist at the Berlin Academy of Music, and like the bossa nova musicians that influenced Naná early on, Eicher became taken by the contemplative jazz of Miles Davis and Bill Evans. He began ECM with an ear for the possibilities and constraints afforded by both written and improvised music, and worked to make recordings that rose to the demands of both. In Eicher's words:

> For me it's very good to bring the demands of written music—phrasing, intonation, dynamics—to improvisational recording, where the approach is looser and more spontaneous. And vice versa, to bring some of the spirit of an improvised music session into a recording of written music, to get some empathy into it, so that it doesn't become an academic-circle record. I'm trying to make an exchange, to bring one to the other.[2]

Beyond the nuances of phrasing and dynamics, many ECM albums have a sense of narrative arc and flow from one section to the next, as opposed to simply offering a random collection of songs.

Eicher's vision for ECM extends beyond the playing itself to the recording process and studio production as well. As a production assistant for the Deutsche Grammophon label in 1969, he noticed a gap in how much care was taken in the recording of classical music when compared to the recording of jazz.[3] He remained committed to having ECM right this wrong, finding ways to record jazz with "unusually transparent sound-mixes in which the nature of the musical interaction was newly illuminated" and "every nuance and timbre lovingly registered."[4] In 1971, Canadian magazine *Coda* dubbed ECM mixes as "the most beautiful sound next to silence."[5]

Unlike many major record labels that release a variety of music to a range of audiences without curating a cohesive sound or process, both supporters and detractors of ECM agree that the label's Eicher-produced records share a signature sound. Steve Lake hears the fundamentals of this sound being based on reverb and microphones: "He has a poetic grip on the parameters of Lexicon's reverb machines, a good sense of the character of diverse microphones—Neumann and

Schoeps preferred—and an intuitive feeling for microphone placement."[6] In conjunction with carefully calibrated artificial reverb, Eicher has sought out locations, such as monasteries and concert halls, to create an atmosphere for the recording, a sonic setting that doesn't simply invoke the sterile and neutral recording studio.

Jon Pareles, in the *New York Times*, writes that "across styles, the label's hallmark has been the contemplative detail of its music, a kind of acoustic enhanced realism."[7] Robert Hunt argues that Eicher's aesthetic is "immersive, not analytical … Microphones are not ears, and every step of the recording process is some sort of 'compromise' from being there in the room, during the performance. Good recordings are illusions. I prefer the immersive illusion that ECM creates over some attempt to capture the 'perfect' rendition of a performance, room reflections, coughing, and all."[8] While seeking out good-sounding rooms, Eicher doesn't believe in recreating the room sounds faithfully, instead seeking to reproduce the atmosphere of the music as it is played in the new room of the listener, with its own reverberant idiosyncrasies. In Eicher's words, "The crucial thing is for a tone or mood to be created—an atmosphere that sincerely expresses what one wishes to convey."[9] With this goal in mind, during a time when sound production and recording technology were transforming dizzyingly quickly, the ethos of the label was to retain much of the standard restraint of the last decades of jazz-recording practice by spending days or even just hours on recording sessions, rather than months, as was becoming the process for many rock acts who made the multitrack studio their instrument. At the same time, Eicher wasn't against the use of technology, as his reliance on high-quality microphones and electronic reverb make clear. And while the label focused on extended performances recorded without undue splicing, some multitracking allowed multi-instrumentalists like Naná and Don to sound more than one of their instruments at once.

Listeners' responses to ECM studio production, often phrased in a language of hot and cold, express an ambivalence surrounding the emergence of European jazz in the 1970s. Critics have described it as "cold and humorless," "baleful Nordic starkness," and "seductively austere."[10] Steven Feld referred to it as "a particular technological aesthetic featuring crystalline audio transparency, a brittle if ice-clear sound, marked by hauntingly stark reverberation," shaping "one of the significant aesthetic spaces of global improvisational avant-gardism in the late 1970s, intensifying atmospheric presence and focusing attention on audio resonance."[11]

This focused attention on atmosphere and audio resonance facilitated Naná's transition from being literally and figuratively turned down in the mix as an accompanying percussionist, to becoming a central participant and collaborator with an ensemble. The sonic microscope of fine microphones provided a showcase for Naná's efforts to find melodies in the overtones of instruments that had been so often relegated to timekeeping. Naná ended up performing on over a dozen records on ECM: three with Codona, three with Egberto, and several with Pat Metheny, Ralph Towner, Pierre Favre, Jan Garbarek, and Arild Anderson. This partnership between Naná and the label makes sense when considering that so many of Eicher's priorities were Naná's longtime priorities as well: bringing together Afro-diasporic and European music, exploring the stereo field, linking the sonic to the visual and the narrative, and wedding the complexly arranged to the spontaneous.

Underlying this alignment between Eicher's vision for ECM and Naná's vision for transforming the role of the percussionist, however, there is a fragility to the partnership. In an essay titled, "The Center and the Periphery," Eicher himself outlines his cosmopolitan openness to musical exploration outside the realms of jazz and Western concert music that contributed to the emergence of world music as a genre.[12] At the same time, his view is firmly based on the subject position of a white European traveler:

> Genuinely knowing ourselves always involves knowing how others see us. Those who are serious about culture will try to position themselves at the periphery and see how they are mirrored from there. The meaning of a culture reveals itself in its plenitude only through encounter and contact with a culture different, even alien to it. The dialogue that develops between them by far transcends the realm of the self-contained and unambiguous. We ask an alien culture questions it would not ask itself. And in doing so, we look for answers to questions that are our own.
>
> But we must never settle too comfortably at the periphery—the margin should only be a source, a spot from which to grasp the essence of the center. The moment we realize that there are no frontiers, distance becomes light.[13]

While in one moment Eicher announces that there are no frontiers, in another he is clear in his contention that "the margin should only be a source,"[14] not a means to fully decenter the center-periphery axis. In a sense, while celebrating the musical cultures of the economic periphery outside of Europe, their role, in his view, is to provide raw sonic materials. This sentiment echoes what anthropologist Shelly Errington calls "avant-garde artists' celebration of and inspiration by the primitive as a magical resource for the modern."[15]

Recording for ECM, Naná, as an Afro-Brazilian, is perhaps an unlikely participant in creating the soundtrack to particular geographies of whiteness in 1970s–80s jazz, where his atmospheric, arranged, "painting through sound" approach to percussion put him in high demand among his labelmates. Although largely kept from the center of the mix, Naná contributed to the atmosphere of Jan Garbarek's refiguring of Nordic folk songs and Pat Metheny's pastoral jazz invoking the wide open road in rural spaces of the United States, in albums such as *As Falls Wichita, So Falls Wichita Falls* (1981).[16] Explorations of the present so often require a glimpse of the past, at least for contrast, as the *New York Times* described Naná's playing and vocalizing as "inarticulate tribal murmurs" at the beginning of the vaguely science fiction record with the Indigenous word "Wichita" in the title.[17] Pat himself, in a eulogy he posted when Naná passed away, mirrors Eicher's admonition to encounter the periphery without decentering oneself. Pat places Naná in a counterbalancing role of maintaining a "natural sound" within a contemporary electric ensemble. "As I moved towards using more and more electricity in the music, I really felt it was important to balance that with natural sound and Naná was able to offer that in a perfect way; including the way he used his voice."[18]

Interlude: Creative Music Studio (CMS)

ECM records proved to be an important node in the career trajectories of both Naná and Don. After they moved back from Europe to New York in the late 1970s, however, another institution expanded their community of musicians, the range of instruments they played, and the musicians with whom they would gig in years to come. Naná's friendship and collaboration with Don Cherry also led him to the Creative Music Studio (CMS), a crucial site for improvised music that disregarded genre labels and engaged with musical systems from around the world.

Naná was not the only player affected by Don's journey. Vibraphonist and pianist Karl Berger sought out and played in Don Cherry's quintet in Europe in the mid- to late 1960s. By 1971, while Don was assigning students parades as exams at Dartmouth, Berger was also considering ways to rethink music education. But instead of doing like Don and seeking to change music education from within an established institution of higher learning, Berger felt compelled to start a new kind of music school, or rather a site where players' musical horizons could be transformed. Berger later explained in an interview: "What we did with Don Cherry was so groundbreaking. In the 60s, the doors just opened up and a flood of new music started happening. It was almost uncontrolled. There came a time in the 70s when we were basically asking, what is it that we're doing and how can we convey it to anyone else?"¹ Inspired by Don Cherry's musical egalitarianism, deep listening, and openness to other musical systems as he traveled, Berger and Ornette Coleman decided to open a music school at a camp in Woodstock outside New York City. For Berger, the rural setting was key in that, in order to understand sound, one had to start with silence, a perspective in line with his days visiting Don in his Swedish retreat.

A *New York Times* profile refers to the Creative Music Studio as "the unmusic school" and compares it to Black Mountain College, the progressive school in North Carolina so important to experimental writers and artists from the 1930s to the 1950s. CMS offered an immersive approach to learning music, aiming to free players' own voices over the consumption of the "frozen information" of the last generation's masters, as Wadada Leo Smith put it.² One guiding artist per week would lead the workshop, not focusing on their instrument only, but working up material together for a concert at the end of the week (student groups on Friday, and the visiting artists on Saturday). Naná saw the value of CMS for its opportunities to "learn more with your own body" rather than simply through book learning. "When you learn it with your own body, you have the possibility to never forget. When you learn it by the book, you have a tendency to forget. With your own body, it's like learning how to ride a bicycle; after twenty years go by, you get on a bicycle and your body remembers."³ According to Naná, what happened outside of the scheduled workshop was the most exciting part:

> When I was there, I was playing twenty-four hours; we played almost all the time. I would do my workshop for a couple of hours, and after that I would just go outside; the place was beautiful in the woods. I would just be playing all the time with musicians who were there. It was an incredible way to learn!⁴

In Woodstock, Naná forged new connections with musicians such as percussionists Trilok Gurtu from India and Aïyb Dieng from Senegal. During the late 1970s and early 1980s, when Naná was participating in the CMS, new instruments such as the talking drum started to appear in his recordings and live arrangements, and other instruments, such as the tabla, that he had taken up in Paris in the early 1970s, fell away, leading certain collaborators to speculate later that after hearing Trilok's mastery, Naná felt that he wasn't doing justice to the instrument. During CMS after-hours jam sessions, Naná was learning new instruments and watching the technique of virtuosos on their respective instruments. Several musicians whom he had performed with in the past, as well as several whom he would soon perform with, were a part of the CMS community (although not necessarily in Woodstock at the camp at the same time). In addition to Trilok Gurtu, Aïyb Dieng, Karl Berger, and Don Cherry, that long list included Oliver Lake, Abdullah Ibrahim (Dollar Brand), Mark Helias, Jack DeJohnette, Ed Blackwell, Janet Grice, Adam Rudolph, Cyro Baptista, Carlos Ward, and Pat Metheny.

5 Naná and Egberto Gismonti

Even before Naná recorded three Codona records, his first recording on the ECM label marked the start of a longstanding collaboration with Brazilian composer, multi-instrumentalist and arranger Egberto Gismonti. It is tempting to flatten the story of Naná Vasconcelos and Egberto Gismonti's musical chemistry into a story where oral tradition meets written tradition—non-Western folklore in an encounter with Western art music. Even Naná himself fell into this narrative to a certain extent when he talked about why they sounded so good together. After all, Gismonti had studied composition with Nadia Boulanger, a student of Igor Stravinsky's, placing him in the distinguished company of others who had been drawn to study with her in Paris, including Aaron Copland, Astor Piazzolla, Philip Glass, and Quincy Jones. Gismonti also studied with Jean Barraqué, a disciple of Webern and Schoenberg who, as Gismonti tells it, once stole and silverplated a rose from Beethoven's grave and hung it on the wall of his house.

But pinning Naná only to oral tradition and Egberto only to written tradition doesn't do justice to either musician. Telling the story that way disavows Naná's already strong love for Brazilian classical composer Villa-Lobos's sound-images and interest in Stockhausen. It also ignores Egberto's ambivalence toward erudition, as heard in the difference between his highly trained style as a pianist, and his self-taught guitar playing that pushes the boundaries of classical technique. The encounter

Figure 5.1 *Naná Vasconcelos and Egberto Gismonti. Photo by Roberto Masotti.*

of music played without a score and music played with a score is certainly part of their story. But that tension already existed within each player before they met in Europe and began working together, first on the acclaimed record *Dança das Cabeças* (Dance of the Heads) in 1976, on *Saudades* three years later, and on several other records as well.

According to Gismonti, when his lessons ended, Nadia Boulanger told him to return home to Brazil, warning him that if he didn't, he was going to become a mediocre European composer. In his words, she told him to seek out the music from his country, "because it is alive. Here [in Europe], it is dead." She urged him to "be a little irresponsible" with music, "just trust and break the rules."[1] Playing with Naná allowed him to counter his elite European musical palette with sonic markers of Brazil, both Indigenous and Afro-Brazilian. It fit Egberto's efforts to remain harmonically adventurous while breaking certain rules, moving toward a difficult-to-categorize sound tied to twentieth-century Western art music, jazz, rock, samba, and Northeastern Brazilian styles, either alternately or all at once. For Naná, playing with Egberto fit Naná's efforts to bring his musical vision—forged by Afro-Brazilian religious and carnaval music, Afro-Latin dance music, African-American jazz, and European concert-band repertoire—into ever more erudite settings. At the time, neither of them knew much about Eicher's ECM records. What Egberto and Naná together brought to the recording session, however, resonated with Eicher's efforts to record, with impeccable sound quality, music that was "free" but engaged with and possessing the same complexity as Western art music as he understood it.

Naná and Egberto's first record, *Dança das Cabeças*, came together after the Brazilian military government imposed exorbitant fees on musicians' travel. Gismonti found himself with a recording date booked in Oslo, and no way to bring his band. Stopping along the way in Paris, Gismonti asked Naná if he would do the session with him, with less than 48 hours notice. Unfazed by the urgency of these constraints, according to Gismonti, Naná simply responded that, well, if they didn't have time to rehearse, they would just have to talk through his vision for the record.

Egberto proposed the underlying idea of two Indigenous boys (*dois curumins*) running through a dense, humid forest, full of insects and animals, keeping a distance of 50 meters from each other. This refrain, found throughout accounts of the story behind the recording, presents the project as an imagining of Amazonian Indigenousness, but not a grandiose, tragic treatise of an entire people. Rather, by focusing on two *curumins*, the sound-image of the record is cast in an innocent register. Innocent, and also immersive, placing the listener alongside the boys as they chase each other, comfortable in a forest that they know like the backs of their hands. Following *dois curumins* in the forest gives the sounds a dramatic setting. The opening track begins with forest sounds made specific by Naná's use of a set of functional Brazilian birdcalls whose makers are confident enough in their verisimilitude that they offer your money back if you don't attract the intended birds. Naná's simulated bird sounds are so realistic that multiple listeners have asked online where the field recording of the forest sounds was made.

After reading Egberto's description, and then listening to the record, my inner cinematographer sets up quite a complex shot of the two boys. They are running, the shot is moving too, and they are separated by a distance, so if both are going to share the shot, it must be a wide angle that gives us a glimpse of the forest. The relative importance of sight and sound in navigating a forest differs from that of a more open field. The density of the foliage makes a bird's eye view impossible, and, in my mind's eye, the boys appear and disappear out of sight, as tree trunks obscure the view. The recording alternates between sounds heard up close and sounds heard in the distance.

Upon the release of *Dança das Cabeças*, and as it rose in acclaim, the refrain of two boys running provided an entry point for hearing the sounds within. There is a power to listening to the record with this narrative in mind. It wasn't, however, how Gismonti grouped the pieces when he first composed them.[2] Gismonti had recently recorded nearly all the compositions, whether his own or other people's works, on his own *Academia de Danças* and *Corações Futuristas*, and Paul Horn's record *The Altitude of the Sun*.[3]

Before unreasonable fees for travel shaped the recording of *Dança das Cabeças*, Egberto had already been exploring new technologies and styles that made his music progressive rock and jazz-rock fusion-adjacent, even if neither of those labels comfortably fit his work. During a trip to Los Angeles, Herbie Hancock had generously granted Gismonti access to his garage of recently developed synthesizers, including various ARPs, and Gismonti had spent several long nights testing their sonic possibilities. The two records Egberto released prior to *Dança das Cabeças*, *Academia de Danças* (1974) and *Corações Futuristas* (1976), with their rock-like propulsion and space-age sounds from the first generation of artist-friendly synths, represented a break from Gismonti's previous arrangements, which had fallen more squarely within the idioms of Western art music or Música Popular Brasileira.

The fact that most of the compositions featured on *Dança das Cabeças* were first recorded during Egberto's Brazilian music-meets-prog/fusion phase immediately prior provides a basis for comparison between what I hereby dub Egberto's *before Naná* (BNE) and *with Naná* (WNE) Eras. Contrasting arrangements of the same compositions make it possible to hear Naná's particular contributions. Gismonti had already been experimenting with a combination of painstaking composition and improvisation. But on *Dança das Cabeças*, Naná and Egberto presented these tunes in a way that places them outside of prog rock and jazz fusion, leading to a hit album that was difficult to classify. Naná describes the shift in Gismonti's music this way:

> when we started to play together, it was a big change for his music. It was something he had never experienced before. He was used to playing with a quartet that had a drumset, bass, saxophone and himself. When he started to play with me, because of my instrumentation and approach, his music took on an Afro-Brazilian quality to it that never had before. Egberto was coming from a schooled concept; he went to

> the conservatory in Vienna to be a classical musician. I come
> from the street. I brought those elements to his music.[4]

Frequently switching instruments, the two musicians share the duet-in-wide-stereo format that Don Cherry experimented with on his "Mu" records. Naná and Egberto, however, take the *Dança das Cabeças* recording further outside of standard jazz-samba-bossa instrumentation. There is no drum set and no synthesizers. These conspicuous absences remove key markers of the time, as drum styles and mixes evoke time periods, and synthesizers offer ever-changing sounds that index the then contemporary. By beginning the record with a forest soundscape featuring sounds resembling birds and frogs, the story of the two boys plays out in an established setting. By refusing to allow any dead space between compositions, the entire 25 minute first side of the record has the quality of a cinematic soundtrack to a film that hadn't yet been made.

Dança das Cabeças features very few electronic effects and little studio wizardry beyond overdubs and reverb. Ever since the 1973 *Africadeus* record, Naná had been experimenting with sound without any electronics other than a stereo pair of microphones, whether on berimbau, or on shakers that he himself made. While on the record, one can occasionally hear an electronically produced flange or phase-shift effect on Gismonti's guitar, Naná produced a similar effect simply by scraping a stick on the gourd of his berimbau. The careful placement of sounds throughout the stereo field was the result of microphone choreography, rather than just the mixing board. Naná would the move the berimbau within the stereo field created by two mics placed a meter apart.

During the *Dança das Cabeças* recording sessions, Egberto knew the tunes inside and out, while Naná was going in cold.

A few days before the session, he didn't even know that he would be doing the recording. This circumstance, which in lesser hands could have easily resulted in a disaster, instead led to a career-making record for both artists. Working as a duo gave them lots of space in the stereo field at a moment when sound recording and playback technology were reaching higher standards of fidelity. Breaking away from conventional jazz instrumentation freed them from rote arrangements, and their mastery of several instruments each gave them a multitude of options in filling the available sonic space. They pivoted away from the conventions of the album, with its discrete tracks and stand-alone themes. Throughout the recording, their egalitarian interplay, a value that Naná also shared with Don Cherry, allowed Naná to serve not as a sidelined rhythmic timekeeper, but as a crucial purveyor of timbre and melody, occupying front and center alongside Egberto's guitar and piano.

The title composition "Dança das Cabeças" offers an opportunity to compare Egberto's *before Naná* and *with Naná* eras, as well as his *before Eicher's* and *with Eicher's* distinctive arranging and production choices. On the version of "Dança das Cabeças" found on the 1976 album *Corações Futuristas* that Egberto had just released, an electronic phase-shifting effect that shimmers with drummer Robertinho's hi-hat and ride cymbals transforms the frantic opening guitar part. A buzzing synthesizer glides in, playing runs at breakneck speed with a filter creating a wah-wah effect. Soon after this proggy *futurista* intro, two overdubbed flutes enter in harmony in a gesture to Gismonti's source material. The flutes are playing in the style of the Northeastern pífano bands that so fascinated both Gilberto Gil and Sérgio Ricardo in Caruaru, Pernambuco, in 1967. While the guitar effects and synthesizer sounds date the track as produced during the mid-1970s, the melodies, harmonies, and rhythms are drawing from older *banda de pífano* repertoire but adapted to a Brazilian music-meets-prog/fusion context. Close listening to the guitar part reveals that it too nods to rural Northeastern tradition, without any interest in reproducing the style outright. In this case, Egberto references the *cantoria de viola* troubadour tradition of improvised song duels. As the next section begins and the guitar builds rising tension by moving a dense chord fret by fret up the neck, Nivaldo's soprano sax solo reminiscent of John Coltrane further sets the recording in either a jazz/rock club, or a recording studio. Egberto is working with the same kinds of juxtapositions indexing the modern and traditional and local and transnational that Caetano, Gil, and other Tropicalists played with. But, at this point, Egberto was working outside of the antagonistic Brazilian nationalist context, and musical explorations were his focus.

A year later, when the song became the title track of Egberto and Naná's *Dança das Cabeças*, the arrangement, the instrumentation, and the studio production all shift dramatically to reframe reception of the tune. The forest setting provides narrative justification for the breakneck pace as Egberto tests Naná to see if he can keep up (which he can, without breaking a sweat). As opposed to the masculinist one-upmanship of prog rock or fusion displays of speed and dexterity, their virtuosity is put in the service of painting a sonic picture. The section that raises tension by rising by half-steps, that in the *Corações Futuristas* version of the track felt like a standard prog device, becomes on the ECM record the imagined chase between the two boys. Naná's chattering vocalizations zoom in and out of the sonic space, providing the sounds of insects buzzing around them.

One emblematic section in particular, later on the album's first side, suggests an encounter between imagined European notions of the primitive (a la Stravinsky's *Rite of Spring*), and Brazil's Afro-diasporic national-popular music. At around 21 minutes (the transition to a piece called "A Porta Encantada" on the vinyl releases of the record), Egberto plays thrashing parallel tone clusters on his guitar, pushing the perceptual boundary between dissonant harmony and harsh timbre, pointing to the Stravinsky-to-Boulanger lineage in his training. The dense chord stabs filled out on multiple guitar tracks are punctuated with timpani, only to give way to a recognizable samba rhythm. While the dissonant cluster in the guitar continues stubbornly unresolved, it shifts into an asymmetrical samba timeline. Spread throughout the left and right speakers, the timpani becomes a surdo part, shakers and a cuíca friction drum appear, and even a tabla drum can be heard keeping time. This moment is key to understanding the recording. Renato de Barros Pinto put it this way:

> The improvisation and the strict notation, the complex rhythm and the folkloric roots, atonality and samba mingle here with ease. But, although their spaces interpenetrate each other, the elements and practices remain identifiable and traceable to the history to which they belong. The artistic syncretism establishes a close and comfortable cohabitation between two unlike entities, without suppressing their differences.[5]

After "A Porta Encantada," the record shifts markedly, as Gismonti switches from guitar to piano for most of the record's second side. This change in instrumentation takes the setting outside of the forest and back into the concert hall. While Gismonti's approaches to both piano and guitar are percussive and urgent, his touch on piano feels more controlled and erudite when compared to his self-taught ferocity on guitar. Naná sits out the first half of the second side, which consists of solo piano pieces that flicker between modern jazz, MPB and contemporary European art music, in the same vein as Keith Jarrett's recordings on ECM from around the same time. Unlike the stereo painting through sound that happens throughout the rest of the record, the piano stays stationary within the stereo field. After 13 minutes of solo piano, the play of sounds associated with the center and the periphery, the European and the non-European returns, with Naná accompanying Egberto on a gong as Egberto plays a Chinese sheng, an instrument that resembles a bundle of bamboo and metal flutes, or a miniature version of the pipes from a church pipe organ. The player blows into one mouthpiece to sound several pitches at once, offering the possibilities of playing tone clusters with the breath articulation and phrasing of a flute or a saxophone. Gismonti tongues this acousmatic or mysteriously not-quite-recognizable instrument (is it a melodica? an accordion? a gaggle of oboes? almost, but not quite) in lopsided, zigzagging Brazilian *baião* and *ijexá* rhythms before returning to guitar.

Listening to *Dança das Cabeças* now, it feels quintessentially ECM, but at the time it wasn't easily recognizable as a particular musical genre. Gismonti cites the categories of the awards it won in different countries as evidence of how audiences in that country considered it: pop music in Germany, MPB in Brazil, folkloric music in Japan, experimental music in England, and jazz in the United States. It won the Grosser Deutcher Schall plattenpreis, an important prize for a German record, received the highest rating in *Downbeat* magazine, won best record of the year by *Stereo Review* in the United States, and *Melody Maker* called it one of the best albums of 1977.[6]

Amazonian and Central African Flutes

After touring on the heels of the international success of *Dança das Cabeças*, Egberto returned briefly to Brazil, spending forty days in the Xingu region with the Yawalapiti, living with the musician and shaman Sapain. They did not share a common tongue, and communicated through music. Egberto became fascinated with the way that polyrhythmic jakuí flute music went in and out of phase, as tempos were displaced between players. When he first heard the music, he couldn't make sense of the sounds: "I thought to myself: 'This here was much richer than *The Rite of Spring*.' I panicked because I learned the extent of my ignorance."[7]

By the end of the forty days, Egberto was very aware of how little he knew about the jakuí flute. Sapain gave him a small beginner's flute, as the jakuí flutes proper can only be played by the initiated. Egberto learned to reproduce certain melodies on this beginner's flute, but he didn't feel comfortable using them both because he knew he still lacked competence, and also because he learned that the jakuí was more than just music. The practice was interwoven with everyday Yawalapiti life, and if he were to extract it, "it loses its purpose and becomes only music."[8]

Egberto deliberately chose not to incorporate jakuí melodies on his subsequent album *Sol do Meio Dia* (ECM, 1978), on which Naná appears. He decided instead to commemorate his time in the Xingu through the track names rather than through Yawalapiti melodies. He added song subtitles invoking Yawalapiti life to works he had written and recorded before his pilgrimage such as "Festa da Construção" (Celebration for the Building of the Village), "Procissão do Espirito" (Dance of the

Spirits)," and "Voz do Espirito" (Voice of the Spirits). The record features the beginner's flute that Sapain gave him, but the melodies that he plays on it aren't based on Yawalipiti songs.

With this project, Egberto Gismonti ventured into contradictory terrain with his 1970s rethinking of 1920s nationalist modernist uses of Indigenous songs and dances by composers such as Villa-Lobos. Egberto felt uneasy representing the Yawalapiti in their absence, and sought to distance his project from earlier efforts that treated Indigenous melodies as "raw materials" to be "improved" through orchestral arrangements. His conviction that forty days wasn't enough to do justice to such a complex performance could be seen as praising Sapain. But this claim is also convenient for Egberto, granting him the same freedom to stray from the constraints of tradition that Naná granted himself on the berimbau. Yawalapiti rules around initiation as a precondition to playing the jakuí flute help Egberto justify not remaining beholden to tradition. Yet, casual listeners most likely still hear the resulting album as representing Indigenousness.

So, if Egberto wanted to invoke forest life without playing Indigenous melodies, what did he use instead? That's where Naná came in, momentarily swapping the Amazon for the Central African rainforest. During "Sapain (Sol Do Meio Dia)," one of the only compositions that Egberto hadn't written before spending time with Sapain, Naná performs hindewhu, a Central African technique of one person alternating between their voice and a one-pitched flute acting as a pedal tone. Naná also accompanies on body percussion and plays a steady pulse (Indigenousness in many Brazilian contexts such as carnaval is indexed musically as steady beats of less- or not-at-all-polyrhythmic drums with flute). He plays melodies on a West African talking drum, and doubles them with his voice, and he chants, "Sapain yeh ah, Sapain yeh," in a gesture toward Amazonian vocal practice.

Naná's performance provides vivid sounds of "that which came before," merging South America and Africa. It evokes an imagined time before so much musical specialization, where singers were also dancers were also players, and people struck their bodies as well as drums. By this point in the 1970s, technological advances in the recording studio, such as the ability to overdub countless tracks, shape sounds with reverb, and use highly precise top microphones, make it more possible than ever to represent on record the immediacy of body percussion and less familiar percussion instruments. The new makes it possible to vividly render the old.

Anthropologist Steven Feld, in an influential 1996 article, traces the use of hindewhu in a wide range of recordings from the 1970s to the present, including "Sapain (Sol Do Meio Dia)." He sees the trope as "romantic and patronizing renditions of an old theme," that fixes Central Africans as a "timeless primal other." Feld goes on, decrying that "a complex humanity is thus fixed in a tape loop in the machine of both postcolonial devastation and primitivist fantasy."[9] Naná participated in three of the musical projects that Feld cites. Hindewhu became a part of Naná's vocabulary as a percussionist soon after Herbie Hancock made it famous when his drummer Bill Summers performed it with a beer bottle on the 1973 record *Headhunters*. Naná's first wife Merrie remembers when they were living in Paris and he brought home a record of field recordings of Central African music, and how he had it on heavy rotation in their apartment.

Naná's placement of hindewhu within "Sapain (Sol Do Meio Dia)" tests the assumptions of the listener. If one hears Naná's use of hindewhu alongside Don Cherry's restless desire to learn about musical systems throughout the African diaspora, imagining life outside the strict time and profit motives of the city, the choice is laudable and sincere. Glauber Rocha's turn to Black and Indigenous cultural forms as enchanting and revolutionary in an anti-imperialist context also supports this conclusion. But a listener could also easily hear the slippage not just between Afro- and Indigenous Brazil, but Africa and the African Diaspora as well, as treating the Global South as interchangeable primitivism.

Musicologist K. E. Goldschmitt, in their work on Brazilians in the international music industry, provides a broader context for Indigenous-themed records that are deliberately not Indigenous in their musical elements. Goldschmitt describes how the ethnic and racial identities of Brazilians were somewhat illegible as they performed and recorded outside of Brazil. In many cases, they were received as not white (even when they were considered white in Brazil), yet not quite Black (in the sense that African-American US jazz musicians were Black), and not quite Latinx (in the sense that they weren't heritage speakers of Spanish and players of genres such as salsa).[10]

The reception of Milton Nascimento by international audiences, mediated through his collaboration with Wayne Shorter on the 1974 record *Native Dancer* serves as a case in point. Milton has dark skin and an almost operatic singing style, reconciling European bel canto with the intimacy of bossa nova vocals. Yet, this didn't stop Shorter from praising him by saying: "He's got more of an Indian or Amazonian or African element."[11] As the title *Native Dancer* suggests, Shorter mediates Milton's breakout international success by "mapping the índio onto Blackness," joining "the timelessness of primitivism with the Afro-modernity of Pan-Africanism."[12]

6 Utopia, Caricature, Satire, and Therapy: Naná in France

When Naná arrived in Paris, he did so at a moment when France was in the midst of redefining the primitive "other" as notions of multiculturalism emerged in the wake of the hard-won independence of several former African and Asian colonies during the mid-twentieth century. Naná walked the streets with his one-stringed bow on his shoulder, poised to demonstrate how an apparently simple, handmade instrument could reveal such complex sonic possibilities. In France, he piqued the interest of multiple cultural gatekeepers, each with their own particular agenda, each hearing Naná's sounds as a means to evoke and/or refigure narratives about cultural and musical origins.

Naná's percussion was heard as spiritual, therapeutic, kitschy, or a means to mock bourgeois close-mindedness, depending on how a particular project framed him and his work. And as Naná navigated these opportunities—some alienating, some liberating—he found a robust community of Brazilians and non-Brazilians—some old friends, some new. Naná's time in Paris between 1973 and 1978 was a fertile period for him, where many of the musical ideas and techniques that he would use for the rest of his long career coalesced. It was a time in which he found increasing success in occupying the stereo field and refiguring the role of the percussionist. My goal for this chapter is to strike a balance between describing what French cultural gatekeepers wanted from him, and emphasizing the vision that Naná himself was pursuing, and the networks that he was building as he moved forward.

Pierre Barouh

Actor, documentary filmmaker and record producer Pierre Barouh became a key figure in welcoming Naná to Paris and supporting him as he found his footing in France. Barouh had spent time in Brazil and produced a documentary film *Saravah* with virtuoso Brazilian guitarist Baden Powell featuring rare footage of aging samba icons Pixinguinha and João da Baiana. Barouh did many things, but was most famous for acting in the hit film *Un Homme et une femme* and writing the lyrics to its main theme.[1] The theme to *Un Homme et une femme* is a breezy French interpretation of bossa nova. It has proven to be an earworm so catchy, and, in time, so emblematic of bourgeois innocence and 1960s French romantic comedy kitsch that it now has been used in over 20 films and television programs through the years, ranging from the earnest *Growing Pains* to the darkly ironic *House of Cards* and *Nightmare on Elm Street*. With the money earned in his successful acting and songwriting career, he started Saravah records. For Barouh, Naná represented post-bossa nova authenticity—an artist as comfortable with Afro-Brazilian tradition as he is compatible with psychedelic experimentation. Barouh befriended Naná and, not only produced his solo record *Africadeus*, but also found him opportunities to make money playing on the records of other artists and recording music for advertisements and a TV movie.

Africadeus

A key breakthrough in Naná's efforts to center himself within the stereo field, literally and metaphorically, came in France in 1973, when he recorded the solo album *Africadeus*. On *Africadeus*, Naná proposes, through his berimbau playing, a spiritual and utopian Afro-future that hears the multiple in the singular, and the complex in the ostensibly simple. It also resonates with and challenges contemporaneous studio production, demonstrating the possibility of making psychedelic sounds without multitracking or studio effects. Naná mesmerized listeners with an epic 19-minute opening track recorded with just one string. By physically panning the instrument between a pair of microphones, Naná creates an expansive and hallucinatory stereo field. By scraping the gourd resonator, he creates acoustically the phaser and wah-wah effects in popular music studio production at the time. On this record, he is not merely a groove provider, focusing rather on timbre, melody, and even Foley artistry and sound effects, finding as many sounds as he could out of the miked berimbau. *Africadeus* showcases Naná's unique vocabulary of extended techniques on the berimbau, standing as a key piece in the puzzle of understanding the later *Saudades* record. Much of *Saudades* is the material from *Africadeus* interacting with an orchestral string arrangement, creating a kind of berimbau concerto. The later ECM studio production on *Saudades* teases out sounds from the instrument that can't be heard on *Africadeus*. But in contrast to the more majestic, wide open spaces that *Saudades* evokes, *Africadeus* invites the listener on a psychedelic inner journey, the record cover featuring a close-up of Naná's face, with his eyes closed in meditation. In *Africadeus*, inner and outer worlds blur. The almost binaural recording, when listened to on headphones, sounds as if it were emanating from within the listener's skull.

A Chrysler Commercial Called "Jungle"

Even though *Africadeus* foregrounds what was in the early 1970s an unfamiliar and exotic instrument in Europe, the record is contemplative and serious—a far cry from previous caricatured musical representations of the so-called "primitive" other. Musicologist Phil Ford, in writing about the shift from 1950s–60s exotica to 1960s–70s psychedelia, suggests that: "In the 1950s, those enthralled by exotica representations drew a frame around their encounter with otherness, but in the 1960s they sought to step through that frame."[2] The difference was that: "in the 1960s, a primitive of an unknown culture is not only what you dream of; it is what you say you are."[3] This contrast between exotica's distanced, kitschy take on the other and the depiction of immersive and spiritual proximity in *Africadeus* is illustrated vividly by a Chrysler commercial titled "Jungle" that Naná recorded when he needed money in Paris.[4] The difference between this commercial and, say, *Dança das Cabeças*, recorded around the same time, serves as a testament to how the use of the same musical elements can lead to such different ends.

In "Jungle," Naná provides the soundtrack for a campy sales pitch for a proto-Range Rover with pseudo-4-wheel drive. The 1976 ad features the markers of 1950s–early-1960s exotica, which cheekily promised that hi-fi recording techniques could bring close contact with the primitive into a modern bachelor pad. Using state-of-the-art multitrack recording techniques, Naná's Foley artistry renders jungle sounds that commingle with vocalizations in line with how Phil Ford describes 1950s exotica records like Les Baxter's "Jungle Jazz," in which "a pop obedience to clean intonation, is nevertheless dirtied with growls, chirps, mutters, and screams."[5] A man and woman move through the jungle, on a thrilling adventure, not sure what they'll encounter next. Their senses heightened by the unseen noises around them, they whisper about the Chrysler Matra Rancho Simca. The same descending rustling sounds scraped on the berimbau that appear in *Africadeus* within the listener's head, and sincerely depicting two boys running through the forest in *Dança das Cabeças*, are played here for laughs alongside the screech of a bird and a reverberant cackle that wouldn't be out of place in a haunted house amusement park ride.

Naná accompanies this safari with a polyrhythmic 12-pulse pattern—a timeline more characteristic in the Americas of ecstatic religious music than popular dance styles. He marks 4 beats on a shaker for each 6 of the drums. But the drums aren't only African in origin—in one ear, he plays the lopsided timeline on congas, but in the other, he plays a variation on South Asian tabla drums. In contrast to the humanism of the East-meets-West fusion that Naná performed with Don Cherry, here the collapsing of African and South Asian styles dismisses cartoon jungle-dwellers as all the same. The surrounding context frames musical elements as laughable that can be heard elsewhere as solemn or even elegiac.

Allowed Into the Center, and Relegated to the Side

Most of the projects in which Naná participated in Paris were located somewhere on the broad spectrum between the proud achievement on *Africadeus* of recording a solo record that centers the berimbau, and the alienated labor, exceptionally executed, of a caricatured jungle-themed Chrysler ad. One of Barouh's stated goals for his Saravah record label was to mix musicians and styles and to multiply musical encounters, and Naná's skills as a percussionist fit within a wide range of mid-1970s Saravah releases, from the prog rock of Mahjun to the poetic spoken-word storytelling of bohemian fixture Jean-Roger Caussimon.[6] Admittedly, there are records where his contribution as a session musician on a straight-ahead singer-songwriter's project appears to be just to pay the bills. There are, however, other records on which the musical chemistry is audible. On the album *Nandipo* by Gabonese musician Pierre Akendengué, for example, Naná adapts Afro-Brazilian grooves to Akendengué's gentle acoustic guitar-driven songs as Akendengué began to formulate his vision for a Pan-African music.[7] During this period, Naná developed a subtle shaker-driven way to complement acoustic guitar-based songwriting without overpowering a quiet song's delicate foundation.

In addition to the recordings on Barouh's Saravah records, Naná was also active during his time in Europe with free jazz musicians whose sounds were sharply distinct from, say, a country waltz by Saravah singer-songwriter David McNeil.[8] Baikida Carroll treated Naná as a full collaborator on his memorable album *Orange Fish Tears*.[9] The title track begins with an unsettling non-metrical soundscape of bells, thundersheet, bird calls, and rustling sounds underneath atonal piano, a celesta-like electric piano, and bamboo flute. The track takes its time. It is over halfway through the recording's 8 minutes before saxophone melodies eventually rest on this insomniac's bed of sounds only appearing over halfway through the recording's eight minutes. The next track, however, is hard-hitting right out of the gate. Naná nails down a 12-pulse timeline on cowbell and tabla as the track shifts into a kind of free jazz cubop, the saxophone, trumpet, and piano parts rudderless and at the mercy of an overwhelming layer upon layer of multiple clashing sounds. What makes this track stand out as it does is that Naná gives the furious groove an authoritative but relaxed core that provides a backbone for the other players and allows their jagged melodic lines to stand out.

A couple of years earlier, during Naná's first extended stay in Europe, he recorded *The Day After* with jazz clarinetist Rolf Kühn, his brother Joachim Kühn on piano and Phil Woods on alto saxophone.[10] In contrast to the incandescent fury of Baikida Carroll, this notable record has a subtlety to the sound production that allows Naná's range of timbres and melodies to shine through. Of the hundreds of recordings that I've tracked down on which Naná appears, *The Day After* represents one of the finest examples of a jazz musician fully realizing what Naná could contribute to a record if given free rein. Rolf Kühn is a versatile player who is able to move between freer and more straight-ahead jazz styles with ease, and like Milton Nascimento, cedes Naná significant terrain within the stereo field—most of the right channel—treating him as an equal in the mix. On the non-metrical title track, Naná is a Foley artist as he switches between the berimbau, shakers, iron bell, congas, gong, flexatone, and whispering vocalizations. But despite switching instruments constantly, his playing never steers the contemplative tune into caricature, ably complementing Oliver Johnson's brushes and mallets on drumset. The careful mix of this MPS Records release strives toward ECM's standards of high fidelity and microscopic nuance, allowing the listener to hear how intently the musicians are following each other's cues at any given moment.

The final, eleven-minute track on the record, "Sonata for Percussion, Piano + Clarinet," represents another step closer for Naná to his goal of placing his playing on equal footing with forms of Western art music that he later achieves on the *Saudades* record. The drummer, sax player, and bass player all sit out, giving Naná ample negative space between the Kühn brothers' skittering pointillistic staccato lines interspersed with sustained chord voicings. Naná darts between the left and right channels, utterly attuned to the improvisations on piano and clarinet, each note (or lack thereof) carefully placed. As Naná dropped into other people's projects as a session musician or a featured special guest, some players could hear the possibilities he brought and nimbly pivot to embrace his contribution, while others simply forged ahead, only permitting him to keep time.

Naná's Brazilians in Paris

While Naná remained in demand with cultural gatekeepers, he sought out community both within and outside the circles of Brazilian exiles in Paris in the 1970s. Like Naná did in New York City in 1971 when he lived with Glauber Rocha, and in the 1980s when Arto Lindsay and his brother Duncan lived with him off and on, he felt at home not only with other Brazilians, but Brazilians specifically from his Northeast region.

The 1976 album *Visions of Dawn* that Naná recorded with fellow travelers Joyce Moreno and Mauricio Maestro from the Rio de Janeiro scene, as well as their stint in Mexico City as part of La Sagrada Familia, represents the continuity of community that Naná was able to maintain on three continents.[11] *Visions of Dawn* is a Joyce record, with her voice and songwriting featured, but it is also a trio record, with space for all three to interact with a friendly intimacy. Unreleased until 2014, it is a terrific album that foreshadows the sound of many female MPB artists in the 1990s–2000s such as Marisa Monte, on whose records Naná would later appear. The album ends with Naná's wordless composition "Chegada" ("Arrival") that plays on the parallel pleasures of arriving at a geographical destination and arriving at orgasm.

In Paris, Naná's most enduring friend and musical collaborator was singer Teca Calazans, with whom he played in Grupo Construção in Recife before moving to Rio de Janeiro. Teca was in exile in Paris, principally because of her husband Ricardo Vilas' links to the armed struggle to overthrow the Brazilian dictatorship, and has lived most of her life there to this day. Brazilian ethnomusicologist Carlos Sandroni brought me to meet her outside of Paris, and she generously shared a scrapbook chronicling both her days with Grupo Construção in Recife and her later career in France. Two records of the husband-and-wife duo of Teca & Ricardo during Naná's time in Paris showcase their long-term friendship and collaboration.

When Naná played with Teca, it was like old times. In the same mid-1970s when Naná recorded *Caminho das Aguas* and *Cadê o Povo*[12] with Teca & Ricardo, he was reshaping the role of recorded percussion in *Dança das Cabeças*, *Africadeus*, and adventurous jazz records with Rolf Kühn, Baikida Carroll and others. His contribution to Teca & Ricardo, however, feels like a more polished continuation of the work they did in the mid-1960s in Recife with Grupo Construção. Teca's voice is dexterous, forceful, and lyrical, and Naná's accompaniment (together with the rest of the band) complements her like only an old friend can do. In their home state of Pernambuco, traditional genres are taken seriously, and when Teca sings a ciranda, a coco, or a maracatu, Naná knows what he is supposed to do and doesn't stray far from these established rhythms. When Naná brought his vast knowledge of percussion as a Pernambucan to a session with, say, Egberto, Don Cherry, or Rolf Kühn, it served as a vocabulary or a starting place, without the expectation that he would stay within the parameters of given traditional genres. In sessions with players unaware of the rhythms of his home region and/or uninterested in staying true to them, Naná would treat these rhythms like Dizzy Gillespie's cubop treated Afro-Cuban clave. Dizzy with Chano Pozo would play around *with* clave while not necessarily playing *in* clave throughout a given tune. Similarly, when Naná played with Teca, he was playing *in* clave, or rather its Northeastern Brazilian equivalents.

Naná was legible to Teca to an extent that he wasn't to anyone from outside of Northeast Brazil. Teca was the one who brought Naná a berimbau from Bahia so that he could play it in one of their Grupo Construção shows. In other words, they went way back. To many audiences in Europe, Naná's berimbau and wordless, timbre-centered vocals were exotic and unnameable, conjuring up stories of a primitive "that which came before." To Teca, however, the local ingredients of Naná's sound—coco, ciranda, reisado, maracatu, berimbau—were simply the musical ingredients that she had been popularizing for decades.

In addition to Naná's longtime contacts dating back to Recife and Rio de Janeiro, he also made new Brazilian friends in Paris. There is no more stark contrast during this period between Naná's work as a timekeeper accompanying mainstream French crooners, and the joyful Marcelino Buru album *Sessão Cabidela* that Naná produced and played on.[13] Buru, a Brazilian from the state of Minas Gerais also known for his work as an actor on stage and screen, had a sound based on traditional samba de roda but unafraid to add jazzistic touches, dramatic ominous bass riffs, and baritone sax solos. This record provides much of the template for Naná's later solo records from the 2000s when he returned to Recife: buoyant and groove-driven, with lots of layers of percussion, and a commitment to vary the instrumentation and the feel of each song. A stand-out track on the record is a playfully satirical lounge bossa jazz tune called "Ovo Há," a title that means "There are Eggs" in Portuguese, but that, when spoken, sounds like *au revoir* in French. The sophisticated piano and whispery sax of the tune sound ridiculous in contrast with the roots samba de roda of the rest of the record. While Naná plays a sleepy cuíca, Marcelino recites a word salad of common phrases that a beginning French student would learn. The awkwardness of going through life as a foreigner navigating another language provides fodder for Marcelino and Naná to poke fun at the absurdity of their everyday existence as Brazilians in Paris.

Naná *Épate les Bourgeois*

While Marcelino and Naná were poking fun at French airs of sophistication and spoofing not being able to express themselves effortlessly in a language they didn't grow up speaking, filmmaker Jacques Rozier and his star actor Pierre Richard deployed Naná and his percussion in an absurdist cinematic context that indexes a rethinking of French notions of the primitive. In the 1974 French new wave film *Les Naufragés de l'île de La Tortue*, Naná stands as a primitive exotic for hire in a film about a packaged "extreme" tourist experience simulating a shipwreck.[14] The figure of Naná's character exposes the tourists' antiquated notions of the primitive in order to mock the bourgeoisie for not recognizing his humanity. In the film, Pierre Richard is a semi-competent travel agent who thinks up a scheme in which people might pay to visit what is touted to be an undeveloped island where they will be forced to survive as modern-day Robinson Crusoes. By the end of the film, as Pierre Richard's character is put in jail for stealing bananas off of someone's private property in order to eat, it becomes evident that the island is also part of the contemporary world—a fact that would have been clear if the tourists had only spoken to Naná rather than adhering to their own fantasies.

When the tourists in dinghies approach the larger sailboat, they hear the unfamiliar sounds of the berimbau before seeing Naná and realizing that the sounds are being played on the sailboat by a human being. Director Rozier plays with expectations of an off-screen soundtrack, only to reveal that Naná's character has been hired to play this soundtrack on the deck of the ship as part of the packaged experience. Considering Wes Anderson's interest in French Cinema, it seems very possible that Naná's character in *Les Naufragés de l'île de La Tortue,* a Brazilian absurdly hired to provide an on-screen soundtrack to a maritime experience, served as a model for Seu Jorge's character in *The Life Aquatic with Steve Zissou*, who plays bossa nova versions of David Bowie songs from the deck of the ship of a Jacques Cousteau-like maritime adventurer.

The bourgeois adventure-tourists on the boat treat Naná as part of the scenery, awkwardly avoiding speaking to him, with the exception of one pair of tourists at the end of the film. When this couple finally does listen to him, Naná sits on the beach and tells them the ridiculous story of their intrepid tour leader being put in jail for stealing bananas. It is one of the only public recordings I could find of Naná speaking French during this period, and although it is thickly accented and contains some Portuguese words interspersed, he is an effective and animated communicator. The speech is a key part of the denouement of the film. It is the moment when the curtain is pulled back, and reveals the island the tourists so desired to be primitive to be part of the contemporary world—this, too, is a place with private property, police, and jails, after all. This moment in the film, as a register of Naná's French-speaking abilities at the time, reinforce the extent to which during his time in France, his accent and non-standard grammar were a part of the performance of racial and cultural difference within which he was received there.

Musical Participation as Therapeutic: Dr. Tony Lainé

Another important cultural gatekeeper for Naná in France, psychiatrist Dr. Tony Lainé, saw very different possibilities in Naná. After watching him play his berimbau on the set of a children's television program centered on the theme of dreams, Lainé was impressed by Naná's ability to captivate children largely wordlessly. The psychiatrist hired a painter, a dancer, and a musician to work full-time at l'Hopital de Sainte Genevieve des Bois in the south of Paris. As part of Lainé's experimental treatments for autistic and schizophrenic children, he saw Naná's musical practice as a restorative balm. Naná offered a kind of music therapy freed from the strictures of traditional music education, with no set methods, structure, or schedule. He was available to the children all day, whenever they wanted to play with him. Naná described it this way:

> The kids could come in anytime to my room; you didn't have to say, "Can I go there," or "Can I touch that," or "Can I go to the painter" ... they didn't establish the time to do music, or to paint, or to dance; the kids were free. The kids always went straight for my studio to listen to music or to ask me to play. I played and sang, and they'd say, [in a demanding tone]: "More!" And I'd play and sing, and they'd say, "More!" And I'd play and sing, and they'd say, "More!" [chuckles]. So I'd say, "Come on, sing with me!"[15]

The two years that Naná worked at the hospital proved important to him in multiple ways. It provided him with a steady paycheck that allowed him to be choosier about the musical projects he accepted. In addition, it gave him ample time to consider how body percussion and wordless vocals could draw people in, regardless of their language skills.

Even later, throughout the 1980s, when he would tour with his project Bush Dancers, whenever he had a free afternoon in a new city, he would seek out opportunities to make music with kids in hospitals. According to his bandmate and fellow percussionist Cyro Baptista, wherever they played, be it in continental Europe, London, or Manchester, they would go to a children's hospital or a community center in the afternoon. Sometimes buses full of children would arrive to see them. Naná would bring the instruments, and "create a situation." He would make berimbaus with them, and they would sing together. He would place shakers into the hands of even the most catatonic and sometimes succeeded in getting less responsive kids to interact with him through the sounds. He would bring a mic and a speaker, and the kids would really perk up when they heard their voices and their instruments amplified. According to Cyro, sometimes a nurse or doctor would comment that a child wouldn't usually move or talk, but would respond in the context of the "situation" they orchestrated. One kid who didn't usually talk spoke up to request specific songs, and when Naná and Cyro faked being able to play them, he called them out on their playful deception.

To a range of French cultural gatekeepers, Naná's percussion served as a restorative balm, a spiritual and utopian Afro-future, a campy sales pitch, and a means to criticize the bourgeoisie. Taken together, these uses of Naná index a 1970s refiguring of notions of the primitive. Anthropologist and art theorist Shelly Errington, in her witty and insightful book *The Death of Authentic Primitive Art and Other Tales of Progress*, situates this period as a moment when new ideas about the primitive were emerging. In what she dubs the narrative of "New Age spiritual evolution,"[16] anti-progress counternarratives were reclaiming previously rejected notions of "the irrational and the intuitive (long linked disparagingly to the natural and the primitive)."[17] This narrative counters the pernicious idea that Europe is the pinnacle of civilization and all others are at various stages of becoming as civilized. But as Errington spells out, even the counternarrative fails to question the either/or thinking upon which it rests. The 1970s–80s tale flips the older Eurocentric tale, but without dismantling its pairs of terms, such as primitive and modern, nature and culture, reason and intuition, and male and female. As a result, it ends up reinforcing what it seeks to overturn.[18]

Part of what happens is that, as bell hooks describes it, "ethnicity becomes spice, seasoning that can liven up the dull dish of mainstream white culture."[19] Beyond merely offering spice, the music of racial and ethnic others is often treated as therapeutic. Together, these contrasting uses of Naná's sounds outline how life in Paris offered an opening for him to narrate his own story, while partially foreclosing his efforts by filtering his sounds into notions of the primitive. Granted, certain gatekeepers were more uneasy with these primitivist representations than others—Chrysler's exotica was bald-faced, for example, while the film with Pierre Richard portrayed the French tourists as the fools and humanized Naná. Naná gracefully found his way through a shifting but still perilous set of work opportunities, and vexing terms of audience reception.

Interlude: Naná's Place Within the *Fourth World*

The influential 1980 album *Fourth World, Vol. 1: Possible Musics*,[1] was recorded within a year of *Saudades*. *Possible Musics* provides an example of how Naná continued to be sought out for projects that morphed the primitive and the exotic rather than fully overthrowing these conceptual straitjackets. American trumpeter Jon Hassell and British producer Brian Eno teamed up to record the album in New York and Toronto soon after Naná returned to New York City to live. The project is a thought experiment inspired by Hassell's time studying with composer Karlheinz Stockhausen (alongside classmates Holger Czukey and Irmin Schmidt, who went on to form the band Can, bringing minimalist notions of repetition from the avant-garde into a rock context). The album was important enough that the online electronic music publication *Resident Advisor* ran a feature article for its fortieth anniversary, to take stock of how it shaped subsequent ambient electronic music featuring elements from the Global South. It is a testament to Naná's career that an album that he participated in could have such a lasting impact, and yet be just another blip in his musical life. *Possible Musics* was released during the same period that Brian Eno teamed up with David Byrne (much to Hassell's chagrin) to produce a variation on the *Possible Musics* concept called *My Life in the Bush with Ghosts*, as well as the Talking Heads' influential albums *Fear of Music* and *Remain in Light*.[2]

Hassell and Eno's speculative album imagines a reordering of the past leading to alternate sounds in a fictional future. In this imagined world, the consolidation of European concert music and its imperial reach had never taken place. His soundbite description of the record is "coffee-coloured classical music of the future."[3] In Hassell's *Fourth World*, the boundary lines and hierarchies between ethnic/folkloric, commercial popular music, and classical music never crystallized the way that they demarcate today's musical world. He asked: "What would music be like if 'classical' had not been defined as what happened in Central Europe two hundred years ago? What if the world knew Javanese music and [Central African forest] music and Aborigine music? What would 'classical music' sound like then?" The "as if" question of possible music allows Hassell to create a fictional and indeterminate mental and geographical landscape: "not Indonesia, not Africa, not this or that. I thought I was more successful in trying to create something that COULD HAVE existed if things were in an imaginary culture, growing up in an imaginary place with this imaginary music."[4]

Hassell's teacher Stockhausen believed that world music could create a new unity between folklore and electronic music. In the chapter, "Beyond Global Village Polyphony," of his book *Towards a Cosmic Music*, Stockhausen proclaims that: "The musical means are microphones and magnetic tape. That is the beginning of universalism." Stockhausen found "the possibility of telephoning Africa to order a tape recording, parts of which I then combine with electronic sounds I produce in Tokyo"[5] to be exciting and unprecedented. Aware of the fear of "cultural greyout," he offers the caveat, "I am not striving for a 'synthesis' where everything is swallowed up in a gigantic mishmash... I want to preserve the autonomy of the individual phenomena within the polyphony achieved."[6]

Hassell took this call to heart, studying with Pandit Pran Nath in India, where he learned, among other things, that there were many more ways to move between one pitch and the next than he had ever imagined. His trumpet melodies bear the imprint of this immersion in the kirana gharana North Indian classical tradition. But Hassell transforms his "quasi-raga" lines, as he describes them, with an early electronic harmonizer effect allowing him to play the melodies in parallel fourths and fifths, creating music he considers "diagonal," in that it lies somewhere in between harmony that is vertically stacked at a given moment, and melody that horizontally moves through time.[7]

On the record, Naná and Senegalese drummer and percussionist Aïyb Dieng lay down muted, controlled but relaxed, looped drum grooves repetitive enough to be reminiscent of minimalism. The parts have been mixed such that they are shorn of their familiar timbres. Great pains are taken to make the sounds acousmatic, obscuring the sonic signature of a well-known instrument in the service of the album's speculative premise. Naná's parts have been slowed down, mixed with watery reverb, or played on a glass version of a ghatam, a South Asian clay-pot instrument, instead of congas. Naná and Aïyb play with a measured swing, with combinations of duple and triple pulses that point toward sub-Saharan African or Afro-diasporic drumming, their parts sometimes veering toward rhythms more akin to Indian classical music as well.

To anthropologists and economists in 1980 when the album was released, the term "Fourth World" was an extension of the Cold War-era descriptor "Third World" that was such an important rallying cry for Glauber Rocha. "Fourth World" referred to the most economically marginalized populations, often non-industrialized Indigenous people. Hassell's use of the term diverges from this use in the contexts of international development, connoting instead an imaginary, reordered, alternative musical world. Before coming up with Fourth World, Hassell's original term for his music was future/primitive, a descriptor that he picked up from Albert Goldman's book *Carnival in Rio* that interprets Brazil.[8]

Hassell is unabashedly fascinated with the exotic, commenting:

> The exotic is central to me. I don't understand why the "exotic" doesn't have the automatic appeal for everyone that it does for me... It's not as though I have a "real life" with glimmers of exoticism—like living in a Victorian house with exotic trophies around the room—it's more, "If something really feels good, then why don't you do it all the time instead of only doing it on Saturdays?" Fourth World is an entire week of Saturdays. It's about heart and head as the same thing. It's about being transported to some place which is made up of both real and virtual geography.[9]

The exotic slips into the erotic in his pleasure-centered view when he describes his music as post-orgasmic in its lack of goal-orientedness, claiming that: "It's about a beautiful girl and a beautiful situation at the same time."[10] Inviting Naná to this project makes sense, considering Hassell's notion of Brazil in particular: "Brazilian music, there's always something there in that culture that is very sexy, that gets to the primacy of their music," he said. "Fourth World—or any of the other ideas I've been promoting—all basically cloaked in one basic idea and that's the primacy of the female."[11]

Clearly, Hassell is blithely unconcerned with critiques of exoticism. If only Rocha, who so famously decried nostalgia for the primitive, hadn't died close to the release of *Fourth World, Vol. 1: Possible Musics*, so that he was alive to respond to Hassell's breathless statements. First, Hassell claims that dabbling in a fascination for the exotic during the height of late-nineteenth-century European imperialism doesn't go far enough in treating difference as a source for pleasure. Next, he indulges in a sex tourist's equation of other places, recreation, and women. During the same year, 1980, Rocha grapples with representations of inequality in his "Third Worldist" cinema in his final film *Idade da Terra*, using Naná's track "Amazonas" as the film's sonic exposition of the bloody history of settler colonialism in the Americas. Meanwhile, Hassell's "Fourth World" music frames non-European musical practices within a timeless, mythic realm that removes them from the imprint of history and politics. That Europe dominated (and continues to hold economic advantages over) the same India, Africa, and Brazil from whose sounds he derives exotic and erotic pleasure is of little consequence to him. His insistence that "the primacy of the female" is behind his ideas fits within Errington's tale of New Age Spiritual Evolution, where older hierarchies such as male and female are reversed without being dismantled.

For Naná, however, this was just a gig among many. When an interviewer asked him, just months before his death, what his five most important collaborations were, it didn't make the cut. Merrie describes the downtown scene that Jon Hassell was a part of at the time as one of minimalists such as La Monte Young and Terry Riley, and their guru Pandit Pran Nath, doing concerts on the exchange floor of the enormous Mercantile building, with huge ceilings and the whole floor covered with white wool rugs. She remembers that, for Naná, Jon Hassell's music was borderline, but generally, the scene was "a little too white for him—not that he would ever say that—but it was too cerebral, too thin, it was not his thing."

7 Race, Primitivism, and Counterculture

There is a passage in the memoir of Márcio Borges,[1] an important lyricist and songwriter within Milton Nascimento's Clube de Esquina circle of musicians, that provides a glimpse of how audiences and fellow musicians alike often received Naná within a primitivist register. The passage below indicates that this was the case not only when he traveled outside of Brazil, but within his home country as well. In it, Márcio narrates as primitive and mystical the way Naná used his voice to complement the berimbau, placing Naná within a story of the origins of music and language. In countercultural, late-1960s Rio, the songwriter describes Naná as "super Black with rumpled hair, like a medusa with little black worms," arriving in a flowery shirt, holding his berimbau and explaining, "I'm barefoot so that I can feel the energy of the earth, man," and entering into "lofty conversations of an esoteric nature, involving stories of proven reincarnation and the materialization of spirits."[2]

In Márcio's account, Naná's vocalizations, which include clicks, gargles, and sibilant, vowel-less sounds, are heard not as timbral sounds that complement his musical instrument, but as the primitive language of a proto-human trying to speak before phonemes were fully developed:

> He was spectacular on the berimbau. He hit the gourd of the instrument against his belly, spun the stick around the

outside of and within it, playing it, playing it some more, striking it and striking it again, singing sacred spirit possession songs. Suddenly, he grimaced, let loose with a series of clicks with his tongue and his throat, accompanied by some rhythmic gargling sounds as if he were speaking a primitive homo erectus language, inarticulate, without vowels. From there, he jumped around with laughable gestures, the rhythm changed and then the sounds produced by his body turned more gentle: Didina-Dina-Diná, dadina dina diná.[3]

Like many stories of "that which came before," multiple past timeframes pile up without adding up. One moment he is a shaman, the next a proto-human working out the first language. The next paragraph in the passage moves from the cave to the kitchen, imagining a time when functional objects were first converted into dedicated musical instruments, just

Figure 7.1 *Naná Vasconcelos, Paris, August 1976. © Alécio de Andrade, ADAGP, Paris 2021.*

as, it is assumed, happened when a bow and arrow was first transformed into a berimbau:

> "I'm going to do some research into your pots and pans." He wasn't referring to food, but rather to the sonorities of said items. Mom, notoriously guarded regarding her kitchen and the stuff in it, that she maintained shined and without blemishes, made an extremely rare exception for Naná—no one understood why—and gave him her precious pans. Just then I noticed that he, as he asked, hissed his S's and looked like that snake that hypnotizes little birds. The fact is that he immediately put the pots and pans around him, seated in the lotus position, just like a holy man (he was very skinny), and started yet another remarkable spectacle...[4]

The passage alternates between admiration and envy. Márcio grudgingly acknowledges Naná's neighborhood fame for being able "to propel rhythms and give acoustic impulses to absolutely each and every element given in nature, from one's chest, to the most miserable tin can abandoned on a street corner...," shifting Naná's knack for finding sounds in everyday objects from a musical skill to an expression of spiritual animism, as if Naná were making inanimate objects actually come alive as he strikes them and finds their resonant sweet spots.[5]

This alternation between admiration and envy should be familiar to anyone who has heard the stories of how white British rock guitarists responded to Black guitar icon Jimi Hendrix during this same late-1960s countercultural era. When I first learned that Naná considered Jimi Hendrix as one of the artists who most influenced him, it made sense in that Naná took inspiration in Jimi's ability to coax such a broad range of sounds out of his instrument. But, just as importantly, both Jimi and Naná navigated a particular form of dehumanization tied to late-1960s–early-1970s counterculture in the way that audiences and critics received their performances. This dehumanization was veiled as and bundled up with a kind of celebration of wildness of the kind that Errington flags as retaining racialized notions of savagery and civilization even as it purports to celebrate savagery and denigrate civilization. This was the era of "wild thing/you make my heart sing"—a casual and sometimes ironic discourse of wildness that accompanied the new musical rules of the rock n' roll era.

When Jimi first arrived in London, the press called him "The Wild Man of Borneo" and, despite his now celebrated virtuosity, dismissed his music as useless noise.[6] When Naná arrived in New York City, he was similarly received as "jungle man," and with his unfamiliar bow-and-arrow-like instrument and then beginner's English, he faced this caricature constantly. His method for dealing with this was, as Eric Galm details, to draw in audiences with primitive assumptions surrounding the berimbau, only to argue, through his fluid melodic, rhythmic phrases, for listeners to acknowledge the instrument's sophisticated possibilities. Naná himself explained that: "They used to call me jungle man because they thought the berimbau was from the jungle, the Amazon. Also, for example, in the middle of concerts, I'd do a solo for berimbau and I realized it didn't look like anything they'd seen played before."[7] In an interview with N. Scott Robinson, Naná elaborated on a critic's confusion:

> I remember this famous writer from *The New York Times*, Robert Palmer. We finished playing, and he came backstage, I

didn't speak any English, and he said, [*in a highly agitated voice*]: "What is this? What kind of music is that? And this guy up there with this bow an arrow" ... because I had my *berimbau* [*chuckles*]. He was so confused, because he didn't know what he was going to write in the newspaper because he had to do a review. He wrote a very good review, but he didn't talk much about the music. He mentioned more about the gentleman, who was me, who had these strange instruments because it was very unusual for Americans. Earlier, there were percussion players that would just play congas, bongos, *timbales*, cowbells, *guiro*, *claves*, and maracas with Dizzy Gillespie in Afro-Cuban jazz.[8]

Naná arrived in New York City one generation after Afro-Cuban percussionist Chano Pozo transformed the form and the rhythmic foundation of Dizzy Gillespie's modern jazz, creating mambo-adjacent cubop in the late 1940s–early 1950s. Chano and Dizzy's creative partnership was hugely important for future generations of African and Afro-diasporic musicians whose music engages with jazz. They emblematized the play of musical proximity and distance between jazz and various versions of Afro-Latin music in New York. Jason Stanyek lays out several precedents that Gillespie and Pozo together established for subsequent Pan-African collaborations in jazz: "an emphasis on co-composition with simultaneous affirmation of improvisation; the insertion of nonjazz repertoires into jazz; the accommodation of instruments not typically found in jazz ensembles; the use of non-English and multilingual texts; the highlighting of African spirituality."[9]

While acknowledging how groundbreaking their work together was for intercultural performance, music scholar and bass player Jairo Moreno also sees Dizzy not quite treating Chano as a full equal as he envisioned the role of Afro-Cuban music within jazz. Moreno argues that Dizzy's relationship with Chano represents Black North Americans' contemplation of a Black other.[10] He considers an off-the-cuff comment when Gillespie spoofed Chano's English as primitive, ventriloquizing Chano's voice with the words, "Deehee no peek pani, me no peek Angli, bo peek African," as ultimately revealing what Cuba meant to Dizzy.[11] In that moment, Dizzy was treating Chano, and by extension, Cuba, as a connection to an African past, while positioning himself as the one who could usher these sounds into the modern world. Dizzy's gesture relegated Latin Jazz music by reframing Black North American and Black Caribbean traditions as an encounter between the modern Black North American and unfiltered "African" tradition, rather than a convergence of two contemporary musical idioms.

Dizzy's slippage here from Afro-Cuba to an imagined Africa marks a refusal to fully acknowledge a formidable and constantly transforming Afro-Latin musical reserve with parallel traditions as weighty as jazz.[12] Instead, his framing treats Black sounds from other parts of the Americas as "that which came before." This "interested misreading"[13] on Gillespie's part clarifies how primitivist reception maintains hierarchies of musical genres, as well as hierarchies in the division of labor within particular musical genres. It contributes to the celebration, dismissal, and hierarchies of prestige of instrument types and the musicians who play them.

Listening to Unruly Voices

Ana María Ochoa Gautier's work clarifies the broader history that underlies these gestures that casually relegate musicians like Chano, Jimi, and Naná to a premodern past. In her groundbreaking book *Aurality*, Ochoa Gautier traces conceptions of the boundary line between what is understood as human-made music, and what is understood merely as sounds from nature. She situates the discussion by examining early musicologists' attempts to transcribe clear musical pitches and separate them from "impossible to transcribe howlings,"[14] arguing that by centering their definition of music around pitch, early musicologists relegated less readily transcribable vocal and instrumental forms to a subordinate position. Clear, steady pitch and recognition as a human being had become entangled: "The identity of the comparative musicologist as a worthy scholar is thus based on his ability to identify pitch, while the identity of the Indigenous peoples as (cultivated) persons with music is based on their ability to produce one."[15] In this conception, rhythm is placed alongside "howlings," as in music critic Eduard Hanslick's writing from 1885, where he insisted that rhythm only becomes music by accompanying harmony and melody. According to Hanslick, without harmony and melody, "they are performing natural music, that is, *no music at all*."[16] That same year, Carl Stumpf countered that the actual thing that was "wild and tenuous" wasn't the vocalizations perceived as howlings themselves, but the idea that a strict separation between European concert music and so-called "natural music" could even be made.[17]

Ochoa Gautier uses a vivid scene from Colombia's history to trace how definitions of proper, in-tune music, and correct spoken grammar serve to tame or "immunize" voices in a process that separates out who counts as a full human and, by extension, who counts as a full citizen.[18] In the scene she analyzes, European travelers mishear the vocalizing and body percussion of riverboat workers of mixed African and Indigenous descent in soon-to-be Colombia. Even though the scene takes place in the early nineteenth century, the enduring division between proper and improper voices continues to resonate strongly with the 1970s reception of Naná, as Márcio Borges' account attests. Transportation options in the Viceroyalty forced Europeans such as Alexander von Humboldt, a naturalist documenting flora and fauna, to travel by a type of boat moved by men with long sticks standing on the roof of the boat's cabin. For weeks, despite his privilege, Humboldt was trapped in the cabin below, subject to the sounds of the men, known as bogas, as they stomped their feet on the roof and vocalized in time with the exertion of their work. Travelers' journals feature several descriptions of disgust at these loud sounds. Humboldt described the sounds of the bogas as a "bellowing ruckus," an "unbearable racket," and even "blasphemy." One moment, he complains of "barbarous, lustful, ululating, and angry shouting," and the next he describes a range of emotions expressed, as it is "sometimes like a lament and sometimes joyful." Almost grudgingly, he concedes that the rhythm of the work leads to what he would categorize as "a song and even a dialogue."[19]

Are the bogas shouting? Are they singing? Are they making lewd noises? Are they having a conversation? Or are they simply grunting with the physical exertion of the work? Are they inventing music on the spot? Humboldt lacked an interpretive frame for making sense of what he was hearing: "It was a sound that was impossible to inscribe onto a genre or an emotion, its untraceability begging for classification in Humboldt's ears."[20] Reading against the grain of accounts written by the bogas' reluctant audience of travelers, Ochoa pieces together an acoustic practice that blurred the boundaries between speech, melody, and shout. The bogas were identifying and calling to people they knew far down the river. They were synchronizing their work rhythm. They were reciting prayers in multiple languages that combined Catholicism with Afro-diasporic and Indigenous beliefs (much like the religious practices Naná witnessed growing up). They were engaging in an improvisatory practice that accompanied labor, yet was described as "tremendously irreverent, unruly, and with exaggerated bodily contortions."[21] When the bogas vocalized to both humans and nonhumans, both spiritual and animal, they were engaging in "sensorial tuning to species and spatial acoustics," a kind of knowing of the world through sound.[22]

This description of the bogas hews closely to the "wild, unidentified chant"—as film scholar Randal Johnson called it—of Naná's track "Amazonas" that Glauber Rocha found so pivotal to summing up the colonial Latin American experience.[22] When Naná arrived in Rio, or in Harlem, or in Paris, in the 1970s, with his musical bow on his shoulder, he challenged his listeners to be less like Humboldt and more like Ochoa Gautier in their reception of his unfamiliar sounds. He gave listeners a choice to either fall back into old categories separating song, speech, and screams and dismiss him, or to embrace the rethinking and reordering of these categories. In his case, the questions were: Is that a musical instrument being played, or is it a functional object? Should that vocalization be considered to be singing, or is it just reinforcing the sounds of the instrument? Is that speech or song? Is that language or just sounds? Is that music or is it noise? Does the judgment of being in-tune or out-of-tune apply here? Is that the sound of one instrument or several? Is that the sound of one voice or a crowd?

These are questions that ECM records adjudicated in the 1970s when Eicher released records such as *Dança das Cabeças*, with its Foley artistry, less recognizable timbres, and wordless vocalizations interspersed with more familiar instruments and song forms. The label's output during this time expanded the scope of contemporary European music to incorporate certain heterodox and difficult-to-classify forms of performance. Eicher celebrates the global margins, refusing to reject musicians like Naná outright as an unbearable racket the way that Alexander von Humboldt heard the bogas. Eicher's move—and by extension, ECM's—is instead subtler, incorporating elements from outside of Europe but, nonetheless, ultimately upholding genre hierarchies with the belief that: "the margin should only be a source, a spot from which to grasp the essence of the centre."[24] The label's offerings disavow certain Eurocentric definitions of musical value, while letting others persist.

Racial Animosity and *Jogo de Cintura*

Just as Jimi Hendrix was unafraid to cover the rock n' roll ditty "Wild Thing" and lean into the racialized and sexualized ways that audiences received him, Naná also embraced his exotic image at times. Thinking pragmatically, Melvin Gibbs sees a side to exoticism that can be less corrosive and dehumanizing, as traveling reveals one person's ordinary to be another person's extraordinary. Melvin makes the point that traveling can distinguish a player and provide them with valuable cultural capital in the new setting:

> If I had a Japanese friend walk in and pull together a meal, to me it would be an exotic meal, right? But for the Japanese person, it would just be what they eat every day. That we are contextualizing it, in and out of itself, it creates certain value … I think the good thing about that is you learn that your culture is valuable. It reaffirms your decision to value your culture.

Melvin spent enough time with Naná "to know that there's just certain walls that can't be climbed, even today in Brazil." As a Black musician playing risk-taking music who has spent time in Norway, Melvin figures that Naná's decisions to travel were made for the same reasons that many Black jazz musicians left the United States:

> I mean, that's why we all leave, right? At least that's why all the jazz musicians went to France. Their experiences had respect in France. I imagine [Naná] went to them and people were kind of "oh you did X, you did Y, you did Z." That's valuable to us as opposed to, "you're just the guy who goes *doh-een doh-een doh-een* [he gestures playing the berimbau]." They deal with all these things they dealt with in the States, and they get on a plane and go to another country and everybody is more or less worshipping these guys.

Naná's first wife Merrie agrees, explaining that when they arrived in Paris after a difficult few months in Rio de Janeiro, personally and politically, "he suddenly was valued, he was loved, he was respected, he was recording with a lot of people. There was Don Cherry that would come down and stay with us. And he got work." She describes how he deftly disarmed racist animosity when they lived in Paris on the market street

Rue Montorgueil, using the Brazilian expression *jogo de cintura*, that describes the way capoeiristas and top soccer players gracefully maneuver around their opponents:

> I just want to answer one thing about the racial thing. It illustrates how Naná dealt with it. There was this cafe downstairs. Hardly anyone was in it during normal hours and Naná would go and get a beer. There was this woman who would sit in the back corner all the time, who drank something green, like chartreuse. She was really old and had a million wrinkles all over her face. Naná walked in and ordered a pint. It was just him and her at the cafe, and she said, "J'aime pas les nègres" ("I don't like Black people"). Naná turned around and with this incredible "Encore un pour la madame" ("Another drink for the lady on me") and she was totally stunned and they became friends. They didn't hang out together but every time he went in, she greeted him, "Bonjour." I think that that illustrates a little bit, I think he held in his feelings.
>
> A friend once said: "we as Black people laugh because it's so horrible, it's so harsh, and we crack jokes to *superar* (overcome)." Naná had this laugh that he was famous for. He was very outgoing, very engaging, and he didn't let the racial thing intrude into his *joie de vivre* and his need to connect. That was the gift that he had to overcome all these things. However they would respond to him, he would just ignore it and move on, but he would be pissed about things. I remember a situation we had in Toulon that was really scary and in Paris too, he was really angry and pissed off.

Just as Louis Armstrong used his horn to win over racist whites as he paraded through hostile New Orleans neighborhoods during the Jim Crow era,[25] Merrie emphasized how playing the berimbau that was so often tucked under his arm was Naná's principal means for winning people over. But at what cost? Naná succeeded in finding where, as Melvin described it, his melding of "high art" and the "street folkloric thing" were mesmerizing. But, even then, the racial formations he thrived within were treacherous, and his status within them remained precarious, whether he was in Brazil or abroad. Naná joked that as a Black person in overwhelmingly white countries such as Sweden and Norway, where he recorded, toured, and visited Don Cherry, he felt like a "fly in a bowl of rice," amending the expression, "fly in the buttermilk," which is itself a riff on the expression, "fly in the ointment," altered to refer specifically to racial awkwardness. This unease is an understandable response to "hostipitality," the coexistence of hospitality and hostility toward people racially marked as outsiders that Ryan Skinner discusses in depth with a range of Black ex-pats and citizens living in Sweden in the 1970s in his forthcoming book, their stories unsettling Swedish self-understanding as a "moral superpower" where "foul racial theories have never gained purchase."[26]

8 Voice, Body, Rhythm, and Special Effects

Percussionist Marcos Suzano, commenting on Naná's early- to mid-1970s recordings, wrote that they were the work of "a complete percussionist," clarifying that: "There is voice, body, rhythm, and special effects."[1] Writing specifically about *Dança das Cabeças*, he claims that, "It wasn't virtuosic percussion"—a statement that strains credulity, but sets up his actual point: "the virtuosity was in the context, in the way that he chose the instruments and added other elements." Writing about *Amazonas*, he mulls over how it wasn't just what he was playing, but also how his overall sense of the role of percussion, and by extension the percussionist, was more expansive than the instruments are customarily used in a composition:

> Without a doubt, the concept of percussion at the time was very different from what he presented on this record. It is clear that he used his body as percussion, the voice is the backbone of the entire album. The percussion, as such, is arranged almost as if they were violins, a brass section or a guitar solo. That's how percussion instruments work here.

He goes on to praise Naná's ability to elevate lowly noisemakers into viable music:

> Naná uses a flexatone, which is something of an undignified toy, normally used to make spacey sounds. But in this case,

his playing actually transforms it into a percussion instrument. He takes an instrument that is an antenna and plays it such that he makes it into art. This is very difficult.[2]

There is voice, body, rhythm, and special effects. Suzano's comment structures this chapter. With the aim of gearing up to listen to *Saudades* in detail in the next chapter, I center how Naná created his own body of gestures, techniques, and processes. Expanding the possibilities of percussion, he used voice, body, rhythm, and special effects on stage and in the recording studio.

Vocalizing (not Singing)

Naná was adamant that he was not a singer. Instead, he called himself a vocalist who treats the voice like just another instrument. Throughout his recordings, he uses his voice to reinforce the sounds that he produces with his instruments. Berimbaus can make sounds homologous to vowel sounds, such as the wah-wah effect produced by the distance of the gourd resonator from the belly of the player. Naná would emphasize this instrument/human connection with his voice. The sounds he utters shift focus to a particular detail within the complex overtones he produces on the berimbau—as if to say, "listen to this part right now. Do you hear that detail within the sound as a whole?" Or, less nobly, in the case of the cuíca friction drum, several of his old friends and fellow musicians claimed that he just didn't have a very good cuíca, and/or wasn't the best cuíca player. By doubling the cuíca's squeaks in an exuberant falsetto, Naná made the sounds work in tandem, hiding the faults of the instrument and his playing.

Naná's vocalizing sometimes complements percussion that he plays not on another instrument, but on his own body. Halfway through the second side of *Dança das Cabeças*, the difficult-to-identify timbre of Egberto's Chinese sheng—somewhere between the sound of a melodica, an accordion, and an oboe—gives way to the sound of multiple overdubs of Naná's handclaps spread throughout the left and right channels, a stomped bass drum pattern, mid-frequencies thumped on his chest, and vocalized hi-hat/shaker sounds. Naná credits his work with children in Paris in teaching him the possibilities of the body percussion and working wordlessly. His 1983 record *Zumbi* explores compositions built in the studio around vocalizing together with a range of sounds of produced by striking his body.[3]

Audiences heard Naná's vocalizing differently, depending on the project it was a part of. In *Dança das Cabeças*, the vocals evoked all sorts of forest sounds, from birds and monkeys to buzzing insects. In his playing with Pat Metheny, Naná's not completely "immunized" voice returned vocals to Metheny's instrumental jazz, bringing spontaneous-sounding utterances not always conforming to Western-tempered tuning to Metheny's tight, orchestrated sounds.

Naná utilized overdubbing, tape loops, and delay effects in the studio to create chattering crowds made up of several of him speaking or singing. Many of the syllables that he would use were actually words even when they sounded like onomatopoetic nonsense. Naná would blur meaningful words with sounds chosen for their rhythm. Like *acabou, acabou, acabou, acabou*, a word in Portuguese that means, "it is done." Or *já caiu o cajá*, which means, "the cajá fruit already fell" (from the tree). These rhythmic spoken utterances would spread to fill the stereo field, moving from channel to channel.

Wordlessness in Milton Nascimento's *Milagre dos Peixes*

One of the most significant examples of Naná's wordless vocals was his contribution to Milton Nascimento's *Milagre dos Peixes*.[4] The release of the record situates Naná's wordless vocals within both a film soundtrack and the circumstances of the Brazilian dictatorship. During the few months in 1973 that Naná was back in Rio de Janeiro before returning to France for five years, the lyrics for all but three of the eleven songs that Milton was prepared to release were censored. Milton later explained that it was Naná who convinced him to go ahead with the record anyway, replacing the censored lyrics with wordless vocals, heightening the protest while circumventing the military.[5] Lyricist Fernando Brant explained the decision:

> All of a sudden, we thought, since there really won't be lyrics anymore, the idea is to carry them in the singing, to protest, to send a message with the voice. I remember that the recordings were very emotional, very strong. Bituca [Milton] wanted to let out everything that they were impeding him from saying in words.[6]

Replacing the censored lyrics with wordless vocals fit with the record as it was, since several of the tracks that weren't censored were already wordless because they were first recorded as part of the soundtrack to an experimental Ruy Guerra film *Os Deuses e os Mortos* (*The Gods and the Dead*), an experimental Brazilian film about the ghosts of history where the dead silently walk among the living.[7] The tracks' beginnings in this radical and violent film—a reviewer claimed: "your stomach may turn, but you will never forget"—followed by its inclusion later on the censored record, create several layers of significance.[8] Naná and Milton's wordlessness invokes the people disappeared by the dictatorship, circumventing censors to scream a protest.[9]

On the track, "A Chamada" (The Call), Milton Nascimento's falsetto serves as the siren song of a river mermaid. Meanwhile, swirling around Milton's voice is a swarm of Naná's vocal effects and whistling paired with berimbau, triangle, atabaques, reco-reco, and what sounds like a thunder sheet whipping around too hard to realistically sound like thunder. The tempo isn't steady—it stretches and flows as the "taunting mutterings, pained shouts, moans, squawks, and squeals"[10] swing between the left and right channels in a state of disorienting flux. Birds, monkeys, insects, and ghosts are all possible interpretations of the unsettling, circling sounds that envelop the mermaid and her call. The only comprehensible words uttered are multiple Miltons pleading, "*Eu estou cansado, me salva, estou cansado!* [I am tired, save me, I'm tired]" and the expression of exhaustion with the predicament that the censors have put them in: "*Como é que nós vamos gravar?* [How are we going to record?]"[11] Here, wordless utterances, in their "kaleidoscopic movement and aleatoric pace are deliberately unnerving; howls and monkey-like calls provoke the body to a state of alarm, disorientation, and unease."[12]

The Sound Box and the Sound Stage

As Naná's artistic trajectory took shape in the late 1960s and into the 1970s, audio-recording technology was undergoing a deep transformation. The mixing boards in recording studios grew exponentially as multitrack recording quickly expanded from 2 tracks to 4, 8, 16, 32, and 64 or more tracks, even before the arrival of digital technologies. A convergence of advances brought higher fidelity recordings, the transition from mono to stereo, and further development of electronic effects beyond echo and reverb.

Naná's first recordings, such as the 1967 Agostinho dos Santos EP, are all mixed in mono, which was the dominant format at the time. Stereo was on the rise but still not the most common way that people were listening to records. Pop music scholars Ruth Dockwray and Alan F. Moore identify the late 1960s as a moment of transition between thinking of an auditory space as a *sound stage*, and thinking of it as a *sound box*.[13] The idea of the sound stage already existed in the late nineteenth century, before radio, when opera performances were transmitted via telephone wires. The layout of a theater stage, with its separation between performers and audience, became the accepted model for imagining a broadcast or a recording, giving the listener the "best seat in the house."[14] The transition to stereo mixing and multitrack overdubbing facilitated moving away from reliance on an imagined theater stage and audience configuration. This more realist staging gave way to a virtual space that is no longer modeled after a performance in a theater. The multitrack studio became an audio playground, free from the idea of capturing a "real" performance. Rather than "the best seat in the house," the listener could be placed inside a drum, a mile away, or on a rocket together with the recorded musician on their way to the stratosphere. Quick cuts, cinematic montage-like effects, and the superposition of multiple settings and spaces all became possible.

Within this new range of possibilities, Naná thrived as someone whose playing developed during the mono era of the sound stage, and who figured out how to translate that playing into the stereo era of the sound box. He excelled within the traditional jazz-recording process—not too many takes, don't spend too long on a record, capture what happens in the room. But he could also play with those expectations, refusing to be yet another jazz musician anchored in place in a standard mix. Instead, he got up close to the mics and choreographed his instrument. Through moves like the parallax gesture, he established an expansive stereo field, placing the sound throughout a full three dimensions. He understood the power of the stereo headphones that had just started to proliferate—the kind that are huge cans that envelop your hearing—and experimented with using the sound box to create virtual spaces that, like certain Jimi Hendrix tunes, could be either set in the outer space or the inner space of one's mind. By exploring

Figure 8.1 *From left to right: Naná Vasconcelos, Manfred Eicher, Pat Metheny, and Jan Erik Kongshaug. Photo by Deborah Feingold.*

the possibilities of both the sound stage and the sound box, Naná provided a bridge between older jazz practices and the multitrack era (see Figure 8.1).

Microphone Choreography

Sound engineers who have worked with Naná, such as Pat Dillett and Pablo Lopes, noted that he wouldn't necessarily ask for fancy microphones (although Manfred Eicher used high-end mics when he recorded with ECM). What ended up being key to his sound, according to them, is that he would often ask for a stereo array 3–4 feet apart, and that all of his positioning within the stereo field was done by him as he performed, in contrast to the stereo panning most often done from the mixing board in pop music. According to Dillett, "he really had the control of an orchestral player" in this regard.[15] Although this two-mic array was often his standard recording setup (and what he would customarily use live on stage), sometimes his choreography led sound engineers to take more drastic measures. When recording with saxophonist Rev. Dwight Andrews in 1979, the engineer ended up using 8–10 mics or more, to be able to capture anywhere that Naná might dance as he played his parts in the studio. The lightness of the berimbau allowed him to gracefully move between the microphones as he explored the instrument.

Dillett would often have no idea what Naná was trying to do after he had recorded tracks 1, 2, and 3. Naná's arrangement would instead cohere little by little, like a photo slowly emerging in a darkroom. Only after he had recorded the final tracks (tracks 10, 11, and 12, say), each sound would appear in its interlocking place in the mix. Subtle fills would serve as cues to himself, so that he would remember the transitions from one overdubbed track to the next:

> So, what would happen, is that Naná would come in and listen. You would prepare tracks for him and then he would build this thing where he would play an entire song on one channel and then another channel. And then you would go, "this is really weird" and it was just such a strange thing. It was like watching a photo develop. And by the time that you would get through all of his tracks, you would be like "oh wow!" [laughing] … He was arranging and orchestrating himself with a complete picture already in his head when he would go out there, there was no doubt.[16]

Geraldo Azevedo, one of Naná's earliest collaborators in Recife, suggests that this focus on form, arrangement and orchestration was one of Naná's strengths even back in the mid-1960s. *"Tem que aprender a formatar,"* Geraldo recalled Naná advising. "We have to learn how to arrange our music: the first part, the second part, etc." Gibbs agrees that "it was definitely well conceptualized, everything he did. He was never just like virtuoso to be virtuoso, there was always something behind it." He describes the parts that he would add as a "composition on top of a composition," that would crystallize in his mind after just listening to the song once or twice. "The level of thought and the level of compositionality of what he was doing with the instrument was just incredible … He is not just a percussionist, there was a lot going on with him." As Chico Amaral put it in his book about the music of Milton Nascimento, "Vasconcelos is more than a collaborator; he is a coauthor."[17] Naná himself phrased it this way:

> Percussion, for me, is an orchestra of timbres. I use percussion as if it were an orchestra. Percussion isn't about who plays fastest or loudest. I seek to make music with percussion, that's the difference. I seek to tell stories through sound, so I entered this area of sonority, and ended up exploring it as if it were an orchestra.[18]

Percussionist and improvisatory bandleader Adam Rudolph acknowledges that Naná thought compositionally and orchestrally, at the same time insisting that this should not be understood necessarily as a move toward Western musical practice. Rudolph hears in Naná's choices just as much a turn to sub-Saharan African and Afro-diasporic musical practices of "weaving the fibres" of multiple interlocking rhythmic parts. Gibbs agrees, adding that: "the thing about African instruments is that they are all separate instruments that are making this combined sound, and the psychic trick of it is: it sounds one way when the things are at a whole, and when you can hear each piece separately then it becomes symphonic."

Naná's Time "Illuminates Everything Around It"

Naná's superb time surfaced in several conversations. Arto Lindsay sang his praises, noting that: "Naná has this kind of crystal clear time. It illuminates everything around it. It's the time itself that is just glorious … It breathes, but it never lets you down." Gibbs thought that: "It was kind of healing. It always made everything better. Naná's time always served to make whatever musical situation work better. If you called Naná, whatever you would put down was going be better after he finished working." Gibbs finds that one of Naná's strengths was the ability to treat time feel and tempo so independently of each other. "Naná to me always very consciously manipulated the grid. Regal isn't the right word, but a feeling that his time kind of transcended his tempo." Underlying this praise is the fact that the beginning of Naná's career—from the 1960s forward—corresponds to the rise of the click track, a metronomic pulse that anchors most multitrack recording projects with stopwatch precision. Naná could easily work without a click track, or dance around the pulse of a click track, producing parts that don't feel pinned down by its tyranny. Even during his early-1980s stint playing music for breakdancers, he preferred to play his electronic beats with his fingers, without quantizing himself to a machine pulse, like J Dilla would later become famous for. This ability to breathe musically played out in situations where Naná was faced with reconciling the clashing feels of two previously recorded tracks, or mending an arrangement recorded by another musician with a shakier sense of time. Dillett heard this as the ability to listen and constantly give and take:

> With Naná it's always a conversation and he's listening to everything else. He's not just listening to the click or the beat or even the other rhythms, and he definitely would listen just as much as he would play ... He would listen and find that flow throughout the entire thing and be able to keep it in his head as if it's like a 120-bar phrase that he could play.

Part of what struck Melvin Gibbs when he listened to Codona records was that: "There was a certain kind of manipulation of breath that he was doing and I think it was conscious. That was really the beauty of what Naná was doing." As a bass player who has played with a wide range of African and Afro-diasporic musicians from around the globe, Gibbs locates Naná's strength in almost ineffable questions of microtiming and feel: "He would play these rhythms, but he would play them in a way that would make them sound open instead of sound like a restriction. It was elastic enough, so it could be multicontextualized." For Melvin, this openness meant that he and Naná were together playing "in the gap between Brazilian music and African American" grooves. In other projects, such as *Saudades*, Naná plays in the gap between his berimbau practice and Western art music. Gibbs sees Naná's ability to seamlessly mediate between feels/grooves as a key strength: "He could go play with a bunch of European guys and you wouldn't have that clash that you usually have ... somehow what Naná did, managed to transcend that war. Again, going back to his ability to shape shift what the era is, and where the time is at, you know?" These questions of microtiming and rhythmic feel often escape notation and analysis, while remaining instantly noticeable to a listener:

> You won't know why you feel in a certain way when you hear the track. But that was the genius of what Naná did. It's a very specific thing that people who play rhythmic instruments, percussionists, understand about manipulating time, and manipulating this instrument that doesn't have pitches and western sounds so that it has a kinesthetic effect on people.

And this is the fundamental task of the percussionist. "The percussionist's job is to make you breathe a certain way, to make you move a certain way."

Gibbs points out that: "You can't really get the kinesthetic aspect of percussion across in a recording. I mean, people can't really feel it and then read the reflections in the room." He sees this as connected to the fact that percussion instruments are "made to be played outside. They are made to communicate, to be heard by crowds. They are not really meant to have a mic close up to them; that's not what they were designed for." Microphone choreography, as well as the judicious use of reverb, compression and mixing, all helped Naná convey this kinesthetic dimension, linking up sound and bodily movement. Melvin compares this effect to the way a make-up artist helps the contours of an actor's face show up vividly to the camera: "with percussion, the movement is what gives you the illusion of what it would sound like if you were actually there, hearing what he was doing."[19]

Naná as Foley Artist

There is voice, body, rhythm and *special effects*. In the recording studio and on stage, Naná incorporated Foley artistry into his musical practices, using squeaky toys, thunder sheets and vocal effects as mimesis of anything from storms to forest sounds. When Egberto proposed the idea of recording an album about boys running through the forest, Naná asked: "Which forest? The forests of the Northeast sound different than the forests of Amazónas, which are different from the forests in South Brazil," suggesting a specificity to his forest sounds that included the mimesis of birds, insects, and monkeys. One of the last projects that Naná recorded, *Boy and the World* (*O Menino e o Mundo*),[20] which was released in 2013, illustrates the porosity between music, sound effects, and noise in Naná's work, all carefully placed to suggest proximity, distance, and movement. Calling his work merely part of the soundtrack for the wordless feature-length film falls short, as certain animated scenes were tailor-made to work with Naná's sounds, rather than the other way around.

The "making of *The Boy and the World*" video offers a glimpse into his process by switching back and forth between the moment of recording, and the final product of the film, where the animation is joined with the sounds.[21] The video begins with a producer's off-screen description (in Portuguese) of what they need: "forest atmosphere—add more instruments as animals in nature." Naná tries out a hindewhu-style one-note flute and other whistles. The shot switches back to the film, showing a simple stick-figure boy running through a vivid, sketched forest landscape. Cut back to a montage of Naná playing huge caxixi-style basket shakers, bundles of cowry shells, and a glass sphere with a hole in the top that he plays like a ghatam, finding a watery groaning thump. Return to the boy, running up an oversized vine to the canopy of a tree, a hummingbird, and insects interested in his ascent. Naná leans into the microphone, continuing his rhythmic buzzing, droning vocables, before backing away to create a manual fade.

He then rummages through the kitchen of the recording studio for household objects with resonant sounds. He finds a suitable cooking pot, leaves the lid behind, flips the pot over, returns to the booth and plays it with his hands. His cooking-pot rhythm serves as a transition to a much less idyllic scene of two sketched birds fighting in mid-air. Naná squawks, shouts, and mutters, carefully calibrating his proximity to the microphone to create several perceived distances from the listener. As stylized tanks, helicopters, and submarines fire at the birds, his staccato muttering becomes a stream of tank fire.

Binaural Biriba Berimbaus

The berimbau solo that begins *Saudades* has many recorded predecessors, as the instrument had become the centerpiece of his work. Naná's vocabulary of gestures and techniques was cumulative—once he added a way of playing to his palette, chances are it would show up somewhere else later. That said, his recorded berimbau solos varied both in how they were recorded, and what he actually played. In March, 1971, Naná recorded *El Increíble NANA con Agustín Pereyra Lucena*,[22] during a quick stop in Buenos Aires immediately before moving to New York City and honing his berimbau techniques in the echo-y East Village loft he shared with Glauber Rocha. For me, listening to his playing on that earlier record, and contrasting it with the berimbau-centered pieces on his 1973 records *Amazonas*, recorded in Brazil, and *Africadeus*, recorded in France, charts his accumulation of techniques, and helps me to know what to listen for on *Saudades* (Figure 8.2).

Because *El Increíble NANA* was recorded a week or so before Naná moved to New York City, it gives a clear sense of what he had and hadn't figured out when he arrived in the US. In line with the spontaneous arrangement of the session during Naná's quick visit to Buenos Aires to play a concert with Gato Barbieri, it is not as tightly rehearsed as the later extended tracks on *Amazonas* and *Africadeus* that showcase his berimbau chops. Here, the parallax gesture runs throughout. He allows ample negative space in the mix, and right away establishes a wide dynamic range, from quiet whisperings and rustlings to loud strikes. But there are certain techniques that he tries out that he will later jettison. The most evident is that on the 1971 *El Increíble NANA* record, the 17-minute track is a duet with himself that moves back an forth between berimbau and

Figure 8.2 Saudades *back cover detail of Naná playing berimbau and tabla. Photos by Roberto Masotti. Courtesy of ECM Records.*

conga, and his conga playing ends up feeling like an unnecessary crutch, like he's not quite ready to fully move into the role of berimbau soloist, and feels the need to fill in some of the space. Also, when he does the parallax gesture and reinforces it with his voice, he is still settling on the syllables to use, experimenting with a variety of gibberish sounds, when later the voice/berimbau gesture would become more fixed, with *oh oh oh ah ah ah … wow wow wow …* and *pssiussiu*, but no *cah dah coo doo la oo* and *key dee cah ree key dee cah ree la oo*.

Two years later, in early 1973, on the album *Amazonas*, the track "Espafro" (Amphibian) showcases the results of Naná's day-in, day-out exploration of the instrument. The track is more atmospheric and disorienting than the berimbau tracks on *Africadeus*, recorded a few months later in France, and on *Saudades*, recorded six years later in 1979. "Espafro" consists of a dizzying blend of more than one berimbau at any given moment. The microphone choreography is more precise, and the location and movement of each sound is more deliberate.

Overdubs of multiple berimbaus allow for chords moving chromatically, and microphone placement brings out the instrument's microscopic nuances, even when he plays as hushed as possible. Careful manipulation of the distance between the open side of the gourd resonator and his stomach adds a filter effect that heightens the sense of shifting distance and proximity. I hear this effect as an important part of how Naná conveys the spatial and kinesthetic aspects of percussion, creating the illusion of what it would sound like if you were actually there.

Berimbau players hold in the same hand both the caxixi (a small wicker-basket shaker) and the baqueta (a stick used to strike the string). In New York City, Naná refined how independently he could play both, becoming an expert at muting the caxixi at will even when he was swinging the baqueta to strike the string. The extent of his independence opens up polyrhythmic possibilities, freeing the caxixi rhythms from being tied to each baqueta hit, allowing Naná to play nearly as independently as a skilled trapset drummer can. During several moments in "Espafro," the caxixi part plays a steady pulse that creates tension with the asymmetrical baqueta rhythms played on the string. This may be an overdub on the recording, but it is around this period that he begins to explore this type of caxixi/baqueta independence in his live performances as well.

The opening track of *Africadeus*, "Africadeus (Concerto pra Mãe Bio)," shares its subtitle with the opening track on *El Increíble NANA*, but the recordings reveal a leap in his conception of the piece, both in berimbau technique and recording quality. The track on *Africadeus* is a true solo, with no apparent overdubs or superfluous congas. Every strike, scrape, or shake feels deliberate and in place. There is a clear sense of arranged sections, mostly structured around gestures and techniques, from the phaser effect of swishing the baqueta inside the gourd resonator, to the vocal+berimbau version of the elastic "parallax" gesture. Naná's confidence in holding the listener's rapt attention can be heard in a luxurious amount of negative space in the arrangement. With the microphone levels turned up to the point that microscopic details of the sound can be heard, there are moments that are quiet enough to hear Naná breathe.

Both the manual stereo panning of Naná's microphone choreography, and the filter effect of the gourd against his stomach can be heard with a high level of control. By varying the gourd distance, vowel sound-like overtones emerge from the vibrating string, foreshadowing the actual whispers that follow. The precision of the sounds' travels throughout the stereo field make it feel binaural, as if it were happening inside listeners' headphoned heads. Although it is evident that certain sounds are being produced by a kind of shaker, and others are being produced by somehow striking a string, many of the ways that Naná manipulates the sound remain obscure to the average listener. Even when he played live, for example, the source of the filter effect of the gourd against his body was not easy to detect. Nor that the several timbres he could coax out of the string depended on how hard he pressed a stone against it.

For the climax of the track, what is most dazzling is the way that Naná keeps multiple contrasting parts going at the same time. Once again, the single becomes multiple. He takes full advantage of caxixi/baqueta independence, playing the lopsided drum patterns of Afro-Pernambucan *maracatu nação* and their distinct shaker patterns. He reaches back to his samba school days, teasing out the interlocking drum parts of Rio's carnaval *samba de enredo*. By this third iteration of his berimbau showcase, many of the techniques that will be heard on *Saudades* are already in place. What shifts so dramatically on *Saudades* is that he places the sound of these extended techniques in conversation with the strings of a chamber orchestra.

9 *Saudades* and Saudades

The album *Saudades* came about during an extended tour throughout Europe on the heels of the *Dança das Cabeças* album. Egberto gave me a detailed account of the process. He and Naná rode in a tour bus "maravilhoso," with beds and lots of space. After each show, they would eat a late dinner, and then leave for the next city around midnight, or one in the morning. When they arrived the next morning at the hotel, they would sleep, eat breakfast, sound check, play the show, pack up, rinse, and repeat. At a certain point in the tour, Egberto couldn't take the monotony of the road any longer, commenting that they should take advantage of the six or seven hours a day they were spending on the bus. When they first met, Naná had talked to Egberto about his dream of recording a work for berimbau and orchestra. He gave Egberto an "are-we-doing-this?" look, and Egberto went to get his staff paper.

After hearing Naná's berimbau solo night after night, Egberto knew it inside and out, and they had names for each improvised section. For example, "*palha agarrada no sapato*" (piece of straw stuck in a shoe), later shortened to "*palha*," was Egberto's term for the swishing sound of the baqueta stick around the gourd resonator which sounded remarkably like an electronic phaser effect. Realizing the futility of transcribing such a timbre-centered part, Egberto placed these headings on the top of the page and sang Naná's berimbau parts back to him so that Naná could sing to Egberto the accompanying parts that he had worked out in his mind. Egberto would then write down Naná's melodies, allowing the Stuttgart Radio Symphony Orchestra to be cued by Naná's berimbau:

> I said "I'm going to sing to you your berimbau part. And you sing back to me everything that you are hearing, the part that the orchestra will have." So I sang and he knew right away what I was singing from his berimbau solo. I was writing quickly what he was proposing. The whole thing. I was writing, writing, writing. It wasn't only for one day, it was for fifteen or twenty days. I had lots of notes and then I said "Now I need a whole day. Go to bed, stay on the bus, just leave me alone here so that I can make sense of this thing." I worked on it, worked on it, worked on it, always annotating which part the berimbau part should do.

Naná Undid the Orchestra (At Least for a Moment)

When they arrived in the recording studio, Manfred Eicher suggested that they start with "O Berimbau," because he considered it the subtlest piece on the record, and the piece that the orchestra knew the least, so they'd have to spend more time on it. Egberto's role was confusing to the orchestra members—it wasn't his composition. He had just written it down:

> My friend has many musical ideas, and he is an expert in something that we aren't. And he hears things that we don't.

For example, he succeeded in communicating to me an idea that he had about what he would like to accompany the berimbau that he is about to play. That's the principal instrument. This orchestra here has a very important function, but it has a function ... and I gave examples. I knew these examples at the time, because of my study of music: "This here, for example, is compared to the piano in the piece *Petrushka* by Stravinsky. It seems like a soloist, but it isn't. He fits within the orchestra! We seem like soloists in the orchestra, but we aren't. The berimbau is the soloist."

In Egberto's telling of the story, conductor Mladen Gutesha and the orchestra were baffled when they realized that the work prominently featured a solo instrument that didn't even appear on the page beyond a cryptic shorthand code. At this point, the orchestra members became fascinated with Naná's mysterious musical instrument. Egberto describes it in a way that echoes a colonial encounter:[1]

"Berimbau, what is that?" I said, "ah, it's an instrument ...," and I started to explain, while Manfred listened. Then Manfred said, "Excuse me, excuse me, Egberto, wouldn't it be better to call Naná in here to demonstrate the berimbau," I said, "of course." Then Naná entered, with that way that he has, he entered and said "What's up?" I said, "They want to see the berimbau, they want to know what it is."

The orchestra was there, sitting. Naná started to play and the 21 of them or so kept moving forward to the edge of their seats, because they couldn't figure out how those things came out of that instrument, that sound from that thing there. Because for the Germans, it was a bow and arrow. If someone arrived with an arrow and a bow in their hands, BOOM, they would shoot the arrow into the people.

And then Manfred interjected, saying, "wait there, forgive me, Naná, wait a second. Everyone, please, place your instruments on your seats, get up, and let's make a circle around Naná. If you are holding your violin, viola, cello, you won't see anything. Put down those instruments and you'll be able to see Naná up close." This broke the ice, dispatched with any formalities, undid the orchestra and everyone was in a circle, or rather, a half-moon around Naná playing.

And after a while, Manfred said this: "Do you understand now? I think that's enough." And they said some things that I didn't exactly understand, but I presume they were things like "But how could it be, that there is just a bent stick, where does the sound come out from?" And Manfred laughed, and then said "If I knew that, I would be playing it there. But no one knows how to play it—only he knows how to play that damn thing."

Naná's berimbau "undid the orchestra," calling the musicians into a circular *roda*, or rather, a half-moon around Naná. He momentarily broke apart the orchestra's fixed spatial configuration, with its intricate hierarchy of first chairs, second chairs, and so forth, everyone pointing toward the all-hearing conductor with their (usually his) back to the audience. Naná had managed to reconfigure everyone into an arrangement closer to what Don Cherry insisted upon in the Organic Music Theatre days, or berimbau's traditional setting of capoeira.

During the session, Egberto served as a translator of the conductor's formal musical practice. When the conductor said, "Let's turn to measure such and such," Egberto would say,

"Naná, it's *palha* time," or "it's time for you to do the sequence of harmonics," and they'd all go from there:

> It was difficult to begin this session, because the musicians were playing and looking at Naná, and that didn't work. At one point, Manfred stopped the session to ask the orchestra members to return to their written scores and stop gawking: "Excuse me, sirs, could you look at the score, please? Otherwise, this won't work." Finally, they pledged to only look at the score, and we started to record. They started to get the hang of it and realized that they didn't need to follow Naná rhythmically. They understood the reach of Naná's musical perception.

According to Egberto, Naná was beaming for a long time after the recording session, having fulfilled one of his life's dreams:

> I was very pleased because I had never seen Naná playing with an orchestra. And he had never played with an orchestra. And while he played, and heard what we had figured out while we were on the bus, he was smiling the whole time for me. He would look over and smile. So happy. Just picture it! It was his life's dream to make a record with berimbau and orchestra. And all of a sudden, it was happening there, well played, with me there. Because we had this thing of our friendship—he had told me about this dream when we first met.

Naná mirrored this sentiment in a 2015 interview, where he stated that in composing and recording *Saudades*, he succeeded in doing his greatest work, elevating the berimbau as a solo instrument for the whole world.[2] Although the piece doesn't follow the formal conventions of the concerto, Naná describes as such because it shares the format of placing a solo instrument in musical conversation with the collective voice of an orchestra.

In nineteenth-century European art music, concertos gave virtuoso soloists a key avenue for the advancement of their careers, providing a showcase for their technique. But the form became more than just a vehicle for showing off speed and dexterity. Concerto form also came to provide a way to explore the relationship between the individual and the collective: "Mood, expression, the stirrings of the soul and even a sense of melancholy could be realized as a solo instrument worked against, resisted, displaced, led and triumphed over orchestral sound. The concerto's solo instrument functioned as a metaphor of the individual's engagement with the conflict between freedom and order."[3]

The ECM press release for the record seems not to know exactly how to categorize the record in order to sell it. It describes "mixed idiom sequences" that are neither Western classical nor Brazilian traditional music. It acknowledges Egberto's "straight music" credibility, while the next moment falling into describing Naná as exotic, and blurring the cultural distance between the Afro-Brazilian coastal Northeast and the more Indigenous Amazon rainforest:

> The music for strings on *Saudades* was written by Egberto whose "straight music" credibility stretches back to tutelage by Nadia Boulanger and twelve-tone composer Jean Barraqué. However, nothing in Egberto's classical past quite prepares one for Saudades, where overlapping strings, percussion and multi-layered voices suggest some new kind of hybrid music ... out of the jungles of the Amazon ... and the conservatory!

A problem with this juxtaposition of the jungle and the conservatory (*et tu*, ECM?) that remains even if more neutrally phrased as the Afrological, the Indigenous, and the Eurological, is that everyone involved were all interested in "mixed idiom sequences," while describing it this way (and presenting the orchestra members as dumbstruck by anything other than a recognizable orchestral instrument) echoes a story of first encounter. The bona fides of conductor Mladen Gutesha, for example, were located as much in the jazz world as they were in Western classical tradition. Not only had he arranged the strings for several Keith Jarrett records on ECM, but he had also done arrangements for jazz greats such as Miles Davis, swing clarinetist Benny Goodman, Lee Konitz, and the Modern Jazz Quartet.

Track 1: "O Berimbau"

The track "O Berimbau" begins by moving between various explorations of the capabilities of the instrument: "parallax," "straw stuck in a shoe," "the harmonic series." But it is the moment that the lyrical, orchestral strings enter that gives this experimentation an imagined cinematic and emotional grounding. The strings would fit within a contemplative, melancholy film. Their interaction with the timbral sounds of the berimbau conjure up a vivid feeling of recollection, a flying dream, where the berimbau moves throughout the sonic space shifting in vantage point in order for Naná to best imagine the remembered scene. The skittish scraping sounds strike me as the crackling of synapses, or a chill down the spine and goosebumps upon remembering something specific and fantastic. If the orchestral strings are the heart and the breath in the chest, the swishing and scraping are the nervous system responding in tandem. In this way, it reminds me of Naná's "North Brazilian Ceremonial Hymn" on Don Cherry's *Organic Music Society* album. Naná's playing on that earlier track portrayed the almost rude interjection of thoughts into a meditation session as the mind gradually settles down. In this case, in contrast, his playing feels like electric bodily responses to both the heavy and light of nostalgic saudades.

There is a particular moment several minutes into the extended track where the orchestra and berimbau stop, and Naná unexpectedly shouts a bird call at the top of his voice, repeating the call several times as it fades away, creating an echo with his voice as the strings return. When I hear this arresting moment, I think about how recollections can be evasive, slipping away until suddenly, a particular crystal-clear memory like the bird call can break through the haze. Naná's bird call here is not the call of a generic songbird, however, but the sound of an acauã, a bird closely associated with the Northeastern interior. The acauã, with its evocative onomatopoetic name in Portuguese and its nasalized -ã sound pointing to Tupi-Guarani origins, has a distinctive call that seems tailor-made for expressing the bittersweetness of saudades. Named the "laughing falcon" in English, birders describe its far-reaching call as a human-like "wah-wah" cry suggestive of laughter that changes from joyful to sad.[4]

By 1973, when Naná recorded *Africadeus*, he was adept at reproducing the interlocking polyrhythms of a samba school or maracatu nação with a single berimbau. By *Saudades*, six years later, the arrangement gives this accomplishment emotional justification, rather than simply showcasing impressive extended techniques. By positioning the stone against the string just so, he is able to find the recipe of resonance and noise that is recognizable as a snare drum in the distance. He begins the section without swing, playing straight in a military marching pattern, before moving toward a heavy, swung maracatu nação beat, complete with suggestions of the interlocking snare, shaker, and alfaia bass drum patterns. But the transition isn't immediate. Between the tight, swingless military snare and the thunderous, swung maracatu is an intermediate section of irregular and shifting phrase lengths made up of shards of samba, baião and maracatu. This transition leads toward the moment when he locks into the groove, taking full advantage of the independence between the baqueta and the caxixi that he possessed, playing separate drum and shaker patterns at the same time without overdubs. For a few fleeting measures, the key ingredients of the maracatu groove are all there, but in miniature, like an AM broadcast of a hit song played on a small transistor radio. This sonic miniaturization recalls what it's like to hear a parade far away, or to hear a tune playing back in the mind's ear. Naná teases us more confidently on *Saudades*, giving us less of the impressive batucada we want to hear than he provides on the earlier album *Africadeus*.

Drummers playing snare drums, timpani, and congas factor in gravity to their technique when they let their sticks or hands drop onto the instrument. In order to play the berimbau with the baqueta, in contrast, Naná struck the vertical string by moving the baqueta toward his body at an angle that is closer to horizontal. Hitting the string this way means that gravity affects the baqueta more consistently throughout the stroke, rather than helping the stick fall onto the snare drum, and then hindering it from going back up. The vertical string gives his horizontal strokes a certain buoyancy that is especially noticeable when he reproduces samba or maracatu parts, as if he were playing in a world with slightly different physics.

During the last third of the piece, the orchestra plays a section that, like "A Porta Encantada" from *Dança das Cabeças*, combines Afro-Brazilian styles with the dissonant harmonies of twentieth-century Western art music. While on *Dança das Cabeças*, dense tone clusters keep to a samba timeline, in *Saudades*, the strings play around with fragments of the gonguê iron-bell pattern which was the only part missing from the miniature maracatu drum corps played on the berimbau that was the high point of the previous section. This brief exploration gives way to the orchestra's emulation of Naná's timbre-centred effects. Using glissandos running in contrary motion, the orchestral strings reproduce the phaser effect-like harmonic partials that are isolated when Naná swishes the baqueta around the inside and outside of the gourd resonator. Using trills and precise dynamics in lieu of microphone choreography, the strings match the earlier nervous system twitches of the berimbau, foreshadowing the doppler effect of a swarm of Naná's muttering overdubbed voices simulating insects flying past one's ear that will appear at the end of the next track, "Vozes."

Track 2: "Vozes (Saudades)"

"Vozes" (Voices) skirts the boundary between speech and song, and between metrical and non-metrical utterances. It begins with Naná reciting the syllables "déro não déro Dedé," a phrase so rhythmic that I assumed upon first listen that it was just nonsense syllables set up to follow the accents of the Afro-Cuban tresillo rhythm, but with the final syllable sometimes stretched, adding an extra 2 pulses when desired. The overdubbed multitude of Naná's exclaiming this line remind me of the old drama teacher's trick of having an ensemble cast repeat "*rhubarb rhubarb*" to each other on stage to create for the audience the hubbub of a lively crowd. Learning that *déro* was short for *deram* ("they gave"), "they gave," in this case meant, "they gave freedom to," and that he was talking to someone nicknamed Dedé about Zumbi das Palmares completely transformed how I heard "Vozes."[5] Rather than a dry recording-studio experiment in overdubbed spoken-word polyphony, the track becomes an imagined backyard conversation, discussing whether or not Zumbi, the king of the enduring Quilombo dos Palmares, had been freed. The Quilombo dos Palmares was a maroon community of escaped enslaved Africans and their allies who existed outside of Portuguese colonization for most of the seventeenth century in Pernambuco, back when it was a captaincy. In the context of *Saudades*, the track contemplates from a distance on whether or not, despite the abolition of slavery in 1888, Afro-Brazilians are truly free today.

There is no straightforward sense of being at rest during the track. However, Naná does offer a certain qualified sense of release from the disorienting tension by manipulating less used rhythms in multiples of 5 and 7 to create tension, followed by resolving into the more recognizable cycle length of multiples of 6. The phrase "déro não déro Dedé" scans as 7 syllables on the page, but the stretch and uplift of the final syllable of Dedé leads to a cycle of 10 repeated three times at the start. Although the phrases used throughout the piece have metric regularity, the addition of the words "e" (and) and "diz que" (they say) are used as pick-up notes to lead into the phrase, and the end of Dedé is elastic in its length as it stretches up and fades away. This allows for a transition to "Dedé com Dedé" which leads to a cycle of more or less 14 pulses. The two phrases coexist, one in cycles of 10 and the other in cycles of 14, not precisely on one metronomic grid, but moving in and out of phase like Steve Reich's tape loops. A vocal loop from Naná's days with Don Cherry's Organic Music Theatre then appears, with beat-box-like onomatopoetic drums and shaker based around the sounds *ah tchika um*. This phrase brings the momentum of a 12-pulse pattern, giving the piece the feeling like it is coalescing into a more comprehensible groove before it is once again overtaken by the rarer cycles.

Meanwhile, after nearly 40 seconds of only voices, the orchestra provides an additional, much slower underlying pulse, the strings sustaining chords that hint at standard cycles of tension and release within the classical idiom, but with enough harmonic substitutions and rhythmic displacement to thwart any easy sense of coming to a resolution or feeling at rest (I–VI after a set up leading to the expectation of I–vi to the relative minor, for example). Manfred was known for insisting upon having everyone take an hour lunch at the same time, but this time, as he called a break for everyone else, he had asked Egberto if he could create a loop for the orchestra to play that Naná could later work with. The fact that the loop repeats exactly gives the sense that its melancholic lack of satisfying resolution may be never-ending.

Track 3: "Ondas (Na Óhlos de Petronila)"

Naná began his career immersed in the wordplay of spoken Northeastern Brazilian Portuguese. In the 1950s and 1960s, he was also steeped in the wordplay of both bossa nova and its psychedelic offspring Tropicália—Tom Jobim, Caetano Veloso, Gilberto Gil, Tom Zé. All of these songwriters drew from the Brazilian avant-garde concrete poetry of Augusto dos Campos and others, in which syllables became building blocks, and switching two letters often led to sharp turns of meaning, like the difference between *luxo* (luxury) and *lixo* (garbage). When I first saw "Na Óhlos de Petronila," the subtitle of the track "Ondas," my first thought was that there was a typo on the record, since "olhos" means "eyes" in Portuguese, but "óhlos" isn't a recognized word. But the spelling was retained in the Brazilian edition of the record, and in all subsequent versions of *Saudades*. More likely, it is a deliberate sertão-ese malaprop that signals the reader to be on the lookout for reversed letters. And the reversal of Petronila and Petrolina opens up the floodgates to a very specific context and meaning.

Petronila is Naná's mother's first name. Knowing that, "Olhos de Petronila" becomes "Eyes of My Mother" and the reversal of letters gestures toward mirror images and reflections. But as the title "Ondas" makes clear, the theme is waves, and waves and ripples refract reflections in the water. "Na" in Portuguese is the contraction "in the" for a singular, feminine noun. But here, it clashes with the plural, masculine "óhlos/olhos." Doubled, however, it becomes Na Na—"NaNá with Petronila's eyes." And refracting the "N" of Na and the "-os" of óhlos, you can glimpse a reflection of "NaNá in the pools of Petronila's eyes," since *olhos* has a second meaning—an *olho de agua* is a watering hole or a pond.

Reversing the "l" and the "n" turns Petronila into Petrolina, the name of the city in the interior of Pernambuco that is the hometown of Naná's old friend Geraldo Azevedo. And at the time Naná composed the track, Petrolina had just become the site of the largest artificial lake in the world. "NaNá in the pools of Petronila's eyes" becomes readable as "NaNá reflected in the waters of Petrolina." Parts of the road through the sertão backlands from the coast toward Petrolina can still resemble the backdrop of a Hollywood Western—xique-xique cacti, scrub brush, cattle ranching, and cowboys (albeit with differently shaped hats than their North American counterparts). Donkey-drawn carts continue to share the roads with motorcyclists and bold drivers, albeit less and less in recent years. I remember how, while driving in the interior, it was jarring to come across large artificial lakes alongside the highway in the midst of miles of a dry landscape. A combination of politics, geography, and cultivation techniques have made the area perennially drought-prone. While the reservoirs have often complicated this problem, they were constructed as attempts to regulate water supplies, to generate electricity through dams, and to facilitate crop irrigation.

When Naná recorded *Saudades* in March, 1979, he had just made a major move less than four months before. When Naná returned to Germany to record *Saudades*, he was just starting to settle into his new life in New York City after spending six years in Paris (when he wasn't touring throughout Europe). It seems possible that the melancholic longing of *Saudades* points not just toward Brazil, but extends in multiple directions at once.

In February, 1979, not long after his move, still settling in, belongings plausibly still unpacked, Petrolina began to appear in international newcasts. The timeline set forth by CHESF, the Brazilian national electrical utility, for the Lago de Sobradinho to reach maximum capacity and the hydroelectric dam to begin producing electricity coincided with heavy rains. The São Francisco River rose, and the enormous reservoir overtopped, causing massive floods and displacing almost 50,000 people in the area.

For some of the displaced in 1979, this wasn't the first time. Two years before, in 1977, the rerouting of the São Francisco River deliberately submerged the towns of Casa Nova, Pilão Arcado, Remanso, Sento Sé, and Sobradinho. The military government relocated over 64,000 of their residents to newly constructed communities with the same names, as if nothing were changing. A propaganda reel produced at the time breezily treats this rupture as the inevitable cost of progress, joking that a boat transporting residents and livestock alike before the flood to their new homes was a kind of present-day Noah's Ark.[6] Abandoned, mostly submerged churches, only their bell towers or the tops of their roofs visible above the surface of the artificial lake became an arresting image of rapid and drastic, forced change.

This violent uprooting and forced sacrifice in the name of progress (*ordem e progresso* are stitched onto the Brazilian flag, right?) troubled artists and activists at the time, especially considering its technocratic and authoritarian developmentalist twist on a religious prophecy and promise of radical social change so embedded in the region's history. Near the end of the nineteenth century, millenarian preacher Antonio Conselheiro had famously proclaimed that, "the sertão will become the sea, and the sea, sertão," promising, "an apocalyptic transformation in which evil will be swept away and replaced by goodness,"[7] not long before troops from the new republican government massacred him and his utopian religious community.[8] This same figure of Antonio Conselheiro later inspired Naná's former loftmate Glauber Rocha, who directed the 1963 sertão-themed film *Deus e o Diabo na Terra do Sol* (Black God, White Devil). In Rocha's film, the character Sebastião "promises the faithful a utopia where everything is green, where horses feed on flowers, where children drink milk from rivers, where stones become bread, and where the dust of the land becomes flour."[9]

Guttemberg Guarabyra from Sá, Rodrix e Guarabyra, a Brazilian rock band that started out in the 1970s, wrote and performed the song "Sobradinho," mourning the drowning of the towns and resulting forced relocations. Sá, Rodrix e Guarabyra has ties to Naná in that band member Zé Rodrix had played with Naná in his previous band Som Imaginário accompanying Milton Nascimento in the early 1970s:

> Vem o rio te engolir
> Debaixo d'água lá se vai a vida inteira...
> Vai ter barragem no salto do Sobradinho
> E o povo vai se embora com medo de se afogar
> O sertão vai virar mar

> The river is coming to swallow you
> Under the water, there goes your entire life...
> There will be a dam at Sobradinho Falls
> And the people will go away, afraid of drowning
> The sertão will become the sea

While Guarabyra chronicles the flooding in the plain language of a protest song, Naná, only six years after recording the wordless *Milagre dos Peixes* with Milton Nascimento to evade the military censors, isn't content to simply tell us this story with words. Instead, he wants the listener to feel the dread of the water rising, wordlessly evoking the scene. In particular, Naná adapts elements of the elegiac, reverent atmosphere that Milton deploys so powerfully when he sets his music in the small towns of the countryside of Minas Gerais abandoned to rural–urban labor migration. Through vocal timbre, reverb and soaring melodies, Milton evokes the melancholy of empty small-town churches. Naná takes this formula and adds rushing water to the mix, imagining the moment that water floods the church, and with it, the entire town.

In order to paint this sonic image, Naná takes full advantage of the ECM sound box. Working alone, Naná (or rather, several overdubbed Nanás) occupies as much space as possible. Recurring gong hits and the parallax gesture establish and maintain the expansive horizon that a large body of water creates. But the percussion confirms that this water is not still, but splashing, churning, and moving forward, overwhelming and unstoppable. Naná spaces a pair of tabla drums over the center and the left side of the mix, multiple conga parts over the center and the right channel, and, late in the track, places an iron bell far right and a shaker far left. Descending falsetto vocal parts in parallel harmony invoke waves reverberating within a church. Singing together with his punctuating conga stabs, he explores a wet slapback echo delineating the virtual back wall to the drenched space. The orchestra comes in with an insistent, droning 2 against 3 cross-rhythm that adds dread and urgency as the water level rises.

The combination of the crystalline ECM mix and the fact that Naná pieced together all of these tracks by himself, playing all the parts except for the anonymous orchestral drone, only heightens a sense of emptiness and dread. The image of the flooded church is a haunting one, and I imagine that Naná, hearing about the flooding while living so far away from his home state, was shaken by it.

Track 4: "Cego Aderaldo"

After the intense sonic painting of the flooding of a church in Ondas (Na óhlos de Petronila), the next track, "Cego Aderaldo," starts as if surveying the damage after the water has stopped rising. After three tracks of only Naná and orchestra, Egberto Gismonti appears on a solitary guitar, reverb filling out the ample space between single-note phrases that linger and breathe. Despite a shift in tone from the dread-filled and mournful Ondas, Cego Aderaldo continues to be set in the same area of the Northeastern sertão. Or, at least, it starts there before traveling far and wide. Cego Aderaldo was the name of a legendary cantoria de viola troubadour from Crato, Ceará, a city just to the north of Petrolina. Cantoria de viola is a tradition featuring improvised song duels and ballads in rhyme and meter that narrate and comment on legends and current events.

Beyond the reference to a cantador in the title, the double-coursed strings of what Egberto calls his "Super 8 String Guitar" echo the sound of the signature instrument of cantoria, the 10-stringed viola—a slightly smaller guitar, not a member of the violin family. "Double courses" mean that pairs of strings are placed very close to each other in unison or octaves and played as one. This design creates a kind of reverb without electricity, as the strings create sympathetic vibrations that spur each other on. It is found in many European and Middle Eastern string instruments, from the mandolin to the oud. Detached from the poetic sung forms of cantoria, where the viola caipira provides a sturdy, formulaic structure underlying vocal improvisations, Egberto's guitar evokes and echoes the cantoria de viola sound without mimicking it. In fact, gestures toward cantoria de viola rhythms and melodies in the track are relatively minimal—Egberto was never interested in folkloric recreations.

I hear Egberto's track instead as an attempt to correct the clumsy Orientalism of Baden Powell's 1969 track "O Cego Aderaldo," that links the Northeast region of Brazil with fantasies of faraway lands. In the industrialized Rio de Janeiro–São Paulo axis of Brazil, there is a long history of marking the Northeast and the Amazonian North regions as domestic others. Musically, this draws on the fact that the Northeast, one of the first regions in Brazil to be colonized by the Portuguese (and the Dutch), beginning in 1500, is a place where one can hear aspects of musical systems that are markedly non-Western. Or, more precisely, in addition to musical practices linked to West and Central Africa, and the Indigenous groups of the region, aspects of Iberian musical practices long entangled with the Islamic world are audible there. Aboio cowherding songs, for example, feature a nasal vocal timbre, non-metrical phrases, and sung intervals that often fall outside of the Western-tempered scale. And considering the centuries of Moorish control over what is now much of Spain and Portugal, ending immediately before the European colonization of the Americas began, this is not just a coincidental convergence of sound quality.

Not long after Baden Powell contributed to popularizing the berimbau with his tune "Berimbau," he recorded "O Cego Aderaldo" in 1969. Powell's track attempts to make a connection between the harmony of cantoria de viola—in particular, the ways in which flatted 7th scale degrees sometimes appear where they wouldn't in Western common practice harmony— and a psychedelic-era fantasy of Middle Eastern musical modes. Powell establishes a dissonant drone a second apart (E and D) and then plays a pseudo-oud part that highlights a raised 4th scale degree (G#) before meandering between the major and minor 6th scale degrees, slightly detuned and harshly over-plucking to get a less guitarlike sound. If anything, the end product resembles the riff in the Rolling Stones' "Mother's Little Helper" that associates non-Western scales with drug-induced disorientation more than it has anything to do with actual Middle Eastern music. Powell's "O Cego Aderaldo" is less about any specific aspects of the music systems of the Middle East, and more about performing the Northeast as emphatically "not Western."

In contrast, Egberto Gismonti's "Cego Aderaldo," without the "O," replaces Powell's ambivalent distancing with cultural intimacy. His father immigrated to Brazil from Beirut, Lebanon, and his mother is from Sicily. The mixture of musical systems found in the Levant and the Mediterranean to him are not just a fantasy, but part of his family heritage. I hear Egberto's "Cego Aderaldo" is as a corrective response to Baden Powell, treating aspects of Middle Eastern and Mediterranean music not as a signifier of a cultural other, but as part of a broader story of Brazil.

Gismonti first recorded "Cego Aderaldo" on *Saudades*, but he recorded his most well-known version of the track a year later on the record *Folk Songs* with Charlie Haden on upright bass and Jan Garbarek on soprano saxophone. Tracing who covers a tune and how they go about it can suggest the tune's stylistic resemblances, and versions of Egberto's "Cego Aderaldo" reveal a field of possibilities. The covers suggest a broad range of styles from Italy to India, Eastern Europe and the Middle East. The tune has been performed in flamenco versions; by Italian accordion player Simone Zanchini, who categorized it as a tango; in a vocal version by Polish jazz singer Grażyna Auguścik, who incorporates klezmer into her work;

and by The Magma Project, a group that explores fusions of Middle Eastern and Indian music. When Egberto picked up a sitar at a music shop in India in 1984, *Cego Aderaldo* was the first tune that he immediately gravitated toward on the instrument.

The frenetic Phrygian melody creates a bridge between Middle Eastern and Mediterranean melodic styles. This bridge can be heard in the rhythm as well, as Naná and Egberto find their explosive musical chemistry, feeding off of each other and reprising the running tempo that served them so well on *Dança das Cabeças*. In Naná's overdubs, he accomplishes what Melvin Gibbs referred to as Naná's stylistically open feel that is "elastic enough" that "it could be multicontextualized." A mid-tempo 4/4 bounce of a Brazilian xote played on the West African talking drum coexists with a frenetic 12-pulse cycle played on Indian tablas that can be heard either as a West African-derived asymmetrical timeline, as Iberian/Latin American sesquialtera (3+3+2+2+2 as in "everything's good in A-m-er-i-ca"), or as the kind of additive rhythm found in some Eastern European music.

Cego Aderaldo, the troubadour, was an iconic Northeastern culture bearer, recognized for his quick-witted barbs in the midst of vocal combat, and harsh words are expected in the insult battle format. His most famous battle was against Zé Pretinho, a Black performer, in the 1920s. While Zé Pretinho mocked Cego Aderaldo's blindness, Cego Aderaldo cruelly tore into Zé Pretinho with racial insults and accusations of social climbing. At the end of a lengthy duel, Cego Aderaldo concluded: "I looked for the Black man in the room/He was already in the kitchen/And once again, he wanted to enter/The dressing room door." While Aderaldo disapproves, taunting "A Black man in a room for Whites/Only results in disgust," he is, in his disgust, describing cause for celebration: the accomplishment of breaking a color barrier and finding success in a white-dominant space. It is rich that Naná, as an Afro-Brazilian percussionist, recorded an homage to Cego Aderaldo on his solo record with German orchestral accompaniment on one of Europe's most prestigious record labels. I don't know for sure whether he had heard these specific verses of Aderaldo's, and included the tribute as a gesture of defiance, or whether he didn't, and this was simply a tribute to his home region. Especially when coupled with the question asked in Track 2 "Vozes (Saudades)" of "Has Zumbi das Palmares been freed?," I want to believe that he knew.

Track 5: "Dado"

The last track on *Saudades* returns to the berimbau to bookend the album. Instead of an ambitious exploration of extended techniques like the first track, however, this outro walks along, contemplative, its variations dividing the meter before quickly snapping back to an insistent and steady striking of the string like the ticking of a stopwatch. "Dado" as onomatopoeia matches the track's stopwatch ticking, and "dado" as noun, verb and adjective contain a rich cluster of associations to chance, time, facts, habits, gifts and assumptions. "Dado" means a die (as in dice); a datum (as in data); dated (as in tied to a date); and the action of being inclined to do something. As the past participle of the verb "to give," it shares the various meanings of the word "given" in English: given away, given to, a given (an assumption), granted.

On the *Organic Music Society* record, Naná's first recording with Don Cherry, Don declares: "We can be in tune with time.

We can be a slave to time. We can be in total aspiration, trying to catch time. There must be a fourth way to flow with time." The track "Dado" is humbler than Don's manifesto, but, nonetheless, in it, Naná mulls over the same concern for orienting oneself temporally. The steady ticking, alternating with interruptions in the flow of the pulse, suggests an ebb and flow of steady, quotidian moments and more unpredictable events.

The center of gravity of the berimbau on "Dado" is very different from "O Berimbau." The instrument's lowest pitch is significantly detuned down a step and a half from F to D. This changes the weight and growl of the resulting sound, as well as the physics of the bounce of the baqueta. After the higher fundamental pitch heard in the earlier tracks, the lower pitch almost sets up an expectation of slow motion, yet the strokes continue at regular speed. Through this shift, multiple perceptions of time coexist in tension. It is a tape-speed manipulation effect done without manipulating any tape. As elsewhere on the record, he uses common meters (4/4, 12/8) as points of rest to return to, creating tension and release through rhythm. Orbiting around a refrain, he ventures farther and farther away from home, using all sorts of irregular phrase lengths as long as they are composed along this steady but still breathing timeline.

How does Naná reach the higher pitches that he produces on this track? It doesn't seem possible. I puzzled over this with my editor Jason Stanyek for some time, before finding Naná's explanation for it in an interview with percussionist and scholar Greg Beyer. My initial interpretation of "Dado" was that Naná, with just one word made up of one repeated consonant and two vowels, was taking stock of his life up to that point: the combination of habits, gifts, chance, and assumptions that brought him to where he was right then. And the title does harbor that rich cluster of associations. But beyond the meanings of the word "dado" and its tick-tock stopwatch quality, it was also the nickname of a friend of Naná's who custom-made him a two-stringed berimbau, with the strings tuned a fifth apart (D and A).[10] The track is a conversation that alternates between the two strings. He does a figure on one string, and then repeats it on the other. The tuning for the two-stringed berimbau turned out to be unreliable, so this track is one of the only recordings of the instrument before he stopped playing it.

Saudades and *Saudades*

"Saudades" is not merely the Portuguese translation of "nostalgia"—it is a particular expression of loss and longing, entangled with the stories Brazilians tell themselves about themselves. Brazilian abolitionist Joaquim Nabuco describes the bittersweet yearning of saudade as "remembrance, love, grief and longing," all at once. Anthropologist Roberto da Matta describes it memorably as "an enchanted temporality that contaminates."[11] On the *Saudades* record, the seemingly nonsensical onomatopoetic syllables of "Vozes" were, to Naná, a contemplation on how far (or not) Brazil had come on issues of racial justice. In "Ondas (Na Óhlos de Petronila)," he rendered a vivid portrait of the social and environmental catastrophe of the Sobradinho dam constructed in the name of economic progress. With "Cego Aderaldo," he paid tribute to a hero of his home region's folklore who found it disgusting that a Black Brazilian like him would dare to aspire to seek recognition in dominantly white elite spaces. All of this points to Naná's expression of saudades as one that is more ambivalent and torn than nostalgia is often understood. Svetlana Boym calls this vexing mixture of feelings "reflective nostalgia." Rather than conjure up a rosy idealization of the past, reflective nostalgia opens a space to contemplate migration and exile. Unlike works expressing "restorative nostalgia"—an often politically toxic longing for the "good old days" of a phantom homeland—works like *Saudades* are pitched in a reflective nostalgic mode that acknowledges uprootedness and diaspora, and allows for expressions of doubt and uncertainty. A person filled with reflective nostalgia can be "at once homesick and sick of home."[12]

Jairo Moreno's writing on what Cuba meant to Mario Bauzá as he was carving a niche for himself in the New York City music scene applies here. Nostalgic evocations of a homeland can serve as a double gesture that occupies an individual register—a personal curation of memories—while also occupying a broader socio-musical and economic register, refiguring the field a person inhabits. In other words, like Bauzá's Cuba, Naná's Brazil offers a sincere, conflicted, personal expression of nostalgia for his home that also serves to broadcast how he is reaching beyond these roots. In Naná's case, in line with the stark off-white cover avoiding any caricatured markers of tropical Brazil, it broadcasts that he is substituting his past with his present as a thriving ECM recording artist split between New York City and Europe. Like for Mario Bauzá, for Naná, "it means that the homeland and the past are retained in the present, as its double."[13] This move confirms the musical authority of his Brazilian origins, stamping what he does in the (then) present as authentic. By evoking where he came from while insisting upon his distance from it,

Naná asserted the same individual self-determination and artistic innovation as the European and US jazz players with whom he recorded, while at the same time laying claim to an Afro-Brazilian musical reserve that others in the European jazz scene couldn't as easily access.

Epilogue: After *Saudades*

Saudades was one of the projects that Naná was proudest of, as confirmed by his widow Patrícia, as well as several of his friends. But that was only one of the many reasons that I gravitated toward writing about it. It wasn't his most well-known recording, although it received some positive reviews from critics. I found *Saudades* worth focusing on because, like the lost filmstrip where Naná responded through sound to the resemblance between Picasso's cubism and African masks, *Saudades* showcased the accumulated musical vocabulary that Naná had developed through the pivotal first years of his career.

But other threads also pulled me to write this genealogy of *Saudades* in order to tell the early story of Naná between 1964 and 1979. The end of the 1970s and the beginning of the 1980s were an important juncture, where transformations in music technology (and their attendant anxieties about the loss of older ways of making music) coexisted with a refiguring of ideas of the primitive and the civilized in the midst of shifting postcolonial centers and peripheries. It was the cusp between the analog and digital ages of musical performance and recording, as well as the cusp of independence for many former European colonies in Africa and the Caribbean. For Naná, the late 1960s to late 1970s were a decade of navigating the proliferation of multitrack recording and exploring the transformation of the sound stage to the sound box with its stereo field of possibilities. Recording to a click track had become commonplace, but drum machines were just beginning to explode in popularity. Naná managed to thrive within this shift, asserting a distinctive recipe of timbre, pitch and rhythm, with a mixture of arrangements and improvisation, and the ability to bridge disparate musical feels.

Access is uneven globally to the current state of word-, sound-, and image-reproduction technology at a given time—what Kittler calls the "discourse network."[1] Not every recording studio around the world, for example, has equal access to new recording gear, and that uneven access still often follows the older contours of maps drawn by European imperialism. At the same time, musicians within particular musical genres vary widely in adopting, or refusing to adopt, new technologies that transform how their music is made. Genres possess different logics of change[2]—a bass synthesizer is less welcome in classic country music than it is in electronic dance music, for example. Naná knew the older studio process of the sound stage, where everything (or everything except for the vocals) was recorded at once and mixed in mono. And then he beheld the moment when the possibilities changed, and the stereo field was there for him to explore (as long as the people in charge of the project gave him license to do it).

Individual artists like Naná pick and choose which aspects of their playing remain a constant, and which aspects embrace new possibilities. Naná was comfortable playing without a click track and exploring micro-timing and subtleties of rhythmic feel. He took a bold display of the elegance of premodern technology, restrung it with a piano string and heightened its sound through microphone choreography. In doing so, Naná demonstrated an awareness of current technological possibilities, such as multitracking and electronic effects such as phaser effects and wah-wah, while arguing that many of these sounds could be made without so much pricey gear and self-proclaimed modernity. In Ochoa Gautier's terms, there are projects following a logic of "transculturation," that assert the value of new sonic combinations (think fusions), and projects aiming for "sonic purification," that question what is being lost in these new approaches (think revivals of tradition).[3] But rather than framing this question as one that pits tradition against modernity, Ochoa Gautier lays out how the two are entangled and mutually constituting. Since Naná's story features both tendencies, it serves as a fitting case study of Ochoa Gautier's less either/or framing.

Naná grew up playing and listening to Pan-Latin mambo, cha-cha-cha and bolero; Afro-Brazilian Xangô religious music; European symphonic band repertoire; Villa-Lobos's sonic evocation of the visual; samba, bossa nova; and local Pernambucan genres such as maracatu, ciranda, baião, and coco. And as he became an adult, new genres pointed to new possibilities. In 1967, Gilberto Gil went to Caruaru with Naná's fellow Grupo Construção members—Naná's not in the photo, so I assume he stayed home that day, but, then again, perhaps he didn't appear because he took the snapshot. In Caruaru, Gil heard an alternate modernity in the sounds of the bandas de pífanos. He returned with the conviction that the sounds he heard should be placed alongside globally recognized greats such as the Beatles and Hendrix, rather than being relegated to tell the tale of "that which came before." The kernel of this reordering of the marginal and the canonical, and the local and the global, soon became a key tenet of Tropicália, and Gilberto Gil himself soon used Naná's future signature instrument the berimbau alongside the electric sounds of psychedelic rock to further this argument through song. This tension between how Sérgio Ricardo heard the music of Caruaru as precious premodern vestiges to be fretted about, and how Gilberto Gil heard them, continued throughout the early years of Naná's career that I chart in this book.

As Naná left Brazil, and found success in Europe and the United States, he shared Gil's disregard for stylistic taste hierarchies. He also saw the possible connections between the worlds of popular music and contemporary art. Melvin Gibbs notes that Brazilians like Naná and Arto Lindsay were able to navigate and contribute to what was happening in New York in the 1980s and 1990s, in part because the music scene then was blending with what was happening in the world of contemporary art, and the Brazilians "had their own version of that with Tropicália." Playing music that shared concerns with the visual and conceptual art scene wasn't anything new to them.

A Dialectics of Arto and Pat

It is impossible to do justice to the remaining 37 years of Naná's post-*Saudades* career in an epilogue, but I feel compelled to touch upon at least a few highlights. Let's start by returning to Naná's couch in the early 1980s, where he brought Arto Lindsay and Pat Metheny together to watch the Knicks play the Celtics. Naná used a sports rivalry that matters so much because it doesn't really matter, in order to playfully poke at a musical rivalry that matters so much because it doesn't really matter.

As is so often the case with apparent opposites, closer examination of what Arto and Pat were doing, especially with the benefit of a longer view of the careers of both, leads to a more complex picture, with Naná and Brazil in the sliver where their Venn diagram overlaps. Pat Metheny had long been interested in Brazil, because of how bossa nova appealed both to his love of dense harmony, and also to his interest in cutting jazz swing feels with straight eighths without eschewing polyrhythm. But when he talks about Brazilian music, rhythm is almost ancillary. For Pat, Brazil is "the last place in the world where the pop music was deeply involved in harmony … Brazilian pop music is one of the great vestiges of chordal activity in the world."[4]

In 1980, Pat only meant to visit Brazil for three days, but he ended up staying for three weeks during this first visit, and later in the decade lived in Brazil for a number of years (from 1986 to 1990). Milton Nascimento's lyrical melodies and the dense harmonies of Milton's guitarist Toninho Horta in particular caught his ear. Metheny and his bandmates such as Lyle Mays came to understand Brazilian music as a parallel universe: an example of how the same cultural and musical flows, broadly speaking, that led to jazz also led to another musical system that was distinct and just as rich. "It was an amazing unpredictable combination of cultural influences of the Western classical harmonic sense and the African rhythmic sense, done in a completely different way from jazz."[5]

Metheny's interest in Milton Nascimento led him to learn about Naná, and in September 1980, Pat plucked Naná away from Codona and whisked him off to Oslo to record *As Falls Wichita, so Falls Wichita Falls* for ECM records. The vaguely science-fiction title track was described by critics as "a stream-of-consciousness dreamscape," as well as an example of Pat's pastoral jazz with its expansive spaces evoking the heartland of the United States and the wide open road.[6] The title track doesn't feature drum set at all, just an early Rhythm Ace-style drum machine and Naná with cowry shells in one hand and jingles in the other, or playing talking drum and shaker at the same time.

Polyphonic synthesizers such as the Prophet 5 had become available just before the Pat Metheny Group recorded *As Falls Wichita*, and one of Pat's goals for the album was to take these new synths seriously as tools for orchestration. The electronic textures on the record that so clearly date the album's era were novel in the jazz world at the time. Metheny's stated motivation for bringing Naná into the mix (albeit at a consistently subordinate volume, as to not upset the primacy of harmony and melody) was to supply an "earth factor" counterbalancing the electronics and multiple guitar types.[7] Naná's wordless vocals appealed to Pat in that they reintroduced the voice into Pat's instrumental work without reintroducing lyrics. He heard Naná's vocals as "an effective tactic to get that vocal quality that I think everybody loves, but with still the possibility of keeping it vague in terms of actual textual meaning."[8] Pat and Naná shared certain longtime musical priorities that made them both good candidates to work with ECM records. Both explore improvisation as narrative, and the creation of evocative sonic spaces through overdubbing. Pat heard *As Falls Wichita* as "a very cinematic record. It seems to have a visual aspect to it," explaining that "it almost creates a movie in your mind."[9]

Naná switched off between working with Pat and working with Don Cherry and Collin Walcott in Codona in 1981–2. By the time that he began playing more regularly with Arto Lindsay, Naná had helped Arto to combine his guitar noise with the rhythms, harmonies, and song structures of bossa nova, samba and other Northeastern Brazilian styles, while playing with post-punk electronics and atmospheric studio production as a musical instrument into itself, in the band Ambitious Lovers in the 1980s and in his later solo work from the 1990s to the present.

While Naná contributed to Ambitious Lovers, Arto contributed to Naná's 1987 record *Bush Dance*, on which Naná embraces drum machines and other electronics. Naná recorded *Bush Dance* not long after he was enthused by the emergence of hip-hop, befriending The Magnificent Force breakdance crew and touring Europe briefly with them. *Bush Dance* was recorded by Martin Bisi, who recorded much of the no wave, avant-garde, and hip-hop in New York in the 1980s, including Afrika Bambaataa, Lydia Lunch, and Herbie Hancock's runaway hip-hop-inflected 1983 hit "Rockit." The production style of *Bush Dance* is a far cry from meticulous ECM as Naná worked to combine his percussion vocabulary with drum machines and synths, creating electronic textures while retaining samba, maracatu, ciranda, and other Brazilian rhythmic feels. The relatively lo-fi record was made for the dance floor in a way that retains a sense of spontaneity but severely flattens the stereo field. It doesn't quite sound like anything else at the time. It's both sloppy and in the pocket. Jon Pareles wrote in the *New York Times* about the accompanying live show that Naná "turned rhythms into melodies and tunes into grooves—heady, exhilarating, unpredictable music." He praised Naná's ability to know "just how long a groove can hold attention, just when a change will be most welcome. With Mr. Vasconcelos' sure sense of timing, his complex music always sounded spontaneous and playful."[10]

Arto shared Naná's art of careful spatial placement on his Pat Dillett-mixed 1990s solo records, placing bilingual bossa nova vocals and chord voicings within a loop-based context with subtle, constantly shifting moods. Naná of the 1970s reconciles with Naná of the 1980s on the 1990s records *O Corpo Sutil/The Subtle Body* and *Noon Chill*.[11] One standout track among many is "Whirlwind" from *Noon Chill*. On it, Naná conveys heartbeat and breath with stethoscopic intimacy by transferring Pernambucan baião and maracatu rhythms from their usual zabumba and alfaia drums to a large parade-style bass drum and shaker close miked and played quietly.

Selected Gigs and Recordings

As I gathered published interviews from newspapers, magazines, and academic sources, and studied the liner notes and discogs.com entries for the almost 300 records that Naná played on, I began to scrape specific dates of live shows and recording sessions. This accumulated chronology (drawing on the extensive efforts by Johann Haidenbauer, who relied on the knowledge of José Teles, N. Scott Robinson, and others),[12] helped me to piece together where he was when, what he was focusing on, who he was spending time with, and which projects he was juggling on which continents. Some of the dates are specific to the day, and others are just the month, or even the range of a year. Here are a few of these entries, to give you a sense of the range of what Naná was doing post-*Saudades*, as he made the transition, as Melvin Gibbs put it, from "rock star mode" to "guru mode," and elder statesman of percussion.

February, 1980: Soundtrack to the Al Pacino film, Cruising

In 1980, Naná's berimbau appears on the soundtrack to a murder scene in the controversial Al Pacino film *Cruising*,[13] his sounds yet again framed as savage and exotic. The parallax gesture and phased scraping of the berimbau's gourd resonator signal the heightened listening of prey and predator, as the murderer lures his victim into a wooded area within Central Park in Manhattan. Naná's percussion, combined with the sounds of men just off-screen having sex, and the murderer menacingly asking "where are you?" frames gay cruising as a zone where civilized rules need not apply—a dangerous jungle in the heart of the city.

> *Squat Theatre Nightclub gigs:*
> *November, 1979. Assum, featuring Nana Vasconcelos,*
> *Collin Walcott and Aïyb Dieng.*
> *December, 1979. DNA; Nana Vasconcelos.*
> *July, 1980. "Jam 1980" featuring John Lurie, Bobo Shaw,*
> *Nana Vasconcelos, Arto Lindsay & movie.*

At the Squat Theatre Nightclub in New York City during this time, ECM- and CMS-linked performers played one night, and Arto's no wave the next. John Lurie's big band The Lounge Lizards took shape during this moment, with Arto in the first iteration of the band. The Lounge Lizards played Mingus-meets-noise-meets-world jazz, toying with the image of the jazzman. Naná's proximity to this scene led to later projects. In 1986, for example, he composed and performed the soundtrack to the Jim Jarmusch film *Down by Law* that Lurie starred in,[14] and his playing can be heard in the Tom Waits episode of Lurie's 1991 *Fishing with John* television show.[15]

Naná spent much of 1982 juggling touring with Codona, and touring with Pat Metheny, leaving the Pat Metheny Group by the end of the year. In June–September, he toured with

Codona, playing dates in New York, Norway, France, Austria, and Germany, with a pause in July to accommodate Pat Metheny Group gigs. In July, October, and November, he played US dates with the Pat Metheny group, including Dallas, Philadelphia, Sacramento, and Nacogdoches, Texas. Eventually, Naná went back to Codona, and Pat Metheny opened up auditions in December to replace him.

April, 1984 Naná Vasconcelos with The Magnificent Force at the Sounds of Brazil (SOBs) nightclub in New York City

In 1984, after Naná watched breakdancers in Washington Square Park, he brought his berimbau and attempted to join them, the low-to-the-ground moves perhaps reminding him of capoeira. After the youngsters laughed off the out-of-touch old man, he recorded himself tapping Brazilian-based beats (no quantization or programming) onto drum pads, and brought them a cassette, to which, as the story goes, they responded more positively. He ended up accompanying the breakdance troupe The Magnificent Force on percussion and drum pads at the New York City nightclub Sounds of Brazil (SOBs), before taking the dancers and Indian percussionist Trilok Gurtu on tour in Europe. The Magnificent Force included Mr. Wiggles, of *Beat Street* and *Wild Style* fame, one of the key figures in the development of popping and locking. This brief tour marked Naná's interest in his hip hop-influenced playing with loops and interlocking grooves that could be heard on his *Bush Dance* (1987) and *Rain Dance* (1989) records later in the decade. Although footage of The Magnificent Force tour doesn't exist, to my knowledge, on the open internet, I was able to watch a (sadly non-circulating) copy at the Inathèque national French video archive. The video showcases the depth of the fissure between 1970s and 1980s production styles and their underlying philosophies in the moment after the crossover success of Herbie Hancock's *Rockit*. In an interlude between the routines of the featured dancers (allowing for a costume change?), Naná and Trilok are suddenly back in Woodstock in 1979, jamming at the Creative Music Studio, it seems. In that moment, they are percussionists who refuse to use chrome stands playing atmospheric South American meets South Asian percussion grooves before the teenagers return to the stage and pretend that they are robots.

After Collin Walcott's tragic death in a bus accident at the end of 1984 led to the dissolution of Codona, Naná and Don Cherry joined Ed Blackwell on drums, Carlos Ward on alto saxophone and flute and Mark Helias on bass to form the NU quintet, which toured in 1985 and 1986 in the US, England, Germany, Austria, and Sweden. Throughout the decade, even while living in New York City, Naná continued to record regularly in Europe with ECM artists, including a return to the duo format with Egberto Gismonti in *Duas Vozes* (1984), records with Norwegian saxophonist Jan Garbarek (1980, 1988, and 1990), Arild Anderson (1990, 1993, 1994), Jack DeJohnette (a 1987 LP and a 1988 laserdisc), and *Singing Drums*, a percussion-only project that Swiss drummer Pierre Favre organized (1984).[16]

According to Patrícia Vasconcelos, certain records were especially meaningful to Naná during this period, such as Jim Pepper's *Comin' and Goin'* (1983).[17] Pepper, a pioneer at fusing elements of jazz and rock in the 1960s, was of Kaw and Creek heritage. At the urging of Don Cherry and Ornette Coleman, Pepper incorporated Indigenous musical practices into a jazz framework. The album, described at the time as

"American Indian Jazz" featured many high-profile players, in addition to Naná, such as Don Cherry, Collin Walcott, Bill Frisell, John Scofield, and Hamid Drake.

During this period, as he collected year after year of Best Percussionist awards in *Down Beat* magazine's critics poll, Naná became in demand in New York City as a top-level session musician, called to add to records by Chaka Khan (1980), Talking Heads (1985), Laurie Anderson (1989), and Andy Summers (1991), among many others. In 1980, B.B. King called him into the studio to fortify the rhythms on a "live" recording in postproduction, leading to one of the only recordings of cuíca on a blues album that I believe exist. In 1990, he contributed to the recordings of Simons both Carly and Paul, although in the case of Paul Simon's Brazilian-themed *Rhythm of the Saints*, his participation was reluctant and he refused to go on the tour for the record. Arto remembers his brother Duncan repeatedly cupping the phone to tell Naná that Paul Simon was on the line, only to have Naná make it very clear through silent charades that he wasn't there. During the recording session, Naná laid down one of his trademark meticulous multitrack arrangements, to which the recording engineer thanked him and asked him to do a simplified, one-track timekeeping part, ostensibly so that they would have options when they mixed it down. Naná suspected that it would mean that the simpler part would be their choice, so he excused himself to the bathroom and promptly slipped out of the studio.

During the late 1980s and 1990s, Arto became a producer of high-profile records by prominent figures in Brazilian popular music and brought in Naná to contribute to these records as well. Having established himself abroad to the point that having Tropicalists Caetano Veloso and Gilberto Gil shape his career was no longer a concern, Naná played on Caetano Veloso's *Estrangeiro* (1989) and *Circuladô* (1991) and Marisa Monte's *Mais* (1991), *Verde, Anil, Amarelo, Cor de Rosa e Carvão* (1994), and *Barulhinho Bom* (1997) that were ever present in Brazil in the 1990s.[18] Still living in New York until 1998, Naná strengthened his ties with Brazil, producing, together with Gilberto Gil, the annual Panorama Percussivo Mundial Festival (PercPan) based in Salvador, Bahia beginning in 1994 and continuing to this day under different management. PercPan features several days of percussion-based ensembles from all over the world, combined with workshops for players.

Em Recife, Saudades de Recife

When Naná moved back to Recife, Pernambuco, in 1998 in his 50s, he began a very active chapter in his long musical career. He became an elder statesman who presided over the city's storied Carnaval traditions, conducting hundreds of drummers of the Afro-Pernambucan maracatu groups in an opening ceremony to the festivities each year. He also became a kind of godfather to the innovative new music scene in the city known as mangue beat, which asserted commonalities between maracatu nação and militant global pop styles such as Public Enemy-era hip-hop and Sepultura-style metal. This reordering of styles energized Naná, and he contributed to the records of the younger generation such as Mundo Livre S/A, Maciel Salu, DJ Dolores and Cordel do Fogo Encantado either as a special guest or a producer. It was in this capacity, as the elder statesman and booster of the post-mangue beat scene, that I first learned about Naná when he had just returned to Recife. Ever *antenado*—attentive to new directions—his own records from the period, such as *Contaminação* (1999), his first album recorded back in Recife, worked within mangue beat parameters using his unique palette of percussion and voice.[19]

When Naná returned to Brazil, he became very active doing projects with musicians from all over the country as well. His list of projects was dense in the 2000s, recording not just with younger post-mangue beat artists in their 20s and 30s from Recife's new scene, but also other long-established Brazilian artists such as Itamar Assumpção, Chico César, Alceu Valença, Badi Assad, Zelia Duncan, Martinho da Vila, and Zeca Baleiro. As a musicians' musician who had thrived abroad, Naná had a widespread renown in Brazil even if the sales and availability of his records there didn't reflect it.

Working with orchestras and working with children continued to be priorities for Naná, and he brought them together in the late 2000s in a series of projects. ABC Musical was a 2009 project working with low-income children in Brazilian public schools, in which he complemented more conventional choral conducting with a series of bodily gestures, each representing a sound, either in unison, or in loose polyphony, like his overdubbed spoken/sung vocalizing. The fact that their sequence wasn't strictly choreographed helped keep the kids' rapt attention, since any of the gestures could come at any point in the performance. It was a system with echoes of his interactions with the orchestra on *Saudades*, where the exact placement of the *palha* gesture scrawled on the top of each section of sheet music was up to him, even if the orchestra's part was fixed.

During this phase of Naná's career back in Brazil, he had the clout with government agencies that provide arts funding to launch elaborate projects. Heartened by the success of ABC Musical in Brazil, Naná extended the program internationally, doing a workshop with kids in Scotland and then bringing them to perform together with Brazilian children. The next year, in 2010, to commemorate the fiftieth anniversary of the construction of the federal capital city Brasilia, his project Lingua Mãe (Mother Tongue), brought together a total of 120 children from Brazil, Angola, and Portugal aged 7 to 10 years old to sing in a concert in Brasilia. At the final concert, using his methods from ABC Musical, he conducted the children's singing and body movements, each group dressed in red, blue, or yellow, depending on their Lusophone country.

For Naná, being heard and being acknowledged were one and the same. Being audible within the stereo field correlated with being socially recognized and valued. He went to great lengths to do more than just play "xique xique xique" for pop stars, transforming the possibilities of percussion, and expanding the role of the percussionist in the process. My goal here was to gather up as many voices as I could, each telling a bit of this story of his early life and work. It was a life so tied up in the times, places, and scenes that he thrived within, that telling his story points to the larger stories of shifts in the boundary lines between traditional, commercial popular, and erudite art music; between music, sound, and noise; between Afrological and Eurological approaches to music making; and between notions of the primitive and the civilized. *Eita velho de ouvido atento ao tempo.* Damn, this guy really hears time. Damn, this guy really hears the times.

Notes

Introduction

1 Oliveira, YouTube comment about Naná Vasconcelos.

2 Lewis, "Ventriloquial Acts: Critical Reflections on the Art of Foley," 108.

3 Fischlin and Heble, *The Other Side of Nowhere: Jazz, Improvisation, and Communities in Dialogue*, 88.

4 I have settled on using the term Western art music to refer to Eurological orchestral music. That said, I am leery of the common label's implication, especially in the context of Naná's story, that other musics are somehow not art. The term classical music was another option, but it is imprecise in its use both for a specific style of eighteenth–nineteenth-century music and also for Western orchestral music in general.

5 See Garcia, *Listening for Africa*, for an in-depth treatment of the implications of receiving Black expressive forms as primitive within nineteenth-century social evolutionist progress narratives.

6 Vasconcelos, *Saudades*.

7 Espir, "Naná Vasconcelos: Uma Entrevista Que Remete Saudades."

8 Boym, *The Future of Nostalgia*, p. xix.

9   Os Mutantes, *A Divina Comédia Ou Ando Meio Desligado*.

10 Atlas, *Put Blood into the Music*.

11 Nascimento, *Milagre Dos Peixes*.

12 Simon, *The Rhythm of the Saints*.

13 Anderson, *The Life Aquatic with Steve Zissou*.

14 Vasconcelos and Assumpção, *Isso Vai Dar Repercussão*.

15 Foley artistry, or simply Foley, is the cinematic process of matching sound effects, like the sound of footsteps, gunshots, and the slam of a door, to on-screen action.

16 Sharp, *Between Nostalgia and Apocalypse: Popular Music and the Staging of Brazil*.

17 Beta, "Fourth World in the 21st Century."

18 Feld, "Pygmy POP: A Genealogy of Schizophonic Mimesis," 26.

19 Novak and Sakakeeny, *Keywords in Sound*, 12.

20 Feld, "Pygmy POP," 17–18.

21 Walser, *Keeping Time: Readings in Jazz History*, 8.

22 Crenshaw, *Seeing Race Again: Countering Colorblindness across the Disciplines*, 159.

23 Melvin Gibbs, Brooklyn, NY, 12 July 2018.

24 Fischlin and Heble, *The Other Side of Nowhere*, 94.

Chapter 1

1   Camus, *Orfeu Negro (Black Orpheus)*.

2   Tinhorão, *Música Popular: Um Tema Em Debate*, 25.

3   Vianna and Chasteen, *The Mystery of Samba: Popular Music & National Identity in Brazil*.

4 See Sandroni, *Feitiço Decente: Transformações Do Samba No Rio de Janeiro, 1917–1933*; Hertzman, *Making Samba: A New History of Race and Music in Brazil*; Vianna and Chasteen, *The Mystery of Samba*; Trotta, *O Samba e Suas Fronteiras: "Pagode Romântico" e "Samba de Raiz" Nos Anos 1990*; Browning, *Samba: Resistance in Motion*; Bocskay, "Undesired Presences: Samba, Improvisation, and Afro-Politics in 1970s Brazil," among others.

5 Vasconcelos, *Africadeus*.

6 Hooper, "Not Your Average Family."

7 Bozzo Junior, Carlos, "De Como Juvenal Se Tornou o Fenômeno Naná Vasconcelos."

8 Aretakis, "O Tropicalismo Pernambucano: História de Um 'Tigre de Vanguarda' (1967–1968)," 66.

9 Lewis, "Improvised Music after 1950: Afrological and Eurological Perspectives."

10 Robinson, "Naná Vasconcelos: The Nature of Naná."

11 Freire, *Pedagogy of the Oppressed*.

12 Kirkendall, "Entering History: Paulo Freire and the Politics of the Brazilian Northeast, 1958–1964," 168.

13 Gaspar, "Movimento de Cultura Popular (MCP)."

14 Roser and Ortiz-Ospina, "Global Education."

15 *Cantochão* is the word for "Plainsong," a body of chants or sung prayers in Christian liturgy. The associations of the Portuguese word, which literally translates as "Ground song," are interpretable here as "the song coming from the ground" or perhaps "the song coming from the roots."

16 All of the quotes from the unpublished programs of Grupo Construção come from Teca Calazans' scrapbook.

17 Aretakis, "O Tropicalismo Pernambucano," 66.

18 Azevedo, "Adeus a Naná Vasconcelos."

19 "'Pregão' é Um 'Show' de Música Consciente."

20 Vasconcelos, "Filme Do Dia: Esse Mundo é Meu (1964), Sérgio Ricardo."

21 Unpublished, found in Teca Calazans' scrapbook.

22 Gil, "Depoimento (Musical) de Um Vira-Mundo."

23 Aretakis, "O Tropicalismo Pernambucano," 60.

24 Brazilian terms translatable as "swing," but with differences in feel and microtiming when compared to jazz contexts.

Chapter 2

1 Robinson, "Naná Vasconcelos: The Nature of Naná."

2 Star, "[A Música de] História Pública Da Música Do Brasil."

3 Nuzzi, *Geraldo Vandré: Uma Canção Interrompida*, chapter 18.

4 Vandré, *Geraldo Vandré – Cine Teatro Goiânia 1968 (Completo) – YouTube*.

5 Nuzzi, *Geraldo Vandré*, chapter 18.

6 Alex, "Geraldo Azevedo, o Sobrevivente".

7 Nuzzi, *Geraldo Vandré*, chapter 18.

8 Moreno, *Naná Vasconcelos e Milton Nascimento Em Cantos Do Rio*.

9 Borges, *Os Sonhos Não Envelhecem: Histórias Do Clube Da Esquina*, 205.

10 Nascimento, *Milton Nascimento*.

11 Christopher Dunn, author, *Contracultura: Alternative Arts and Social Transformation in Authoritarian Brazil*, 82.

Chapter 3

1. Pazcheco, "Naná Vasconcelos – Biriba é Pau!"
2. In an interview with Fabiano Canosa, New York, 11 July 2018, he speculated that it is surely partitioned into several apartments now.
3. Bozzo Junior, Carlos, "De Como Juvenal."
4. Gilberto, *João Gilberto En Mexico*.
5. Rocha, *Deus e o Diabo Na Terra Do Sol*.
6. Rocha, *A Idade Da Terra (The Age of the Earth)*.
7. São Jorge in Brazilian candomblé is syncretized, or coupled, with two orixás: Oxossí, the archer, in Glauber's home state of Bahia in Northeast Brazil, and Ogum, a warrior associated with iron, in Rio de Janeiro, and much of Southern Brazil.
8. Johnson, *Cinema Novo x 5: Masters of Contemporary Brazilian Film*, 119–20.
9. Johnson, 118.
10. Ibid., 120.
11. Ibid., 142.
12. Perrone and Dunn, *Brazilian Popular Music and Globalization*, 39.
13. Machín, *El Manisero (Early Recordings 1929–1930)*.
14. Powell, *Le Monde Musical de Baden Powell*.
15. Weiss, *Always in Trouble: An Oral History of ESP-Disk', the Most Outrageous Record Label in America*.
16. Fenton, "Gato Barbieri: Third World Jazz."
17. Ibid.
18. Martin, *New Latin American Cinema*, 39.

19 Rocha, *On Cinema*.

20 Johnson, *Cinema Novo x 5*, 159.

21 Ibid., 158.

22 Ibid.

Chapter 4

1 Lasson, "It Is Not My Music."

2 Ibid.

3 Ibid.

4 Cherry, "Dartmouth College, Dean of Faculty Records (DA-165, Box 10463, 'Cherry, Don')."

5 Weiss, "Don Cherry at Dartmouth."

6 Ibid.

7 Cherry, *Complete Communion*.

8 Cherry and Blackwell, *"Mu" First Part, "Mu" Second Part*.

9 Douglas, "Don Cherry – The Dozens."

10 Lasson, "It Is Not My Music."

11 Allen, "The Humus of Don Cherry."

12 Cherry, *Organic Music Society*.

13 Lasson, "It Is Not My Music."

14 Ibid.

15 Hooper, "Not Your Average Family."

16 Cherry, *Incontro con Don Cherry*.

17 Interview with Adam Rudolph, via video call, New York, 5 February 2020.

18 Cherry, Vasconcelos, and Walcott, *Codona*; Cherry, Vasconcelos, and Walcott, *Codona 2*; Cherry, Vasconcelos, and Walcott, *Codona 3*.

19 Robinson, "Naná Vasconcelos: The Nature of Naná."

20 Ibid.

21 Ibid.

22 Feld, "A Sweet Lullaby for World Music"; Erlmann, "The Aesthetics of the Global Imagination: Reflections on World Music in the 1990s"; Meintjes, "Paul Simon's *Graceland*, South Africa, and the Mediation of Musical Meaning"; Novak, "The Sublime Frequencies of New Old Media"; Stokes, "Music and the Global Order," among many others.

Interlude: ECM Records

1 Stone, "Manfred Eicher: 40 Years of ECM."

2 Williams, "Manfred Eicher: The Sound Man."

3 Lake and Griffiths, *Horizons Touched: The Music of ECM*, 1.

4 Ibid., 2.

5 Ibid., 188.

6 Ibid., 2.

7 Pareles, "ECM's Catalog is Finally Streaming. Here Are 21 Essential Albums."

8 Hunt, "ECM Studio Production Comment."

9 Lake and Griffiths, *Horizons Touched*, 10.

10 Hudson, "How the Austere Producer Manfred Eicher Keeps World Music Cool."

11 Feld, "Pygmy POP. A Genealogy of Schizophonic Mimesis," 17.

12. Lake and Griffiths, *Horizons Touched*, 7.
13. Ibid., 8.
14. Ibid.
15. Errington, *The Death of Authentic Primitive Art and Other Tales of Progress*, 30.
16. Metheny and Mays, *As Falls Wichita, So Falls Wichita Falls*.
17. Holden, "A Winning Mix of Electronic Innovation and Lyricism."
18. Metheny, "RIP NANA VASCONCELOS."

Interlude: Creative Music Studio (CMS): The Unmusic School

1. Berger, "Karl Berger: Freedom in Discipline."
2. Sweet, "All Kinds of Time: Creative Music Studio Celebrates Forty Years of Irrepressible Staying Power," 71.
3. Robinson, "Naná Vasconcelos."
4. Ibid.

Chapter 5

1. ECM Records, "ECM Records."
2. Moreira, "Um Coração Futurista: Desconstrução Construtiva Nos Processos Composicionais de Egberto Gismonti Na Década de 1970," 107.
3. Gismonti, *Corações Futuristas*; Gismonti, *Academia de Danças*; Horn, *The Altitude of the Sun*.

4 Robinson, "Naná Vasconcelos."
5 Pinto, "Egberto Gismonti e a Poética Da Semi-Erudição," 65, my translation.
6 Junior, "A Dança Das Oito Cordas Nas Cabeças de Egberto Gismonti," 27.
7 Pucci, "Cantos Da Floresta (Forest Songs)," 78.
8 Ibid., 79.
9 Feld, "Pygmy POP," 26.
10 Goldschmitt, *Bossa Mundo: Brazilian Music in Transnational Media Industries*, 76.
11 Ibid., 87.
12 Ibid.

Chapter 6

1 Lelouch, *Un Homme et Une Femme*.
2 Ford, "Taboo: Time and Belief in Exotica," 113–14.
3 Ibid., 117.
4 *Gotainer – Poil À La Pub*. Track 10d.
5 Ford, "Taboo," 109.
6 Mahjun, *Mahjun*; Caussimon, *Jean-Roger Caussimon*.
7 Akendengué, *Nandipo*.
8 McNeil, *J'ai Déjà Fait Mon Arche, J'attends Les Animaux*.
9 Carroll, *Orange Fish Tears*.
10 Kühn, *Rolf Kühn Group Featuring Phil Woods – The Day After*.
11 Moreno, Vasconcelos, and Maestro, *Visions of Dawn*.

12. Calazans, *Teca & Ricardo – Caminho Das Aguas*; Calazans, *Teca & Ricardo – Cadê o Povo*.
13. Burú, *Sessão Cabidela*.
14. Rozier, *Les Naufragés de l'île de La Tortue*.
15. Robinson, "Naná Vasconcelos."
16. Errington, *The Death of Authentic Primitive Art and Other Tales of Progress*, 35.
17. Ibid., 35.
18. Ibid., 36.
19. hooks, *Black Looks: Race and Representation*, 21.

Interlude: Naná's Place Within the *Fourth World*

1. Hassell and Eno, *Fourth World, Vol. 1: Possible Musics*.
2. Talking Heads, *Fear of Music*; Talking Heads, *Remain in Light*.
3. Macfarlane, "The Quietus | Reviews | Jon Hassell & Brian Eno."
4. Ibid.
5. Stockhausen, *Towards a Cosmic Music*, 26. This chapter, "Beyond Global Village Polyphony," is a compilation of texts of 1968–76.
6. Ibid., 26.
7. Beta, "Fourth World in the 21st Century."
8. Gross, "Jon Hassell Interview: Interview by Jason Gross."
9. Ibid.
10. Ibid.
11. Beta, "Fourth World in the 21st Century."

Chapter 7

1. Borges, *Os Sonhos Não Envelhecem*.
2. Ibid., 204–5.
3. Ibid., 205.
4. Ibid.
5. Ibid.
6. Whiteley, "Progressive Rock and Psychedelic Coding in the Work of Jimi Hendrix."
7. Galm, *The Berimbau: Soul of Brazilian Music*, 97.
8. Robinson, "Naná Vasconcelos."
9. Fischlin and Heble, *The Other Side of Nowhere*, 88.
10. Moreno, "Bauza-Gillespie-Latin/Jazz: Difference, Modernity, and the Black Caribbean," 83.
11. Ibid., 94–5.
12. See Washburne, *Latin Jazz: The Other Jazz*.
13. Moreno, "Bauza-Gillespie-Latin/Jazz," 82.
14. Ochoa Gautier, *Aurality: Listening and Knowledge in Nineteenth-Century Colombia*, 45.
15. Ibid., 46.
16. Ibid.
17. Ibid.
18. See Avelar and Dunn, *Brazilian Popular Music and Citizenship*, for discussions of this question.
19. Ochoa Gautier, *Aurality*, 32.
20. Ibid., 33.
21. Ibid., 41.

22 Samuels, Meintjes, Ochoa, and Porcello, "Soundscapes: Toward a Sounded Anthropology."

23 Johnson, *Cinema Novo x 5*, 158.

24 Lake and Griffiths, *Horizons Touched*, 8.

25 Brothers, *Louis Armstrong's New Orleans*, 18.

26 Skinner, *Yellow, Blue, and Black: Remembering and Renaissance in Afro-Sweden*.

Chapter 8

1 Albuquerque, *1973 – O Ano Que Reinventou a MPB*, chapter titled, "O Homem Percussão."

2 Ibid.

3 Vasconcelos, *Zumbi*.

4 Nascimento, *Milagre Dos Peixes*.

5 Goldschmitt, *Bossa Mundo*, 80.

6 Holmes, *Milton Nascimento and the Clube Da Esquina: Popular Music, Politics, and Fraternity during Brazil's Military Dictatorship (1964–85)*, 180.

7 Johnson, *Cinema Novo x 5*, 107.

8 Ibid., 109.

9 Holmes, *Milton Nascimento and the Clube Da Esquina*, 199.

10 Ibid., 201–2.

11 Diniz, "'Nuvem Cigana': A Trajetória Do Clube de Esquina No Campo Da MPB," 125.

12 Holmes, *Milton Nascimento and the Clube Da Esquina*, 202.

13 Dockwray and Moore, "Configuring the Sound-Box 1965–1972."

14 Théberge, Devine, and Everrett, *Living Stereo Histories and Cultures of Multichannel Sound*, 5.

15 Interview with Pat Dillett, New York, 9 July 2018.

16 Ibid.

17 Amaral, *A Música de Milton Nascimento*, 136.

18 Espir, "Naná Vasconcelos," my translation.

19 Interviews with Arto Lindsay, Rio de Janeiro, 4 June 2017 and 22 July 2018, and Melvin Gibbs, Brooklyn, NY, 12 July 2018.

20 Abreu, *O Menino e o Mundo (The Boy and the World)*.

21 Gomes, *O Menino e o Mundo #04-Naná Vasconcelos*.

22 Vasconcelos and Lucena, *El Increíble Naná Con Agustin Pereyra Lucena*.

Chapter 9

1 Taussig, *Mimesis and Alterity*.

2 Espir, "Naná Vasconcelos."

3 Hutchings et al., "Concerto."

4 Channing, "The Laughing Falcon."

5 "Naná Vasconcelos," *Enciclopédia Itaú Cultural*.

6 Rozemberg, *Criando Vida Nova (Coisas Do Brasil No. 263)*.

7 Johnson, *Cinema Novo x 5*, 131.

8 Levine, *Vale of Tears: Revisiting the Canudos Massacre in Northeastern Brazil, 1893–1897*.

9 Johnson, *Cinema Novo x 5*, 131.

10 Beyer, "Naná Vasconcelos, The Voice of the Berimbau."

11. Matta, *Conta de Mentiroso: Sete Ensaios de Antropologia Brasileira*, 34.
12. Boym, *The Future of Nostalgia*, xix.
13. Moreno, "Bauza-Gillespie-Latin/Jazz," 89.

Epilogue

1. Kittler, *Discourse Networks 1800/1900*.
2. Straw, "Systems of Articulation, Logics of Change: Communities and Scenes in Popular Music."
3. Ochoa Gautier, "Sonic Transculturation, Epistemologies of Purification and the Aural Public Sphere in Latin America."
4. Cooke, *Pat Metheny: The ECM Years, 1975–1984*, 166.
5. Ibid.
6. Holden, "A Winning Mix of Electronic Innovation and Lyricism."
7. Metheny, "RIP NANA VASCONCELOS."
8. Cooke, *Pat Metheny*, 164.
9. Ibid., 163.
10. Pareles, "Jazz: Nana Vasconcelos."
11. Lindsay, *O Corpo Sutil = The Subtle Body*; Lindsay, *Noon Chill*.
12. Haidenbauer, "Nana Vasconcelos Discography."
13. Friedkin, *Cruising*.
14. Jarmusch, *Down by Law*.
15. Lurie, "Fishing with John: Tom Waits."
16. Gismonti and Vasconcelos, *Duas Vozes*; Garbarek, Vasconcelos, and Abercrombie, *Eventyr*; Garbarek, *Legend of*

the Seven Dreams; Garbarek, I Took Up the Runes; Andersen, Sagn; Andersen, Towner, and Vasconcelos, If You Look Far Enough; Andersen, Arv; Favre, Singing Drums; DeJohnette, Jack DeJohnette's Special Edition – Irresistible Forces; DeJohnette, Jack Dejohnette's Special Edition – Live at the Montreal Jazz Festival 1988.

17 Pepper, Comin' and Goin'.

18 Veloso, Estrangeiro; Veloso, Circuladô; Monte, Mais; Monte, Barulhinho Bom (A Great Noise).

19 Vasconcelos, Contaminação.

List of Interviews

Rev. Dwight Andrews, Knoxville, TN, 24 March 2019.
Nelson Angelo, Rio de Janeiro, 23 July 2018.
Jon Appleton, via video call, Hanover, NH, 7 February 2020.
Helder Aragão aka DJ Dolores and Renato Lins aka Renato L, Recife, 2 August 2018.
Geraldo Azevedo, Rio de Janeiro, 26 July 2018.
Cyro Baptista, New Jersey, 8 July 2018.
Ricardo "Bolo" Bolognini, São Paulo, 17 June 2017.
Marcelino Burú, via video call, Rio de Janeiro, 5 July 2019.
Teca Calazans, Paris, 20 July 2018.
Fabiano Canosa, New York, 11 July 2018.
Sergio Cassiano, Recife, 15 June 2017.
Pat Dillett, New York, 9 July 2018.
Julie Fraad, Brooklyn, NY, 10 July 2018.
Melvin Gibbs, Brooklyn, NY, 12 July 2018.
Egberto Gismonti, Rio de Janeiro, 31 May 2017.
Richard Graham, via video call, Asheville, NC, 15 February 2019.
Janet Grice, Ardsley, NY, 14 July 2018.
Arto Lindsay, Rio de Janeiro, 4 June 2017 and 22 July 2018.
Arto Lindsay and Vinicius Cantuaria, Rio de Janeiro, 28 July 2018.
Pablo Lopes, Recife, 26 June 2017.
Merrie Robin Monroe, Nyack, NY, 11 July 2018.
Joyce Moreno, New York, 14 July 2018.

Edson Rodrigues, Recife, 16 June 2017.
Adam Rudolph, via video call, New York, 5 February 2020.
Vincent Segal, Paris, 18 July 2018.

Audio, Film, TV, and Video

Audio

Akendengué, Pierre. *Nandipo*. Vinyl LP. France: Saravah, 1974.

Andersen, Arild. *Sagn*. CD. Norway: Kirkelig Kulturverksted, 1990.

Andersen, Arild. *Arv*. CD. Norway: Kirkelig Kulturverksted, 1994.

Andersen, Arild, Ralph Towner, and Naná Vasconcelos. *If You Look Far Enough*. Germany: ECM Records, 1993.

Andersen, Arild, Fabiano Araújo, and Naná Vasconcelos. *Rheomusi*. CD. Brazil: Ágata Tecnologia Digital Ltda, 2012.

Assad, Badi. *Verde*. CD. Brazil: Edge Music, 2004.

Baleiro, Zeca, Naná Vasconcelos, and Paulo Lepetit. *Café No Bule*. Brazil: SESC SP, 2015.

Buarque, Chico. *Apesar de Você*. Vinyl 7". Brazil: Philips, 1970.

Burú, Marcelino. *Sessão Cabidela*. Vinyl LP. France: Kinguele Xango, 1978.

Byrne, David, and Brian Eno. *My Life in the Bush of Ghosts*. Vinyl LP. United States: Sire, 1981.

Calazans, Teca. *Teca & Ricardo—Caminho Das Aguas*. France: Moshé-Naïm, 1975.

Calazans, Teca. *Teca & Ricardo—Cadê o Povo*. France: Moshé-Naïm, 1976.

Carroll, Baikida E. J. *Orange Fish Tears*. Vinyl LP. France: Palm, 1974.

Caussimon, Jean-Roger. *Jean-Roger Caussimon*. Vinyl LP. France: Saravah, 1974.

Cherry, Don. *Complete Communion*. Vinyl LP. United States: Blue Note, 1966.

Cherry, Don. *Organic Music Society*. Sweden: Caprice Records, 1973.

Cherry, Don and Ed Blackwell. *"Mu" First Part, "Mu" Second Part*. Vinyl LP. France: BYG Music (SACEM), 1969.

Cherry, Don, Naná Vasconcelos, and Collin Walcott. *Codona*. Vinyl LP. Germany: ECM Records, 1979.

Cherry, Don, Naná Vasconcelos, and Collin Walcott. *Codona 2*. Vinyl LP. Germany: ECM records, 1981.

Cherry, Don, Naná Vasconcelos, and Collin Walcott. *Codona 3*. Vinyl LP. Germany: ECM Records, 1983.

Cordel do Fogo Encantado. *Cordel Do Fogo Encantado*. CD. Brazil: Rec-Beat, 2001.

Da Vila, Martinho. *Voz e Coração*. CD. Brazil: Butiquim, 2002.

DeJohnette, Jack. *Jack DeJohnette's Special Edition—Irresistible Forces*. Vinyl LP. United States: MCA Impulse!, 1987.

Dos Santos, Agostinho. *Agostinho Dos Santos, Yansã Quarteto—África*. Vinyl LP. Portugal: Tecla, 1967.

Duncan, Zélia. *Pré-Pós-Tudo-Bossa-Band*. Brazil: Mercury, 2005.

Favre, Pierre. *Singing Drums*. Germany: ECM Records, 1984.

Garbarek, Jan. *Legend of the Seven Dreams*. Germany: ECM Records, 1988.

Garbarek, Jan. *I Took Up the Runes*. Germany: ECM Records, 1990.

Garbarek, Jan, Naná Vasconcelos, and John Abercrombie. *Eventyr*. Germany: ECM Records, 1980.

Gilberto, João. *João Gilberto En Mexico*. Mexico: Orfeon, 1970.

Gismonti, Egberto. *Academia de Danças*. Vinyl LP. Brazil: EMI, 1974.

Gismonti, Egberto. *Corações Futuristas*. Vinyl LP. Brazil: EMI, 1976.

Gismonti, Egberto. *Dança Das Cabeças*. Vinyl LP. Germany: ECM Records, 1977.

Gismonti, Egberto. *Sol Do Meio Dia*. Germany: ECM Records, 1978.

Gismonti, Egberto and Naná Vasconcelos. *Duas Vozes*. Vinyl LP. Germany: ECM Records, 1984.

Gotainer—Poil À La Pub. CD Compilation. France: Flarenasch, n.d.

Hassell, Jon and Brian Eno. *Fourth World, Vol. 1: Possible Musics*. New York: Editions EG, 1980.

Horn, Paul. *The Altitude of the Sun*. Germany: Black Sun, 1989.

Kühn, Rolf. *Rolf Kühn Group Featuring Phil Woods—The Day After*. Vinyl LP. Germany: MPS Records, 1972.

Lindsay, Arto. *O Corpo Sutil = The Subtle Body*. United States: Bar/None Records, 1996.

Lindsay, Arto. *Noon Chill*. CD. United States: Bar/None Records, 1998.

Luiz Eca & Y La Familia Sagrada. *La Nueva Onda Del Brasil*. Vinyl LP. Mexico: RVV, 1970.

Machín, Antonio. *El Manisero (Early Recordings 1929–1930)*. CD. Tumbao Cuban Classics, 1993.

Mahjun. *Mahjun*. Vinyl LP. France: Saravah, 1974.

McNeil, David. *J'ai Déjà Fait Mon Arche, J'attends Les Animaux*. Vinyl LP. France: Saravah, 1975.

Metheny, Pat. *Pat Metheny Group—Offramp*. Vinyl LP. Germany: ECM Records, 1982.

Metheny, Pat. *Pat Metheny Group—Travels*. Germany: ECM Records, 1983.

Metheny, Pat and Lyle Mays. *As Falls Wichita, So Falls Wichita Falls*. Vinyl LP. Germany: ECM Records, 1981.

Monte, Marisa. *Mais*. Vinyl LP. Brazil: EMI, 1991.

Monte, Marisa. *Barulhinho Bom (A Great Noise)*. CDx2. Brazil: EMI, 1996.

Moreno, Joyce, Naná Vasconcelos, and Maurício Maestro. *Visions of Dawn*. Vinyl, CD. United Kingdom: Far Out Recordings, 2009.

Mundo Livre S/A. *Samba Esquema Noise*. CD. Brazil: Banguela Records, 1994.

Nascimento, Milton. *Milagre Dos Peixes*. Vinyl LP. Brazil: Odeon, 1969.

Nascimento, Milton. *Milton Nascimento*. Vinyl LP. Brazil: Odeon, 1969.

Os Mutantes. *A Divina Comédia Ou Ando Meio Desligado*. Vinyl LP. Brazil: Polydor, 1970.

Pepper, Jim. *Comin' and Goin'*. Vinyl LP. France: Europa Records, 1983.

Powell, Baden. *Le Monde Musical de Baden Powell*. Vinyl LP. France: Barclay LP, 1964.

Simon, Paul. *The Rhythm of the Saints*. CD. United States: Warner Bros. Records, 1990.

Talking Heads. *Fear of Music*. Vinyl LP. United States: Sire, 1979.

Talking Heads. *Remain in Light*. Vinyl LP. United States: Sire, 1980.

Valença, Alceu. *De Janeiro a Janeiro*. CD. Brazil: Tropicana, 2002.

Various. *Baião de Viramundo: Tribute to Luiz Gonzaga*. CD. Brazil: Stern's Brasil, 2000.

Vasconcelos, Naná. *Africadeus*. Vinyl LP. France: Saravah, 1973.

Vasconcelos, Naná. *Amazonas*. Vinyl LP. Brazil: Philips, 1973.

Vasconcelos, Naná. *Saudades*. Vinyl LP. Germany: ECM Records, 1980.

Vasconcelos, Naná. *Zumbi*. Vinyl LP. France: Europa Records, 1983.

Vasconcelos, Naná. *Contaminação*. Brazil: M. Officer Estúdio, 1999.

Vasconcelos, Naná and Itamar Assumpção. *Isso Vai Dar Repercussão*. Brazil: Elo Music, 2004.

Vasconcelos, Naná and Agustin Pereyra Lucena. *El Increíble Naná Con Agustin Pereyra Lucena*. Vinyl LP. Argentina: Tonodisc, 1971.

Veloso, Caetano. *Estrangeiro*. Vinyl LP. Brazil: Philips, 1989.

Veloso, Caetano. *Circuladô*. Brazil: Philips, 1991.

Film, TV, and Video

Abreu, Alê. *O Menino e o Mundo (The Boy and the World)*, 2013.

Anderson, Wes. *The Life Aquatic with Steve Zissou*. Touchstone Pictures, 2004.

Atlas, George. *Put Blood into the Music*, 1989.

Bertolucci, Bernardo. *Last Tango in Paris*, 1972.

Camus, Marcel. *Orfeu Negro (Black Orpheus)*. Dispat Films, 1959.

Cherry, Don. *Incontro con Don Cherry*. RAI Radiotelevisione Italiana. Rome, 1976. Available at: https://www.youtube.com/watch?v=lu3OLnQvl-g (accessed 29 July 2020).

DeJohnette, Jack. *Jack Dejohnette's Special Edition—Live at the Montreal Jazz Festival 1988*. VideoArts, 1988.

Friedkin, William. *Cruising*. Lorimar Film Entertainment, 1980.

Gomes, Huila. *O Menino e o Mundo #04-Naná Vasconcelos*. Available at: https://www.youtube.com/watch?v=eRs58AcGuNI (accessed 31 July 2020).

Jarmusch, Jim. *Down by Law*. Island Pictures, 1986.

Lasson, Urban. "It is Not My Music." Available at: https://www.youtube.com/watch?v=GZHgZ1K7V7s&t=3064s (accessed 28 July 2020).

Lelouch, Claude. *Un Homme et Une Femme*. Les Films 13, 1966.

Lurie, John. "Fishing with John: Tom Waits." IFC The Criterion Collection, 1991.

Pasin, Camila. *Liniker—Fim de Festa (Itamar Assumpção) |FORA DA CAIXA|*. Available at: https://www.youtube.com/watch?v=V3NslziwyoA (accessed 28 July 2020).

Quaresma, Tania. *Trindade, Curto Caminho Longo*. Documentary. Embrafilme, 1978.

Ricardo, Sérgio. *Êsse Mundo é Meu*. Copacabana Filmes 1964.

Rocha, Glauber. *Deus e o Diabo Na Terra Do Sol*, 1964.

Rocha, Glauber. *Antonio Das Mortes*. Mapa Filmes, 1969.

Rocha, Glauber. *A Idade Da Terra (The Age of the Earth)*. C.P.C. Cinematografica, Embrafilme, 1980.

Rozemberg, I. *Criando Vida Nova (Coisas Do Brasil No. 263)*. Documentary, 1975. Available at: https://www.youtube.com/watch?v=Sp0EGxYjSo8 (accessed 13 June 2021).

Rozier, Jacques. *Les Naufragés de l'île de La Tortue*. Callipix, 1976.

Vandré, Geraldo. *Geraldo Vandré—Cine Teatro Goiânia 1968 (Completo)*. Available at: https://www.youtube.com/watch?v=zY0Kq-Kwg4A (accessed 28 July 2020).

References

Albuquerque, Célio. *1973—O Ano Que Reinventou a MPB*. Brazil: Sonora, 2014.

Alex, Pedro. "Geraldo Azevedo, o Sobrevivente." Farofafá, 17 May 2019. Available at: https://farofafa.cartacapital.com.br/2019/05/17/o-sobrevivente/ (accessed 13 June 2021).

Allen, Clifford. "The Humus of Don Cherry." *All About Jazz*, 20 October 2005. Available at: https://www.allaboutjazz.com/the-humus-of-don-cherry-don-cherry-by-clifford-allen.php (accessed 13 June 2021).

Amaral, Chico. *A Música de Milton Nascimento*. Belo Horizonte: Editora Universidade Federal de Minas Gerais (UFMG), 2018.

Aretakis, Felipe Pedrosa. "O Tropicalismo Pernambucano: História de Um 'Tigre de Vanguarda' (1967–1968)," 2016. Available at: https://repositorio.ufpe.br/handle/123456789/18396 (accessed 13 June 2021).

Avelar, Idelber and Christopher Dunn. *Brazilian Popular Music and Citizenship*. Durham, NC: Duke University Press, 2011.

Azevedo, Geraldo. "Adeus a Naná Vasconcelos," 16 March 2016. Available at: https://geraldoazevedo.com.br/adeus-a-nana-vasconcelos/ (accessed 13 June 2021).

Berger, Karl. "Karl Berger: Freedom in Discipline." Karl Berger Music, 2012. Available at: http://www.karlbergermusic.com/karl-berger-freedom-in-discipline.html (accessed 29 July 2020).

Beta, Andy. "Fourth World in the 21st Century." *Resident Advisor*, 12 June 2017. Available at: https://www.residentadvisor.net/features/2984 (accessed 28 July 2020).

Beyer, Greg. "Naná Vasconcelos: The Voice of the Berimbau." *Percussive Notes* (October 2007): 48–52.

Bocskay, Stephen. "Undesired Presences: Samba, Improvisation, and Afro-Politics in 1970s Brazil." *Latin American Research Review* 52, no. 1 (2017): 64–78.

Borges, Márcio. *Os Sonhos Não Envelhecem: Histórias Do Clube Da Esquina*. São Paulo: Geração Editorial, 1996.

Boym, Svetlana. *The Future of Nostalgia*. New York: Basic Books, 2008.

Bozzo Junior, Carlos. "De Como Juvenal Se Tornou o Fenômeno Naná Vasconcelos." *Folha de São Paulo*, 11 May 2013. Available at: https://www1.folha.uol.com.br/ilustrissima/2013/05/1276788-de-como-juvenal-se-tornou-o-fenomeno-nana-vasconcelos.shtml (accessed 13 June 2021).

Brothers, Thomas. *Louis Armstrong's New Orleans*. New York: W.W. Norton, 2007.

Browning, Barbara. *Samba: Resistance in Motion*. Bloomington, IN: Indiana University Press, 1995.

Channing, Keith. "The Laughing Falcon." Hawk Conservancy Trust. Available at: http://www.hawk-conservancy.org/ (accessed 1 December 1996).

Cherry, Don. "Dartmouth College, Dean of Faculty Records (DA-165, Box 10463, 'Cherry, Don')," n.d.

Cooke, Mervyn. *Pat Metheny: The ECM Years, 1975–1984*. Oxford: Oxford University Press, 2017.

Crenshaw, Kimberlé Williams. *Seeing Race Again: Countering Colorblindness across the Disciplines*. Berkeley, CA: University of California Press, 2019.

Diniz, Sheyla Castro. "'Nuvem Cigana': A Trajetória Do Clube de Esquina No Campo Da MPB," 2012. Available at: http://repositorio.unicamp.br/jspui/handle/REPOSIP/278903 (accessed 13 June 2021).

Dockwray, Ruth and Moore, Allan F. "Configuring the Sound-Box 1965–1972." *Popular Music* 29, no. 2 (2010): 181–97.

Douglas, Dave. "Don Cherry—The Dozens." Greenleaf Music, 16 January 2009. Available at: https://greenleafmusic.com/don-cherry-the-dozens/. (accessed 29 July 2020).

Dunn, Christopher. *Contracultura: Alternative Arts and Social Transformation in Authoritarian Brazil*. Chapel Hill, NC: University of North Carolina Press, 2016.

ECM Records. "ECM Records." 2015. Available at: https://www.ecmrecords.com/artists/1435045864/egberto-gismonti (accessed 30 July 2020).

Erlmann, Veit. "The Aesthetics of the Global Imagination: Reflections on World Music in the 1990s." *Public Culture* 8, no. 3 (1996): 467–87.

Errington, Shelly. *The Death of Authentic Primitive Art and Other Tales of Progress*. Berkeley, CA: University of California Press, 1998.

Espir, Guilherme. "Naná Vasconcelos: Uma Entrevista Que Remete Saudades." *La Parola*, 8 June 2015. Available at: https://laparola.com.br/nana-vasconcelos-uma-entrevista-que-remete-saudades (accessed 13 June 2021).

Feld, Steven. "Pygmy POP: A Genealogy of Schizophonic Mimesis." *Yearbook for Traditional Music* 28 (1996): 1–35.

Feld, Steven. "A Sweet Lullaby for World Music." *Public Culture* 12, no. 1 (2000): 145–71.

Fenton, David. "Gato Barbieri: Third World Jazz." *Ann Arbor Sun*, 16 November 1973. Available at: https://aadl.org/node/196089 (accessed 13 June 2021).

Fischlin, Daniel and Ajay Heble. *The Other Side of Nowhere: Jazz, Improvisation, and Communities in Dialogue*. Middletown, CT: Wesleyan University Press, 2004.

Ford, Phil. "Taboo: Time and Belief in Exotica." *Representations* 103 (1 August 2008): 107–35.

Freire, Paulo. *Pedagogy of the Oppressed*. A Continuum Book. New York: Seabury Press, 1970.

Galm, Eric A. *The Berimbau: Soul of Brazilian Music*. Jackson, MS: University Press of Mississippi, 2010.

Garcia, David F. *Listening for Africa: Freedom, Modernity, and the Logic of Black Music's African Origins*. Durham, NC: Duke University Press, 2017.

Gaspar, Lúcia. "Movimento de Cultura Popular (MCP)." Fundação Joaquim Nabuco Biblioteca Blanch Knopf, 29 July 2008. Available at: http://basilio.fundaj.gov.br/pesquisaescolar/index.php?option=com_content&view=article&id=723 (accessed 28 July 2020).

Gil, Gilberto. "Depoimento (Musical) de Um Vira-Mundo." *Jornal Do Commercio (PE)*, 10 May 1967, sec. II Caderno: 4.

Goldschmitt, K. E. *Bossa Mundo: Brazilian Music in Transnational Media Industries*. Oxford: Oxford University Press, 2020.

Gross, Jason. "Jon Hassell Interview: Interview by Jason Gross." *Perfect Sound Forever*, July 1997. Available at: http://www.furious.com/perfect/hassell.html (accessed 13 June 2021).

Haidenbauer, Johann. "Nana Vasconcelos Discography." Available at: http://discogs.darwinmonkey.com/nana.htm (accessed 30 July 2020).

Hertzman, Marc A. *Making Samba: A New History of Race and Music in Brazil*. Durham, NC: Duke University Press, 2013.

Holden, Stephen. "A Winning Mix of Electronic Innovation and Lyricism." *The New York Times*, 5 July 1981, sec. Arts. Available at: https://www.nytimes.com/1981/07/05/arts/a-winning-mix-of-electronic-innovation-and-lyricism.html (accessed 13 June 2021).

Holmes, Holly L. *Milton Nascimento and the Clube Da Esquina: Popular Music, Politics, and Fraternity during Brazil's Military Dictatorship (1964–85)*, 2017. Available at: http://hdl.handle.net/2142/97330 (accessed 13 June 2021).

hooks, bell. *Black Looks: Race and Representation*. Boston, MA: South End Press, 2015.

Hooper, Joseph. "Not Your Average Family." *The New York Times*, 10 December 1989, sec. Magazine. Available at: https://www.nytimes.com/1989/12/10/magazine/not-your-average-family.html (accessed 13 June 2021).

Hudson, Mark. "How the Austere Producer Manfred Eicher Keeps World Music Cool." *The Telegraph*. 14 February 2014. Available at: https://www.telegraph.co.uk/culture/music/worldfolkandjazz/10639577/How-the-austere-producer-Manfred-Eicher-keeps-world-music-cool.html (accessed 13 June 2021).

Hunt, Robert. "ECM Studio Production Comment." 8 November 2016. Available at: https://www.gearspace.com/board/remote-possibilities-in-location-recording-amp-production/54521-any-ecm-slutz-house-5.html (accessed 29 July 2020).

Hutchings, Arthur, Michael Talbot, Cliff Eisen, Leon Botstein, and Paul Griffiths. "Concerto." In *Grove Music*. Oxford: Oxford

University Press, 2001. Available at: https://doi.org/10.1093/gmo/9781561592630.article.40737 (accessed 13 June 2021).

Johnson, Randal. *Cinema Novo x 5: Masters of Contemporary Brazilian Film*. 1st edn. Austin, TX: University of Texas Press, 1984.

Junior, Patreze. "A Dança Das Oito Cordas Nas Cabeças de Egberto Gismonti," 2017. Available at: http://repositorio.unicamp.br/jspui/handle/REPOSIP/330767 (accessed 13 June 2021).

Kirkendall, Andrew J. "Entering History: Paulo Freire and the Politics of the Brazilian Northeast, 1958–1964." *Luso-Brazilian Review* 41, no. 1 (2004): 168–89.

Kittler, Friedrich A. *Discourse Networks 1800/1900*. Stanford, CA: Stanford University Press, 1990.

Lake, Steve and Paul Griffiths. *Horizons Touched: The Music of ECM*. London: Granta, 2007.

Levine, Robert M. *Vale of Tears: Revisiting the Canudos Massacre in Northeastern Brazil, 1893–1897*. Berkeley, CA: University of California Press, 1992.

Lewis, George E. "Improvised Music after 1950: Afrological and Eurological Perspectives." *Black Music Research Journal* 16, no. 1 (1996): 91–122.

Lewis, Matt. "Ventriloquial Acts: Critical Reflections on the Art of Foley." *The New Soundtrack* 5, no. 2 (1 September 2015): 103–20. Doi: https://doi.org/10.3366/sound.2015.0073.

Macfarlane, Clyde. "The Quietus | Reviews | Jon Hassell & Brian Eno." *The Quietus*, 13 November 2014. Available at: https://thequietus.com/articles/16692-jon-hassell-brian-eno-fourth-world-music-vol-1-possible-musics-review (accessed 30 July 2020).

Martin, Michael T. *New Latin American Cinema*. Contemporary Film and Television Series. Detroit, MI: Wayne State University Press, 1997.

Matta, Roberto da. *Conta de Mentiroso: Sete Ensaios de Antropologia Brasileira*. Rio de Janeiro: Rocco, 1993.

Meintjes, Louise. "Paul Simon's *Graceland*, South Africa, and the Mediation of Musical Meaning." *Ethnomusicology* 34, no. 1 (1990): 37–73.

Metheny, Pat. "RIP NANA VASCONCELOS." Pat Metheny, 9 March 2016. Available at: https://www.patmetheny.com/news/full_display.cfm?id=114 (accessed 30 July 2020).

Moreira, Maria Beatriz Cyrino. "Um Coração Futurista: Desconstrução Construtiva Nos Processos Composicionais de Egberto Gismonti Na Década de 1970." Unversidade de Campinas (UNICAMP), 2016. Available at: http://repositorio.unicamp.br/jspui/handle/REPOSIP/321113 (13 June 2021).

Moreno, Jairo. "Bauza-Gillespie-Latin/Jazz: Difference, Modernity, and the Black Caribbean." *South Atlantic Quarterly* 103, no. 1 (2004): 81–99.

Moreno, Joyce. *Naná Vasconcelos e Milton Nascimento Em Cantos Do Rio*. 29 March 2016. Available at: https://www.youtube.com/watch?v=3-Rj-NhMslw (13 June 2021).

"Naná Vasconcelos." In *Enciclopédia Itaú Cultural de Arte e Cultura Brasileiras*. São Paulo: Itaú Cultural, 2020. Available at: http://enciclopedia.itaucultural.org.br/pessoa14511/nana-vasconcelos (accessed 13 June 2021).

Novak, David. "The Sublime Frequencies of New Old Media." *Public Culture* 23, no. 3 (65) (1 September 2011): 603–34.

Novak, David and Matt Sakakeeny. *Keywords in Sound*. Durham, NC: Duke University Press, 2015.

Nuzzi, Vitor. *Geraldo Vandré: Uma Canção Interrompida*. São Paulo: Kuarup Produções LTDA—Kuarup Editora, 2017.

Ochoa Gautier, Ana María. "Sonic Transculturation, Epistemologies of Purification and the Aural Public Sphere in Latin America." *Social Identities* 12, no. 6 (2006): 803–25.

Ochoa Gautier, Ana María. *Aurality: Listening and Knowledge in Nineteenth-Century Colombia*. Durham, NC: Duke University Press, 2014.

Oliveira, Elias. YouTube comment about Naná Vasconcelos. Available at: https://www.youtube.com/watch?v=BJ3mUcfYkwY (accessed 28 July 2020).

Pareles, Jon. "Jazz: Nana Vasconcelos." *The New York Times*, 17 May 1987, sec. Arts. Available at: https://www.nytimes.com/1987/05/17/arts/jazz-nana-vasconcelos.html (accessed 13 June 2021).

Pareles, Jon. "ECM's Catalog is Finally Streaming. Here Are 21 Essential Albums." *The New York Times*, 17 November 2017, sec. Arts. Available at: https://www.nytimes.com/2017/11/17/arts/music/ecm-catalog-streaming-guide.html (accessed 13 June 2021).

Pazcheco, Mário. "Naná Vasconcelos—Biriba é Pau!" *Do Próprio Bolso*, blog, 2014. Available at: http://www.dopropriobolso.com.br/index.php/artes-visuais/51-cinema/1158-biriba-e-pau (accessed 28 July 2020).

Perrone, Charles A. and Christopher Dunn. *Brazilian Popular Music and Globalization*. New York and London: Routledge, 2013.

Pinto, Renato de Barros. "Egberto Gismonti e a Poética Da Semi-Erudição." Universidade de São Paulo, 2015. Available at: http://www.teses.usp.br/teses/disponiveis/27/27158/tde-24112015-165134/ (accessed 13 June 2021).

"'Pregão' é Um 'Show' de Música Consciente." *Jornal Do Commercio (PE)*, 23, no.7 (August 1966): 533–6.

Pucci, M. D. "Cantos Da Floresta (Forest Songs): Exchanging and Sharing Indigenous Music in Brazil," 2019. Available at: https://openaccess.leidenuniv.nl/handle/1887/70037 (accessed 13 June 2021).

Robinson, N. Scott. "Naná Vasconcelos: The Nature of Naná." *Modern Drummer*, July 2000.

Rocha, Glauber. *On Cinema*. London: Bloomsbury Publishing, 2018.

Roser, Max and Esteban Ortiz-Ospina. "Global Education." *Our World in Data*, 31 August 2016. Available at: https://ourworldindata.org/global-education (accessed 13 June 2021).

Samuels, David W., Louise Meintjes, Ana Maria Ochoa, and Thomas Porcello. "Soundscapes: Toward a Sounded Anthropology." *Annual Review of Anthropology* 39 (2010): 329–45.

Sandroni, Carlos. *Feitiço Decente: Transformações Do Samba No Rio de Janeiro, 1917–1933*. Rio de Janeiro: Jorge Zahar Editor, 2001.

Sharp, Daniel B. *Between Nostalgia and Apocalypse: Popular Music and the Staging of Brazil*. Lebanon, NH: University Press of New England, 2014.

Skinner, Ryan. *Yellow, Blue, and Black: Remembering and Renaissance in Afro-Sweden*. Minneapolis, MN: University of Minnesota Press, forthcoming.

Star, Edy "[A Música de] História Pública Da Música Do Brasil," 2019. Available at: https://www.youtube.com/watch?v=nMysSretZRM (accessed 13 June 2021).

Stockhausen, Karlheinz. *Towards a Cosmic Music*. Shaftesbury: Element, 1989.

Stokes, Martin. "Music and the Global Order." *Annual Review of Anthropology* 33 (2004): 47–72.

Stone, Michael. "Manfred Eicher: 40 Years of ECM." RootsWorld, 2010. Available at: http://www.rootsworld.com/interview/eicher10.shtml (accessed 29 July 2020).

Straw, Will. "Systems of Articulation, Logics of Change: Communities and Scenes in Popular Music." *Cultural Studies* 5, no. 3 (1991): 368–88.

Sweet, Bob. "All Kinds of Time: Creative Music Studio Celebrates Forty Years of Irrepressible Staying Power." *Cadence Magazine*, September 2013: 63–71.

Taussig, Michael. *Mimesis and Alterity*. New York: Routledge, 2016.

Théberge, Paul, Kyle Devine, and Tom Everrett. *Living Stereo Histories and Cultures of Multichannel Sound*. New York and London: Bloomsbury Publishing, 2015.

Tinhorão, José Ramos. *Música Popular: Um Tema Em Debate*. 3rd edn. São Paulo: Editora 34, 1997.

Trotta, Felipe. *O Samba e Suas Fronteiras: "Pagode Romântico" e "Samba de Raiz" Nos Anos 1990*. Rio de Janeiro: Editora Universidade Federal do Rio de Janeiro (UFRJ), 2011.

Vasconcelos, Cid. "Filme Do Dia: Esse Mundo é Meu (1964), Sérgio Ricardo." Magia do Real, n.d. Available at: https://magiadoreal.blogspot.com/2017/01/filme-do-dia-esse-mundo-e-meu-1964.html (accessed 13 June 2021).

Vasconcelos, Naná. "Bush Dance." Website comments. Available at: https://www.youtube.com/watch?v=BJ3mUcfYkwY (accessed 28 July 2020).

Vianna, Hermano and John Charles Chasteen. *The Mystery of Samba: Popular Music & National Identity in Brazil*. Chapel Hill, NC: University of North Carolina Press, 1999.

Walser, Robert. *Keeping Time: Readings in Jazz History*. Oxford: Oxford University Press, 1999.

Washburne, Christopher. *Latin Jazz: The Other Jazz*. Oxford: Oxford University Press, 2020.

Weiss, Jason. *Always in Trouble: An Oral History of ESP-Disk, the Most Outrageous Record Label in America*. Middletown, CT: Wesleyan University Press, 2012.

Weiss, Mark. "Don Cherry at Dartmouth." *Plastic Alto with Mark Weiss*, blog, 21 April 2011. Available at: https://markweiss86.com/2011/04/20/don-cherry-at-dartmouth/ (accessed 13 June 2021).

Whiteley, Sheila. "Progressive Rock and Psychedelic Coding in the Work of Jimi Hendrix." *Popular Music* 9, no. 1 (January 1990): 37–60.

Williams, Richard. "Manfred Eicher: The Sound Man." *The Guardian*, 16 July 2010, sec. Music. Available at: https://www.theguardian.com/music/2010/jul/17/manfred-eicher-ecm-jazz-interview (accessed 13 June 2021).

Index

Academia de Danças 102, 103
acauã 176
Africa Canta Agostinho do Santos 48
Africadeus 104, 114, 115–16, 117
   as precursor to *Saudades* 115, 163, 164, 176, 177
"Africadeus (Concerto Pra Mãe Bio)" 31, 165–7
African music 23, 110, 111, 118, 139, 158
Afro-Brazilian music 20, 27–31, 37, 100–1, 103, 114, 194
Akendengué, Pierre 118
Amaral, Chico 157
Amazonas 67–8, 149–50, 163, 164
"Amazonas" 133, 143
Ambitious Lovers 201
American Center (Recife) 32, 34
Anderson, Arild 92
Anderson, Laurie 206
Anderson, Wes 11, 124
"Ando Meio Desligado" 11, 56
Andrews, Rev. Dwight 23–4, 156
Angelo, Nelson 50, 57
anthropocene 22
Antonio das Mortes (film) 62
"Apesar de Você" 52
Appleton, Jon 73
Aragão, Helder 16–17

Arcoverde 16
Armstrong, Louis 146
Artificial Afrika (show) 75
As Falls Wichita, So Falls Wichita Falls 94, 199–200
Assumpção, Itamar 11
Ato Institucional Número Cinco (AI-5) 51
avant-garde 32, 59, 89, 93, 181
Ayler, Albert 76
Azevedo, Geraldo 38, 157
   imprisonment 53
   in Rio 13–14, 48, 49–50, 54–6, 57

Baiana, João da 114
Banda de Pífanos 40, 44, 105–6
Baptista, Cyro 126, 127
baqueta 82, 165, 166, 169, 177, 178, 191
Barbieri, Gato 57, 59, 63–4, 68, 74
Barouh, Pierre 114, 118
Barraqué, Jean 99
Bauzá, Mario 193
Baxter, Les 116–17
Beatles, The 40, 42
Berger, Karl 69, 95–6
berimbau
   properties 1, 8, 71, 84, 150, 156, 169

as solo instrument 165, 169, 171–4
symbolism 44, 61–3, 66
techniques 12, 42–3, 60, 82, 104, 115, 163–7, 175–8, 190–2, 203
traditional use 19–20, 41, 43, 110
unfamiliarity 71, 82, 122, 124, 138–9, 171–2
"Berimbau" 43, 63, 187
"Berimbau, O" 170–4, 175–8, 191
Bertolucci, Bernardo 59, 68
Beyer, Greg 191
bird calls 102, 118, 176
Bisi, Martin 201
Black Orpheus (film) 27, 47
Blackwell, Ed 74, 75, 205
body percussion 77, 110, 111, 126, 151
bogas 142–3
Bohemians of Sítio Novo University of Samba, The (USBSINO) 31
Bolha, A 56–7
Borges, Márcio 135–7
bossa nova 27–8, 32–3, 35, 36, 38, 55, 114
Boulanger, Nadia 99, 100, 107
Boy and the World, The 161–2
Boym, Svetlana 7, 193
Brant, Fernando 152
Brasilia 28, 51, 67, 209
Brazil
    dictatorship 29, 36, 49, 50–4, 101, 121, 152–3

    hydroelectric projects 7, 182–3, 184–5
    literacy campaign 33–4
    1950s 28–9
    Northeast region 29–30, 41, 120–2, 187, 188
    racial inequality 7, 20, 45, 145, 179
Brazilian Communist Party 34
Brazilian Popular Music (MPB) 29, 108, 121, 199
breakdance 159, 204
Brubeck, Dave 32
Buarque, Chico 52
Buru, Marcelino 122–3
Bush Dance 201, 204
Bush Dancers project 126
Byrne, David 129–30

Cadê o Povo 121
Calazans, Teca 13–14, 36, 41–2, 43, 48, 121–2
"Caminhando" 51–2
Caminho das Aguas 121
Campos, Augusto de 181
Can 129
Candomblé 30, 38, 42, 49, 61
Canosa, Fabiano 59, 60–1
Cantochão (show) 36–7, 45
cantoria de viola 106, 186–7
Capinam 67
capoeira 19, 43, 172, 204
carnaval 16, 27, 44, 110, 207
Carroll, Baikida 118–19
Caruaru 39, 40, 43–4, 105, 197, 198
Casa de Xambá 30, 31

Caussimon, Jean-Roger 118
"Cego Aderaldo" 6, 186–90, 192–3
"Cego Aderaldo, O" 187–8
Cego Aderaldo (troubadour) 186, 189–90
Centro Popular de Cultura (CPC) 35
"Chamada, A" 153
"Chegada" 121
Cherry, Don 13, 145, 147, 205
    artistic practices 74–7, 78–9, 172
    drug use 79–80
    family 77, 78, 81, 82, 83
    musical egalitarianism 74, 83, 96, 105
    and new age 24–5
    spiritual practices and beliefs 31, 80, 81–2
    street performance 71–3
    teaching 73, 76–7, 95–6
    and world music 19, 21–2, 69, 73–4, 111–12, 117
    See also, Codona
Chrysler 116–17, 118, 128
classical music 61, 90, 99, 130, 174–5
    See also, Western art music
clave 122
Clayton, Merry 7
click tracks 2, 159, 196
Clube da Esquina 56, 57, 135
Codona 19, 68, 83–7, 92, 200, 203–4, 205
"Codona" 86
Cold War 29, 34

Coleman, Ornette 32, 69, 74, 85–6, 96, 205
"Colemanwonder: Race Face/Sortie/Sir Duke" 85–6
Comin' and Goin' 205–6
Communist Hunting Command (Comando de Caça aos Comunistas; CCC) 50
Complete Communion 74
concerto form 115, 173–4
congas 11, 48, 51, 56, 66, 86, 117, 164, 185
Conselheiro, Antonio 183–4
contemporary art 198
Corações Futuristas 102, 103, 105, 106
Cordel Do Fogo Encantado 16
Corpo, Sutil, O 202
Costa, Gal 39, 56, 57
COVID-19 pandemic 7, 22
cowbells 86, 119
Creative Music Studio (CMS) 14, 87, 95–7, 205
Cruising (film) 202–3
cubop 3, 63, 119, 122, 139
cuíca 82, 86, 107, 123, 150, 206
cymbals 10, 32, 44, 105

"Da Cheio de Ogum" 49
"Dado" 190–92
Dança das Cabeças 75, 101–5, 106–8, 117, 144, 149, 151
"Dança das Cabeças" 105–6
Dartmouth University 73–4
Day After, The 119–20
DeJohnette, Jack 205

Departamento de Ordem Política e Social (DOPS) 52–3
Desmond, Paul 32
Deus e o Diablo na Terra do Sol (film) 61, 183–4
Deuses e os Mortes, Os (film) 152–3
Dieng, Aïyb 97, 131, 203
Dillett, Pat 156, 157, 159, 201
DJ Dolores 16–17
Dockwray, Ruth 154
Don Cherry's New Researches featuring Naná Vasconcelos 81
Douglas, Dave 75
doussn'gouni 71, 74, 78, 82, 84–5, 86
Down by Law (film) 203
drum machines 196, 200, 201
drum-set playing 32–3, 37, 48
Duas Vozes 205
Dyani, Johnny 73

Eça, Luiz 57
Editions of Contemporary Music (ECM) 14, 83, 200
 Eurocentrism 93–4, 144, 174–5
 recording techniques 89–92, 119, 185
Eicher, Manfred 89–91, 92–3, 101, 105, 144
 Saudades 170, 171, 172, 173, 180
"Em Luanda Saudades de Luanda" 48

Eno, Brian 21, 129, 130
Errington, Shelly 93, 127, 133, 138
"Espafro" 164–5
exotica 23, 87, 116–17, 128
exoticism 21, 132–3, 144–5, 203

Favre, Pierre 92, 205
Feld, Steven 21, 22–3, 92, 111
"Fim de Festa" 11
flexatone 149–50
Foley artistry 12, 22, 80, 115, 116, 119, 161–2
Folk Songs 188
Ford, Phil 116–17
Fourth World, Vol. 1: Possible Musics 14, 21, 129–30, 131–3
Franklin da Flauta 50
free jazz 69, 74, 76–7, 86, 118–19
Freire, Paulo 33, 34
Frutuoso, Armando 53

Garbarek, Jan 92, 94, 188, 205
Gardie, Rene 61
Gibbs, Melvin 18–21, 24–5, 75, 144–5, 157–61, 198, 202
Gil, Gilberto 39, 40–1, 43–4, 49, 58, 197–8, 206–7
Gillespie, Dizzy 3, 122, 139–40
Gismonti, Egberto 13
 ECM records 75, 92, 99–110, 151, 161, 205
 Saudades 6, 15, 169–74, 180, 186–7, 188–9
Godard, Jean-Luc 89
Goldman, Albert 132

Goldschmitt, K. E. 112
Goulart, João 29
Grimes, Henry 74
Grupo Construção 41, 44, 47, 48, 121, 197
    activism 36–7, 38–40, 45, 54
    use of percussion 42–3, 80, 122
Grupo Opinião 43
Guarabyra, Guttemberg 184
Gurtu, Trilok 97, 204, 205
Gutesha, Mladen 6, 171, 175

Haden, Charlie 188
Haidenbauer, Johann 202
Hancock, Herbie 103, 111, 201, 205
Hanslick, Eduard 141
Hassell, Jon 21, 129, 130, 131, 132–4
Headhunters 111
Helias, Mark 205
Hell's Angels 11
Hendrix, Jimi 9, 137–8, 144, 155
hierarchies
    of musical genres 20, 23–4, 62, 130, 140–4, 197–8
    of musicians 32, 44, 74, 140, 172
hindewhu 23, 110, 111–12, 162
hip-hop 201, 204
Homme et une Femme, Un (film) 114
hooks, bell 127
Humboldt, Alexander von 142, 144
Hunt, Robert 91

Idade da Terra, A (film) 61, 67, 133
iê-iê-iê 35, 38, 41
improvisation 75, 103, 107, 139, 196, 200
Increible Nana Con Agustin Pereyra Lucena, El 163–4, 165
Indigenous music 68, 109–10, 112, 141–3, 205–6

jakuí flute 109, 110
Jarmusch, Jim 203
Jarrett, Keith 6, 108, 175
jazz fusion 103, 106
J Dilla 159
Jesus, Clementina de 11
João Gilberto en Mexico 61
Jobim, Tom 28
Johnson, Oliver 119
Johnson, Randal 62, 67–8, 143
"Jungle" (commercial) 116–17
"Jungle Jazz" 116–17

King, B. B. 206
Kubitschek, Juscelino 28
Kühn, Joachim 119, 120
Kühn, Rolf 119, 120

Lainé, Tony 125
Lake, Steve 90–1
Lasson, Urban 77
Last Tango in Paris, The (film) 60
Lennon, John 12
Lewis, George E. 32
Life Aquatic with Steve Zissou, The (film) 11, 124

Lindsay, Arto 11, 14, 17, 120, 158, 200–1, 203
   as producer 206
   rivalry with Pat Metheny 8–10, 198–9
Língua Mãe project 209
"Location of Jass, The" (New Orleans *Times-Picayune* article) 23
Lopes, Pablo 156
Lounge Lizards, The 203
Love, Darlene 7
Luiz Eça y la Familia Sagrada 13, 57
Lurie, John 203

Maestro, Maurício 56, 57, 120
Magnificent Force, The 11, 201, 204
Mahjun 118
mangue beat 15, 16, 207, 208
"Manisero, El" 63
maracatu nação 16, 49, 166, 176, 177, 207
Matta, Roberto da 192
meditation 80, 176
Memórias de Dois Cantadores (show) 41, 47, 49
Metheny, Pat 11, 92, 94, 151, 198–200, 203–4
   rivalry with Arto Lindsay 8–10, 198–9
microphone choreography 104, 115, 156–8, 161, 164–5, 166, 196
Milagre dos Peixes 11, 152–3
Milton Nascimento 56

Minas Gerais 55, 185
minimalism 129, 131, 133–4
Ministry of Culture (France) 4
Miranda, Carmen 62
Moki 81, 82, 83
Monroe, Merrie Robin 5, 6, 14, 58, 111, 133–4, 145–7
Monte, Marisa 121, 207
Moore, Alan F. 154
Mora na Filosofia (show) 37, 45
Moreira, Airto 7
Morello, Joe 32
Moreno, Jairo 139–40, 193
Moreno, Joyce 14, 56, 57, 120–1
Movimento de Cultura Popular (MCP) 34, 35, 36, 54
MPS Records 119
Mr. Wiggles 11, 204
Mu 74–5
multitrack recording 56, 92, 116, 154, 195, 197, 206
"Mumakata" 85
musicology 15, 141

Nabuco, Joaquim 192
Nandipo 118
Nascimento, Milton 11, 33, 39, 55–6, 112, 152–3, 184–5
nationalism, musical 35, 39, 41, 42, 49, 106
Native Dancer 112
Naufragés de l'île de la Tortue, Les (film) 11, 123–5
new age genre 21, 22, 24
Noon Chill 202
"North Brazilian Ceremonial Hymn" 80, 176

Northeast Brazil 29–30, 41, 120–2, 187, 188
Novelli 57
no wave 9, 10, 201, 203
NU Quintet 69, 205

Ochoa Gautier, Ana Maria 140–3, 197
Oiticica, Hélio 57
Olinda 29, 30
Om Shanti Om 80, 81
"Ondas (Na Óhlas de Petronila)" 180–5, 192
Opinião (show) 36
Orange Fish Tears 118–19
orchestras 79, 170–6, 178, 180, 185, 208–9
Organic Music Society 77, 78, 79, 80, 190–1
Organic Music Theatre 69, 77, 80–3
Ornelas, Nivaldo 106
Os Bossanorte 33
Os Bubbles 56–7
Os Mutantes 39, 56
overdubbing 104, 151, 156–7, 165, 178, 185, 189, 200
"Ovo Há" 123

Panorama Percussivo Mundial Festival (PercPan) 207
parallax gesture 1–2, 51, 155, 163, 164, 166, 185, 203
Pareles, Jon 91, 201
pastoral music 10, 22, 94, 199
Pepper, Jim 205–6
Petrolina 181–3

Pinto, Renato de Barros 107
Pixinguinha 114
"Porta Encantada, A" 107, 178
postcolonialism 4, 111, 113, 195
post-punk 9, 200
Powell, Baden 63, 114, 187–8
Pozo, Chano 3, 122, 139–40
Pramaggiore, Gian Piero 81, 82, 83
Pran Nath 131, 133
Pregão (show) 38
primitive, refiguring ideas of the 4–6, 14, 23, 62, 113–14, 123–5, 195
primitivism 65, 93, 111–12, 127–8, 135–44
prog rock 102, 103, 105, 106, 118
protest songs 35, 42, 51–2, 184
psychedelic music 114, 115, 116, 181, 198
"Purple Haze" 14

Quarteto Livre 50, 51
Quilombo dos Palmares 179

racism 71, 145–7, 189–90
Rain Dance 204
Recife 7, 13, 15–16, 29–33, 34, 36, 47, 207–8
recording technology, advances in 4, 56, 91, 153–6, 195–7
Reid, Vernon 75
"Relativity Suite No. 1" 78, 79, 80
reverb 68, 90–1, 104, 111, 131, 185, 186

Index

Rhythm of the Saints, The 11, 206
Ricardo, Sérgio 35, 38–9, 43–4, 198
Richard, Pierre 123, 124
Robinson, N. Scott 18, 138
Rocha, Glauber 13, 58, 59–62, 63, 112, 183–4
  Third Worldist perspective 65–8, 131, 133
"Rockit" 201, 205
Rodia, Simon 76
Rodrigues, Edson 33
Rosa, Guimarães 50
"Rosa do Ventre" 56
Royal Museum for Central Africa (Tevuren, Belgium) 5
Rozier, Jacques 123, 124
Rudolph, Adam 78–9, 158

Sá, Rodrix e Guarabyra 184
Salu, Maciel 16
samba 27, 28, 29–30, 31, 37, 38, 107, 166-7, 176-7
Sambossa Trio 33
Sanches, Eleutério 48
Sandroni, Carlos 121
Santos, Agostinho dos 27, 47–8, 154
sanza 83, 84, 85, 86
Sapain 109, 110
"Sapain (Sol de Meio Dia" 110–12
Saravah (film) 114
Saravah record label 114, 118
Saravah studios 74
Saudades 169–194
  origins 169–70
  recording techniques 115, 178–9, 180, 185
  title and themes 6–7, 192–4
  use of orchestra 170–4, 175–6, 178, 180, 185
  See also, individual song titles
Scherer, Peter 11
Sessão Cabidela 122, 123
sheng 108, 151
Shorter, Wayne 112
Silva, Robertinho 105
Simon, Paul 11, 206
Singing Drums 205
sitar 86, 189
Skinner, Ryan 147
slavery 16, 29, 54, 179
Smith, Wadada, Leo 96
"Sobradinho" 184
Sol de Meio Dia 109–11
Som Imaginário 56
"Sonata for Percussion, Piano + Clarinet" 120
Squat Theatre Nightclub 9, 203
Stanyek, Jason 25, 139, 191
Star, Edy 41–2, 48–9
stereo field 68, 80, 108
  recording techniques 1–2, 104, 105, 151, 155, 156, 166, 196
  significance of 8, 92, 113, 115, 119, 209
Stockhausen, Karlheinz 32, 99, 129, 130–1
Stravinsky, Igor 99, 107
Stumpf, Carl 141

Stuttgart Radio Symphony Orchestra 6, 170–3
Summers, Bill 111
Suzano, Marcos 149–50
Sweden 24, 74, 147
synthesizers 22, 103, 104, 105–6, 200, 201

tabla 11, 97, 107, 117, 119, 185, 189
talking drum 86, 97, 110, 189, 200
Talking Heads 130, 206
tanpura 80, 82
"Taratá" 11
Teatro de Cultura Popular 36
Teatro Opinião (Rio de Janeiro) 50
Temiz, Okey 73
Tinhorão, José Ramos 28
Tiravanija, Rikrit 17
Towner, Ralph 23, 24, 92
Tropicália 39, 42, 43, 49, 106, 181
  juxtaposition of cultures 40–1, 44, 106, 197–8
20 Feet from Stardom (film) 7

Vandré, Geraldo 35, 39, 49–50, 51–2, 53, 54, 56
Vasconcelos, Naná
  as an Afro-Brazilian 5–6, 20, 30, 36, 94, 190, 194
  artistic aims 5–6, 8, 24, 101, 120, 173–4
  awards 7, 108, 206
  compositional skill 156–8
  criticism of 22–3, 111
  early life 10, 13, 30–3, 35–6, 44–5, 197
  LSD use 24, 60
  in Mexico City 13
  in New York 8–9, 13, 18, 59–61, 68, 182
  in Paris 4–5, 13, 77, 113–15, 117–28, 145–6
  personal characteristics 8–9, 20–1
  political views 54, 64
  in Portugal 47–8
  as a producer 16
  return to Recife 13, 123, 207–8
  in Rio de Janeiro 13, 33, 48–9, 50, 54–8
  sense of time 1–2, 158–60
  as a session musician 118, 120, 122, 206
  spiritual beliefs 31
  stage presence 37–8
  statue 7
  work with children 76–7, 125–7, 151, 208–9
Vasconcelos, Patrícia 195, 205
Vasconcelos, Pierre 31
Veloso, Caetano 8, 49, 58, 62, 206–7
Vilas, Ricardo 121
Villa-Lobos, Heitor 28, 61, 99, 110
Visions of Dawn 120–1
vocables 78, 162
vocalizations 135–6, 141–3, 150–2, 153–4, 178–80, 200
"Vozes (Saudades)" 178–80, 192

Walcott, Collin 19, 83, 85, 86, 87, 203, 205
Ward, Carlos 205
Watts Tower 76
Western art music 28, 99, 100–1, 120, 160, 178
　See also, classical music; minimalism
"Wild Thing" 138, 144
Wonder, Stevie 85
Woods, Phil 119
wordplay 180–2

world music genre 19, 21, 22, 87, 93, 130–1

Xangô 30–1, 37

Yansã Quarteto 33, 47–50
Yawalapiti 109–10

Zappa, Frank 11–12
Zé Pretinho 189
Zumbi 151
Zumbi dos Palmares 179, 190